Christian Social Ethics

Exerting Christian Influence

ALBERT TERRILL RASMUSSEN

Professor of Social Ethics and the Sociology of Religion
Colgate Rochester Divinity School

ENGLEWOOD CLIFFS, N.J.

PRENTICE-HALL, Inc.

LIBRARY OF CONGRESS
CATALOG CARD NO.: 56-10471

First printing .... June, 1956
Second printing .... July, 1958
Third printing .... June, 1959
Fourth printing ...... August, 1961
Fifth printing .... June, 1964

PRINTED IN THE UNITED STATES OF AMERICA

29440-C

Preface

Christian Social Ethics: Exerting Christian Influence is a study of the problem of what the Christian response should be toward the enormous pressures and intimidations of the world. In this book we shall be concerned with several of the most disturbing questions that earnest Christians are asking:

Why is the Christian church not more influential in a so-called Christian nation?

What is the danger that Christian leadership might misuse its influence in confronting the injustices and materialistic tyrannies of our times?

How can we help more of our fellow Christians to understand the full gospel and what it requires of us toward our neighbors and toward the massive influences that surround all living human beings?

How can we set about the task of making Christian social influence more potent?

What are some of the concrete things that we can do?

Our mood is both appreciative and realistic; "appreciative realism" is its designation. We thank God for the accomplishment of the churches in keeping the gospel alive and in calling men into the fellowship of Christ. We thank God for the good things of the earth.

However, we must be realistic and honest because we believe that under the grace of God the church is the one institution in the world that can be truly self-critical and can at least partly escape the universal human mood of defensiveness. We shall present no exaggerated statements or apologies about the glorious attainments of the Christian church in our times. We suspect that we are often prone to brag about the wrong things—things that reveal the conformity and worldly success of the church rather than its true spiritual influence.

We are deeply concerned that the fires of the Christian witness seem to be burning low. The social witness before the world seems timid and confused. We often misunderstand the full demands of our faith, and we have made excuses in times of crisis. We have let the moral climate of the times invade our attitudes and press us into meek conformity without answering back. We fail to understand realistically the unavoidableness, yet the dangerousness, of compromise. To acknowledge and analyze these pressures and our failures, to attempt to discover how we can revitalize the Christian influence in this time of struggle for the allegiances of men, is our goal.

If you meekly agree with everything we say here, we shall be deeply disappointed. If you grapple with this basic problem and find some clues for discussion and real Christian action, our purpose will be fulfilled.

The quotations from the Revised Standard Version of the Bible are used by permission of the copyright owners, the National Council of Churches of Christ in the United States of America.

The author is gratefully indebted to his teachers, colleagues, and students to whom this book is a response of gratitude and an expression of the faith that has been developed in the common fellowship in Christ. To the many writers whose materials have been quoted, the many publishers who have granted permission to reproduce copyrighted quotations, and those who have helped to prepare and correct the manuscript, the author expresses his deepest thanks.

ALBERT T. RASMUSSEN

Contents

CHAPTER · 4 (continued)

CHAPTER · 5

Weakness of the Churches' Influence   97

CHAPTER · 10 (continued)

CHAPTER · 11

Christian Social Ethics

To *Marion, Terrill Ann,* and *Linda*

CHAPTER 1

What Is Christian Influence?

. . . there is no hope of establishing a more Christian social order except through the labour and sacrifice of those in whom the Spirit of Christ is active, and that the first necessity for progress is more and better Christians taking full responsibility as citizens for the political, social, and economic system under which they and their fellows live. (p. 76.)

No man is fitted for an isolated life; . . . he needs not only what his neighbors contribute to the equipment of his life but their actual selves as a complement to his own. Man is naturally and incurably social. . . . If you take all these social relationships away, there is nothing left. . . . By our mutual influence we actually constitute one another as what we are. This mutual influence finds its first field of activity in the family; it finds other fields later in school, college, Trade Union, professional association, city, country, nation, Church. (p. 47.) (William Temple, *Christianity and Social Order* [New York: Penguin Books, Inc., 1942]).

> *Either make the tree good, and its fruit good; or make the tree bad and its fruit bad; for the tree is known by its fruit* (Matt. 12:33, RSV).

There is a great focal concern that is haunting sensitive Christians today. Dr. Cavert expressed it in the foreword of the 1949 *Yearbook of American Churches;* he called it "the disturbing discrepancy between the numerical size of the church in the United States and its positive influence in the life of our nation."[1] Henry Steele Commager, the historian, in his book *The American Mind,* says, "Never before have the churches been materially more powerful and spiritually less effective."[2]

Why is there such a gulf between the great Protestant tradition of prophetic protest and responsibility and the timidity and inaction of the churches of Jesus Christ? Why so much complacent conformity to the world and so little Christian challenge? Why is there so much talk and so little effective leadership? These questions raise the crucial problem of influence that demands the attention of all earnest Christians. And they can be faced only after the most self-searching review of our basic Christian obligations and methods. What greater need confronts us today than a renewal of the call to Christian social leadership and a fresh consideration of the meaning and methods of Christian influence?

For this task no simple outline of "how to win friends and influence people" will suffice. Mere advertising tricks and attractions to lure a bigger following will not restore the savor to the salt nor return the "bite" of full moral demand to the gospel. Three urgent considerations are necessary to help us make the Christian faith more relevant and more influential in our times: (1) the moral requirements of the gospel; (2) the actual situation in which we are called upon to be faithful servants; and (3) some ways of exerting leadership in the most urgent areas of injustice and neglect. It is the purpose of this study to analyze these three things with the hope that we may intensify the Christian impact in our perilous times.

Does Christianity make a difference in the behavior of those who attempt to live under its spirit and within its fellowship? A labor leader who is a loyal church member said to a group of students recently: "I wouldn't be so discouraged about Christianity if we could deliver just a little performance along the lines that we profess." A business executive declared, in another meeting, that

[1] Samuel McCrea Cavert in *Yearbook of American Churches, 1949,* George F. Ketcham (editor) (Lebanon, Pa.: Sowers Printing Company, 1949), p. vi.
[2] Henry Steele Commager, *The American Mind* (New Haven: Yale University Press, 1950), pp. 167-168.

he had gone to church regularly for forty years and had never heard of the great Protestant doctrine of Christian vocation which calls men to serve Christ basically in their daily responsibilities. Too many churchgoers have apparently never heard nor taken seriously the full gospel of Christ and the decisional type of living to which it calls men.

Do our churches generate concern and action or indifference and escapism? What is the role of religious leadership? Is it the locomotive delivering power and light as we hurtle down the tracks into a hazardous future, or is it the observation car giving its members a cushioned seat from which to view things after they have happened? Are we hindsight critics who merely deplore what other men have done after it is too bad but too late? The early Christians were said to be "men who turned the world upside down." Contrast this to the characterization of churchmen by a group of college students: "The chief output of the churches today is preachers' pious platitudes and laymen's lame laments over even these platitudes." No doubt this is overdrawn, but most friends and skeptics alike agree that the church today is no humming dynamo of influence.

CHRISTIAN INFLUENCE INTERFERES

Surely, it is something added that changes lives and at least deflects events. It is a divine "leaven" that penetrates and raises the "whole loaf." It is interference that knocks our actions out of their well-worn grooves. It is a divine challenge that demands a new response. Those who want a faith of nonintervention have chosen wrongly, or been badly misinformed if they have turned to the Christian way. William Temple quotes the comment of a Victorian prime minister after coming away from a sermon on the Christian life: ". . . if religion was going to interfere with the affairs of private life, things were come to a pretty pass";[3] and another later prime minister made almost the same comment when a

[3] William Temple, *Christianity and Social Order* (New York: Penguin Books Inc., 1942), p. 9.

group of churchmen offered to mediate a coal strike: "It's a 'fine' thing when the church attempts to bring religion into interference in social issues."[4] True influence is always interference. A living God interferes in human lives and in the events of history. He intrudes and the task of the Christian church is to help men to seek to respond to this intrusion, and to be the vehicle of the power of the influence of Christ in the world.

CHRISTIAN ACTION UNDER GOD—PRIMARY TEST OF THE CHRISTIAN

It is repeated over and over in the New Testament, both in the gospels and the letters of Paul, that the genuineness of the Christian's experience is to be tested by the fruits of his living. "The tree is known by its fruit" (Matt. 12:33, RSV). Jesus said of the scribes and pharisees that "they preach, but do not practice" (Matt. 23:3, RSV). Or again, "Why do you call me Lord, Lord, and not do what I tell you?" (Luke 6:46, RSV). Paul declares that "he will render to every man according to his works" (Romans 2:6, RSV). He rebukes those who "profess to know God, but . . . deny him by their deeds" (Titus 1:16, RSV). This emphasis does not contradict the great evangelical doctrine of salvation through faith rather than works. We do not earn God's forgiveness and grace through good deeds, but the direction and quality of our actions do reveal the measure of the power that changes our lives. If there is no difference in the motives and direction of the behavior of those who are touched by the grace of God as compared with those who walk alone, then the light is indeed the light that fails.

Christians are not just passive assenters and yea-sayers, demurely nodding verbal consent to the influences of the world without entering the struggle for righteousness. Every Biblical description of the faithful servant shows him as a doer and practitioner, not just an advocate. He is a witness to the truth not in mere words and claims, but in the active decisions that are the living testimonials of the power of his faith. Christians

[4] *Ibid.*, p. 7 (paraphrased).

are cross-bearers, taking upon themselves the yoke of responsibility to neighbors—responding to the call of Christ to express and reflect the new light of their lives into every corner into which their relations lead. Daniel D. Williams in his Rauschenbusch lectures puts it clearly: "God . . . calls us to respond in action. It is true, therefore, that we discover our moral responsibility as we begin to act responsibly."[5]

But the most significant thing about the Christian is that he is not alone, bravely attempting to face or influence the world with his own strength or his own two hands. Instead he belongs to a fellowship of faith in which he is supported and criticized and in which he joins in the communion of Christ. First and primarily, he is a seeker committing himself to the influence of his Lord. And secondly, he joins the fellowship in Christ, which continually reminds him of his commitment and sustains him with the Holy Spirit. His response, then, is to be a witnessing and expressing Christian within the fellowship of the church and outward into the world.

THREE WAYS OF EXPRESSING CHRISTIAN INFLUENCE

The Hidden Influence

The first type is the distinctly silent type of personal faith that attempts no real outward expression at all. The Christian response is thought by those who hold this view to be an entirely private transaction with God that does not need to be articulated into action. It assumes that the Christian is to withdraw his life and his interests from the world and transfer them to heaven. But it overlooks the fact that the Christian must linger on in the world, living with his fellows and being influenced or influencing others, exactly as do his neighbors. Therefore, his supposed withdrawal is an illusion. The escapist who does not fight back with his own decisions and actions against the pressures of the world will un-

[5] Daniel Day Williams, *God's Grace and Man's Hope* (New York: Harper and Brothers, 1949), p. 156.

knowingly be silently and surely dominated by the moral climate of his community. This view overlooks one of the greatest facts of human nature: human beings are not isolated individuals but are persons-in-community, growing and spending their whole lives in a network of personal and group relations. This point is so significant we shall discuss it more fully later.

This belief—that inner sentiments, kindly intentions, and good feelings are all that is necessary of the Christian—develops an intensely selfish and egotistical perspective that is entirely contrary to the basic New Testament view. It attempts to offer the selfish rewards of eternal life without the cost of the struggle in the Christian pilgrimage. It overlooks the most often-repeated sentence in the New Testament: "He who loses his life for my sake shall find it." Thus the individualistic vices of personal sensuality are allowed to overshadow the basic Christian emphasis on the sins of selfishness and pride, which are relational in character. It is a far worse and more selfish sin to sin against neighbor than to sin against self.

Few Christians in our day openly support such a denial of the requirements of active Christian influence, but those who daily demonstrate this view are legion. They are what George Kelsey calls, "practical atheists." "Practical atheism," he says, "is the belief that our religion has nothing to do with our practical decisions."[6] This reliance on inner influence is the method of personal contemplation without action. This is the attempt to serve Christ through silent piety without responsibility. It is, indeed, "hiding one's light under a bushel" and failing in the attempt to live under the Biblical imperatives of love and justice. It is burying one's talents in the ground. It is running away from active response to the calling of Christ in the arena of actual temptations.

Whatever initial impact the gospel may have had soon withers away in the life that does not attempt to express it in application and decision. The unexercised faith soon dies from misuse. Unattempted religion shrivels into the husks of dry beliefs and formal

[6] George Kelsey, commencement address at Colgate Rochester Divinity School, 1952.

routines or is given up entirely. In short, the person who does not attempt to project the Christian influence that he has discovered in his own life, out into his relationships with others, will soon discover that the influence of Christ has disappeared from his own. In positive terms, response to the love of God issues in response to the love of neighbor, as the joining of the two great commandments has always shown.

Expression of Christian Influence Through Personal Relations

The second way of expressing Christian influence is through personal relations. This is *Christian personal action*. This is the attempt to live by divine grace and by love in all our "face-to-face" relationships—in the family, in local neighborhood contacts, and among those with whom we actually work or deal in our occupations. This is a far truer view of Christian responsibility. This is a necessary concern for all Christians who take seriously the two great commandments "love the Lord thy God . . . and thy neighbor as thyself" (Matt. 22:37-39), or the teachings of Paul who said, "the greatest of these is love" (I Cor. 13:13, RSV). The impact of personality upon personality is one of the most potent types of influence in the world, for both good and bad. But it is always only a partial type of influence, for no one can be isolated from all of the more remote but powerful organized pressures and patterns of existence; ". . . we are constantly dealing with people with whom we have no direct personal relationship."[7]

Many people seem to believe that if enough Christians witnessed through their lives in personal relations this would produce an automatic influence that would build the good society or even bring the Kingdom of God on earth. But being kind and faithful in the family, or pleasant and generous among one's vocational associates, or a friendly next-door-neighbor does not add up to

[7] John C. Bennett, *Christian Ethics and Social Policy* (New York: Charles Scribner's Sons, 1946), p. 19.

effective influence in organizational and political structures that make the policies that determine the patterns of our society. For here, decisions are made in a very different way from those in simple primary relations. In this realm, issues are decided and policies formulated through formal channels by those in authority, or by those who can mobilize effective consensus from within the groups, or by counterpressures from without. Decisions are made within the context of many complex factors and pressures, all of which have bearing on what can be done and what ought to be done.

"Sentimentalism" is the term Reinhold Niebuhr has often used for this overconfidence in personal good will to produce the good social organization, unrelated to organized policy processes. He has warned repeatedly that one of the fatal weaknesses of Protestant pietistic individualism has been the false confidence in the power of "right individual conduct" to produce just social structures.[8] The personal piety of kings does not overcome all of the evils of absolute monarchies; nor the individual good will of slaveholders toward their slaves redeem or abolish the institution of slavery; nor the conversion of an organizational administrator allow him to abandon suddenly the power or policies developed in relation to associates and competitive groups. More extensive treatment will be given to this problem later.

We have been rediscovering that the lone-eagle, let-every-man-change-his-own-world approach is utterly inadequate to influence the kind of organizational world in which we live. Furthermore, it fails to understand the basic interactional character of human personality and obscures the Hebrew view of the "covenant community-under-God," which became in the New Testament "covenant community-under-Christ."

This personal approach draws an arbitrary line around one's own little provincial world and exaggerates the influence of the isolated man to change the coercive patterns of organizations,

[8] Reinhold Neibuhr, "Christian Faith and Social Action," in *Christian Faith and Social Action,* John A. Hutchison (editor) (New York: Charles Scribner's Sons, 1953), pp. 225-226.

institutions, and social movements. Even our personal lives are lived in families, communities, occupational groups, and nations. Our most personal decisions take place under the attitudes that have developed under the social influences of our past and are limited by the actual possibilities of the present. All personal influence is social influence, taking place in the give-and-take of shared experiences. Even the most personal relations are defined and guided by what we have learned to believe is required of us in our roles as husband or wife, son or daughter, client or employer, student or layman, or whatever kind of relationship is involved. These roles are defined by the institutions of our social world.

We are born into and live within a ready-made world; we go to work in offices or factories that tell us what can be done and what can't be done within the rules that are all worked out before we arrive. Often these rules include moral short cuts and unethical discriminations. No organization can measure up to the requirements of Christian love and justice. All fall short of what our Lord requires.

We are indoctrinated in our families and schools and communities by powerful organs of influence that mold us with the prejudices and biases that are always mixed in our traditions. We are subjected to a barrage of influences in newspapers, radio, and television—all designed to sway our opinions and slant our views along lines that will be beneficial to the particular interests of the sponsors. We live in a new kind of world where influence is organized and centralized as never before in our history. As was declared in the report of the World Council of Churches in Amsterdam, one of the greatest problems of the modern world is the problem of the little man living in a mass world.[9] How can he answer back to the pressures that play upon him? In someone else's interest he is indoctrinated, intimidated, educated, surrounded, cajoled, and browbeaten, by all the massive social

[9] Amsterdam Assembly Series, *Man's Disorder and God's Design,* III (New York: Harper and Brothers, n.d.), p. 190.

pressures and all the psychological devices invented to appeal to his "lower nature."

We live in a prevailing moral climate from which none of us can fully escape. This fact is so significant that we shall discuss it more fully in a later chapter.

Therefore, personal influence can be exerted only through social participation, cooperation with others, and effective instruments of communication. Potent Christian influence can be generated only in the fellowship in which we "bear one another's burdens" and unite in the "new covenant" of Christ (Gal. 6:2) (Heb. 12:24). Uncoordinated and undisciplined attempts by individual Christians to do what the Lord requires of them often lead in so many directions that influence is lost in an anarchy of cross purposes. Just because there is agreement that we must live by love and by justice does not mean that we will agree upon what we ought to do to follow this faith when we face actual problems.[10] That is why we must formulate our decisions in the free fellowship of Christian sharing. Then each individual Christian in the freedom of his own conscience must take his stand. The great belief in "freedom of conscience" has often been misinterpreted to mean a sole emphasis on "lone action" and a denial of the necessity for "mutual influence" among Christians. This reason for the paralysis of influence among "free Protestants" is so significant that we shall discuss it later at greater length.

Lone action produces either disillusionment and a sense of hopelessness on the one hand, or selfish pride untempered by mutual criticism on the other. Lone individuals often go off on "queer tangents" and develop neurotic complexes that throw the individual into chaos and confusion within himself. Even the lonely and forsaken prophets like Amos or Jeremiah belonged to a fellowship or "remnant of the faithful" in which they could rise above the fear that the voice they heard was a personal hallucination, rather than the voice of God.

Lone individuals are easily intimidated or pressed into conformity by the temporary hysterias or band wagons of the world,

10 John C. Bennett, *op. cit.,* pp. 15 and 77-82.

unless they are bolstered and enlightened by the divine fellowship of inspiration and support. Much of this intimidation is both so subtle and so pervasive that it is never recognized. Solitary moral action cuts off the Christian from the fellowship of grace in which the Holy Spirit moves and works; this is the fellowship of divine influence—the church of Jesus Christ.[11] The adherence to the method of solitary personal influence, among large numbers of Christians, has resulted in a loss by default to the principalities and powers of the world; to the children of darkness who are often wiser, more determined, and more consolidated than the children of light (Luke 16:8).

Cooperative Influence

We believe that it is crystal clear that nothing short of a cooperative witness can carry the expression of the Christian faith into the world of events and decisions. This is what is meant by *Christian social action.* If Christianity is going to exert genuine influence and guidance in a world of dynamic social movements and of mass communications, it must enter the struggle for men's hearts and minds. Its influence must be vocal and coordinated, but above all it must develop channels of intercommunication in order that the fellowship of Christian concern may produce a consensus in the Spirit. If we are to generate a climate of opinion that abhors corruption and exploitation, that honors mercy and seeks justice, a broad concern and discussion that engages all Christians called through Christ will be required.

Not only must we develop the channels of concern among ourselves, we must also develop channels of influence into our communities and out into the broad context of social life in which our moral climate and our behavioral patterns are formed. Furthermore, these channels must carry a two-way circuit, not just transmitting the Christian impact out into public opinion and to centers of decision, but also in the opposite direction of social impact upon Christians and the church. Unless the real

[11] Emil Brunner, *The Misunderstanding of the Church* (Philadelphia: Westminster Press, 1953), chap. V.

problems and requirements of the community press continuously in upon the church, demanding response, its influence will be irrelevant. This often overlooked aspect of the relation of the church to society is so important that we shall return to it later.

We live in a vast, rapidly changing, interdependent society where crises arise swiftly and are acted upon by those who are in positions of control. Only groups that have developed methods of promoting moral agreement and that have means of registering their concern with vigor, at strategic times and places, can participate in the great decisions that guide our common destinies. Because Protestants have been inclined to rely upon the first two types of expression, personal feelings and personal influence, they very often fall into inaction or confusion when critical situations come to a head. Kenneth Underwood has aptly declared that Protestantism lacks vehicles of influence and comes perilously close to being "a disembodied gospel" in an organized pressure group world.[12] It is curious how many Protestants believe that in the church they ought to remain silent in moral influence when they themselves join in many secular attempts to influence opinion and events. Many cynics call this "keeping the church in its place." This is a way of keeping the Christian influence tied up and paralyzed. The one great need is "gathered Christians," working in the bond of Christ to extend their arms and amplify the sound of their voices to reach beyond the immediate and the local in order to speak audibly amidst the world's turmoil and clamor.

SUMMARY OF CHRISTIAN ACTION

In summary, Christian action, or Christian influence, demands personal responsibility in all decisions and relations. It also requires that this be carried in a fellowship of concern, discussion, criticism and action:

1. Christian action is seeking and caring for those who are lost, in trouble, disinherited, exploited, cut off. It is "doing unto

[12] Kenneth Underwood, "Problems Protestantism Faces in Contemporary Society," *Christianity and Society*, 17:2 (Spring, 1952), p. 10.

the least of these." But it goes beyond this and assumes blame and responsibility for our part in the social forces and injustices that have victimized these our brothers. It is the physician attempting to fight contagion and its causes, as well as treating the sick.

2. Christian action is building unified, corporate concern and moral consensus in Christian fellowship.

3. It is the sharing of each other's burdens in the undergirding communion of grace against vast pressures and temptations.

4. It is facing the principalities and powers of the world, not in silence or in powerless isolation, but as members one of another in the Body of Christ.

5. Christian action is leadership and not just good intentions; and it is leadership in facing actual situations of tension and conflict.

6. Christian action is true evangelism, calling men to a life of witnessing, not only by talk, but also by deeds and expressions in their careers in family, vocation, and citizenship. It is a salvation not by escape from the world but by answering the call of Christ and taking this yoke freely upon themselves in responsibility to God and to neighbor.

This, we believe, is the true Protestant tradition, especially of the free churches whose historical emphasis has been personal decision and responsibility within a free fellowship of those who have made their own response to God and are called to join one another in a mutual witness to the world.

DARE WE INFLUENCE OTHERS?

Influence is a dangerous and awesome thing. As the World Council study book on *The Responsible Society* emphasized, there are great dangers and risks involved when Christians prepare to act on social problems. As men of Christian humility, recognizing our limitations and the selfishness that tinges our interests, do we dare to attempt to lead and influence others?

From the Christian perspective, there is something presumptious in all leadership. How can we know what the real situation is? What we think is right might be wrong! Do we dare let others trust us when there is so much risk? Would it not be best to keep out of things and not stir things up? These are the questions that make sensitive people hesitate and draw back from participation in the decisions of groups and movements. This is the fear of risking responsibility. This is the dread that has made many of our fellows today seek escape and let someone else who is likely less sensitive run things. It is the spirit that allows racketeers or dictators to assume leadership and authority in cities and nations.

However, it must be remembered that someone always leads. Decisions are made whether *we* register our convictions or not. Silence is one of the most effective ways to vote in any situation. It is a vote of approval of the way things are already going. It is knuckling under to those with the most strength or pull. Leadership is inevitable and increasingly so in our specialized, interdependent world.

In government, we must work through representatives. In business, there must be managers; in churches, officers. This places more power and control in the hands of leaders. They make the decisions and gain more prestige. They "know the ropes" and get acquainted with the key people. They make the news in newspapers and have access to the channels of opinion. Even in small groups, they carry more weight and what they say is more often repeated in conversations. Influence leads to power, and power is open to misuse. That is why there is a general cynicism attached to the terms "men of influence," "big wheels," "influence peddlers": people who know the ropes and can pull the wires. Influence is control and manipulation of other people's lives, even when they voluntarily choose to follow. Nevertheless, leadership is indispensable and no group or society can exist without it.

Democracy, whether in politics or in a small church group, is the method of selecting leaders by the choice of the rank and file of members. But more important, it is keeping the channels of criticism constantly open so that leaders act under responsibility and under the threat of challenge and removal from those whom they lead. It holds that no leader is wise enough or incorruptible enough to lead others without their ongoing consent and their criticism. The Christian, above all, recognizes the temptation to misuse influence. He dares to influence only as he struggles to live under the sovereignty of God and humbly submits himself to the counterinfluence of others and to the judgment of God. Even then his most deeply inspired decisions and his most conscientiously held ideals will not be free from bias nor reflect the full will of God. As it has often been put, our relative decisions can never be safely absolutized.

THE NOT-SO-GENTLE ART OF PERSUASION

There are two methods of leadership in inducing action which are commonly distinguished: (1) persuasion and (2) compulsion. Persuasion is the method of moving others to decide by their own free wills to act in certain ways. Compulsion is the method of forcing others to comply with our demands against their own wishes. It scarcely needs stating that the Protestant Christian view favors the method of persuasion and abhors the methods of force. However, this simple distinction is not as easy as it sounds and has often been misleading. There are many kinds of compulsion and many kinds of persuasion, and the two flow together to the point that much so-called persuasion really uses intimidation.

Total compulsion is compelling a man to do something by sheer brute force, but there are many methods that are just as compulsory and more effective than brute force. Also, there are many degrees of compulsion. If a hold-up man sticks a gun in my ribs and demands my money, this is considered compulsion even if I take out my wallet and hand him my money. But is it compulsion if I obey an employer who tells me to overcharge a client or he will fire me from my job? Is it compulsion if an army "calls up" a young man even though he goes patriotically and willingly?

Most of the compulsions in the modern, civilized world are not performed with a blackjack or gun, but are forced with the more gentle art of veiled threats or cajolery. It has been said that action induced by fear is compulsion, whereas that inspired by reward is persuasion. This, too, is an oversimplification. Fear of losing a reward is still fear and may tip the decision. If a man is maneuvered into a practical situation where there is only one way out, when he takes this one alternative is he coerced or persuaded? Underworld characters, at least in mystery stories, even call their guns "persuaders."

Is social custom compulsory? Even fashions intimidate women (and men, too) into wearing all sorts of ridiculous things so they will not "look queer" and be out of style. Is the powerful pressure of fear of gossip compulsion or persuasion? If one succumbs to the crowd enthusiasm of band wagons is he really persuaded? It seems clear that somewhere between compulsion and persuasion there are at least two other methods of influence. Next to compulsion there is intimidation, which includes all types of threats that play upon our fears and compel protesting submission. Closer to persuasion is inveiglement, which induces choice but fails to really convince. Full persuasion and all genuine leadership produces action with sustaining conviction.

It has been pointed out by many writers in Christian ethics in the last few years that middle-class Americans are prone to consider all of the more subtle and silent coercions short of violence as kinds of persuasion that do not curtail free choice. A distinguished industrial leader and church member, quoted by *Information Service* of the National Council of Churches, said, "Freedom is not freedom for this or freedom from that. . . . There is no middle road of freedom. You are either for or against it."[13] This statement utterly fails to understand that all freedom is limited. Most of our decisions are made under attitudes that are biased, or situations that are already restricted in choices offered. It is said that a human being always has some choice. This is

[13] Publication of The National Council of Churches, *Information Service* (January 31, 1953).

true, but very often this choice is limited to conforming or re-signing, giving in or dying. Christian martyrs found that some-times dying was the only way out, short of giving up their faith.

When we meet many situations, it is already too late to exert influence. We have to throw our weight into cooperative proc-esses while they are still in development. The only kind of ethical freedom that ever exists for a mortal human being is the freedom to select available alternatives. No man or group ever creates any situation out of new cloth. He gets into it in mid-passage and throws what weight he can muster into its outcome. By the time a personal temptation reaches an individual and stares him in the face, the answer to it is usually only Yes or No. This zero hour is a poor time to change events. The most significant decisions are made by groups, boards, committees, staffs, or councils who vote for a policy after deliberation. They are not personal deci-sions. The earlier we get into the organized processes of influence the better chance we have to be constructive rather than having to "take it or leave it" after it is policy.

This is the real meaning of leadership: it is entering and helping our fellows to enter the community of decision before compulsion is upon us. This is the true basis for social action. Personal action tends to wait too long, until the situation has jelled and possibili-ties are narrowed.

THE DANGERS ACCOMPANYING LEADERSHIP

The worldly dangers of social leadership are ever present to the Christian as to all other human beings. Let us look at some of these dangers.

1. The kind of good community a man pictures as his goal as he enters the struggle for justice and love will be to some degree a projection of his own ideals rather than the Kingdom of God. It will be partly the kind of world he wants, partly the kind of world that he believes God wants; but in any case, not a carbon copy of a kingdom ruled by divine love or even justice.

As one of the World Council study books asserted, our vision is distorted in some measure by the historical circumstances under which we live.

2. The second great danger is that all the plans of man miscarry, because in striving for a just society he never "starts from scratch." He begins with institutions and ways of doing things that carry powerful momenta. All movements to make a better social order are reforms or rebuilding jobs in which he has to make the most of the situation at hand. He has to steer powerful forces that cannot be halted or remade; they can only be partially directed. He is partly driven, and never just driving. Unpredictable results will arise and fresh evils emerge in the conflicts of men and institutions. No reform ever produces exactly what we hope for. Some good but unrealistic intentions backfire completely. Christians believe that outcomes are in the hands of God, and are not ultimately controlled by themselves.

3. Even social changes toward justice encounter resistance. There are "good men" in favorable positions who conscientiously fight to preserve life the way it has been. Others strive for their favorite changes and there is conflict. There is always a danger that we fight for supremacy rather than justice; for what would be good for us rather than for others, or for God's purposes.

4. Then there is always the danger that the drive behind our struggle is personal aggressiveness and desire to dominate, rather than concern for neighbor and loyalty to God. As Professor Rudolph Heberle says, there are "two types of active participants in any kind of social movement: the enthusiast and the fanatic. The enthusiast is primarily inspired by the ideals of the movement, while the fanatic is primarily concerned with action."[14] It is often said that aggressive domineering personalities make the strongest leaders because of their drive and persistence. The people who make the most "fuss" often get what they want.

Under this definition, the Christian should be neither an enthusiast nor a fanatic. Enthusiasm he must have, to be sure, but

[14] Rudolf Heberle, *Social Movements* (New York: Appleton-Century-Crofts, Inc., 1951), p. 114.

his enthusiasm is based not on final faith in particular ideals but on serving Christ the Lord of love and justice who leads us into paths beyond our capacity to foresee. Heberle also describes the "political type" of person who is dominated "by a will to power for its own sake."[15] The church is not free from the fanatic and the political type of leaders, in fact it often attracts them. Even the church can sometimes provide a splendid stage on which self-centered prima donnas can perform and strong personalities intimidate their fellows in the name of the Lord. We must beware of this danger in ourselves.

5. There is the opposite temptation for leadership. It especially appeals to those who are anxious to be popular and stand well in the eyes of others. It is the attempt to win influence by playing upon the views and fears that people already have. This is not genuine leadership; it is simply mirroring to people the image of what they are. One version of this temptation is shown by those who believe that the highest value in a church is harmony. To avoid conflicts, all disagreement is side-stepped and glossed over with the result that the group is just a fine happy family that stands for nothing, refusing to enter the conflicts for righteousness. Many people are elevated to positions of so-called leadership because they are safe, friendly souls who will never push anything. As an antidote to this we must never forget that creative disagreement is the way in which the spirit moves in the Christian fellowship. The supreme temptation of the church is that it reflects, rather than leads.

6. Another great danger of Christian social leadership in the church is that it may seize upon some single issue or problem and emphasize it so strongly that all the other great moral issues are nearly forgotten. This has served to lower Christian sensitivity about other evils or injustices. It has identified the Church of Jesus Christ, not with the great mission of transformation by grace of men and communities, but with single causes. This is not only an error in strategy in promoting Christian influence, but it is a flaw in our spiritual loyalty. For instance, our churches

15 *Ibid.,* p. 103.

in America have tended to militate so strongly against gambling or alcoholic drinking that victory in one of these fields has been thought to be equivalent to bringing in the Kingdom of Christ. During the intensity of these movements, many Christians were so preoccupied that other causes of human suffering and degradation went almost unnoticed. It is true that we must center our effort on a limited number of areas at any one time, but we must never allow this to blunt our general sensitivity. Unfortunately, in the battle against exploitation and injustice, there are never any final victories in this world.

7. There is always the danger in attempting social leadership that we center our attention on minor problems and forget major problems entirely. This is the problem of "straining gnats and swallowing camels." It is always tempting to concentrate Christian concern on the support of the conventions and decencies of society and to forget the great open injustices that society condones. American Protestants have been particularly prone to emphasize the personal, self-centered sins of sensuality and have neglected the great Biblical sins of selfishness and exploitation of neighbor. It is relatively easy to raise lively concern about gambling, liquor, and vice, which are the sins of personal escape, but much harder to generate concern and action about the powerful social influences that destroy morale and drive men to such escapes.

8. There is always the danger of counter social action—the danger that the church be made a tool by special interests who attempt to mobilize the powerful emotions of religious faith to support unworthy or narrow human goals; that the power of God be distorted into supporting manipulations toward special interests or cynical ends. What greater spiritual travesty could there be than a captive church in the hands of practical atheists who do lip service to God in prayer and protestations, but make it a citadel of worldly defense and complacency or open injustice and special privileges? The church often has been tamed and made to support much of the prevailing culture, rather than struggling to be the "Body of Christ."

When we earnestly face the real dangers of Christian influence, we are sobered but not turned back. We believe that there is a Christian corrective and power that can offset these dangers.

We must approach all attempts to guide the patterns of our community with fear and trembling and with deep Christian humility. We must recognize that only as we live under self-searching Christian judgment do we dare to believe that we can be the bearers of an influence that is worthy of support. We must understand that we are often ourselves involved in the benefits that are created by injustices and that we occupy positions that bring us special privileges. We must struggle to recognize the unwitting blindness and prejudices that have influenced us from without. Our vision is often colored by the one-sided views that we have assumed out of our class and region and nationality background. If social influence is merely imposing my will, or even my personal understanding of God's Will, upon everyone else in society, then I am no different from any non-Christian. Only in a process of continuous reconciliation in love, within the Christian fellowship, and in an interchange of mutual criticism under the judgment of God, may we dare to lead. In fact, we dare not default on our leadership, for we are called in Christ to the life of Christian influence in action.

KEY QUESTIONS FOR DISCUSSION

1. How does the Christian faith influence a person's behavior?
2. What is personal Christian action?
3. How does social action differ from personal action?
4. If men expressed their Christian faith in their personal contacts, why would it still be inadequate to produce improvement in our social institutions?
5. Why is "talk" not necessarily influential? Do you believe that we place too much emphasis on talk as a method of influence?
6. What types of persuasion really rely on intimidation rather than unfettered choice?

7. What are the dangers of social action?
8. Why are the most popular leaders often without any real influence?
9. What makes the Christian more likely to be trustworthy in social leadership than a non-Christian? Or *is* he more trustworthy?
10. Discuss Professor Underwood's warning that "Protestantism runs the danger of being a disembodied gospel in a pressure group world."

RECOMMENDED READINGS

Bennett, John C., *Christian Ethics and Social Policy.* New York: Charles Scribner's Sons, 1946.

"Christian Faith and the Protestant Churches," *Social Action* (May, 1952). New York: 289 Fourth Ave., $.25.

Spurrier, William A., *Power for Action.* New York: Charles Scribner's Sons, 1948.

Underwood, Kenneth, "Problems Protestantism Faces in Contemporary Society," *Christianity and Society,* 17:2 (Spring, 1952), pp. 8-14.

CHAPTER 2

The Sea of Influence Around Us

The world today is experiencing a social crisis of unparalleled proportions. The deepest root of that disorder is the refusal of men to see and admit that their responsibility to God stands over and above . . . any earthly community and their obedience to any worldly power. . . . Two chief factors contribute to the crisis of our age. One of these is the vast concentrations of power—which are under capitalism mainly economic and under communism both economic and political. In such conditions, social evil is manifest on the largest scale not only in the greed, pride and cruelty of persons and groups; but also in the . . . inertia of huge organizations of men, which diminish their ability to act as moral and accountable beings.

Our churches . . . have often concentrated on a purely spiritual or other-worldly or individualistic interpretation of their message and their responsibility. They have often failed to understand the forces which have shaped society around them (Amsterdam Assembly Series, *The Church and the Disorder of Society* [New York: Harper and Brothers, n.d.], pp. 189, 190, 191; Report on Section III).

And his gifts were that some should be apostles, some prophets, some evangelists, some pastors and teachers . . . so that we may no longer be children, tossed to and fro and carried about with every wind of doctrine, by the cunning of men, by their craftiness in deceitful wiles (Ephesians 4:11, 14, RSV).

One of the most dangerous blind spots of our day centers about a need for an adequate understanding of the gigantic powers of social and institutional influence that inevitably play upon all living human beings. The Protestant attitude has too frequently become "soft" toward all of the secular forces that threaten to dominate the loyalties and moral values of men. We live in a moral climate that surrounds us as pervasively as the air we breathe. We are bathed and saturated in it from the moment of our birth till the moment of our death. We breathe it into our lives as continuously and as unconsciously as the oxygen of the physical world. We develop our habits in the collective pattern of society called custom. Institutions organize the various aspects of our lives. Public opinion curtails our behavior and colors and tinctures our outlook. Even our consciences are never simon-pure but reflect the values under which we have developed.

Many people have become so impressed by the power of this sea of influence around us that they say that our lives are totally determined by the social experiences and groups in which we have lived. In the Christian tradition, we believe that man has a freedom to respond to God; but the pressures of the world have always been taken very seriously. Most Christians have held that only the grace of God can extricate us and give us any degree of emancipation from the life of either static acceptance or selfish rebellion.

Early Christians were suspicious of the world that killed the martyrs and persecuted the saints. They scoffed at the penalties of the world and turned their expectations to the coming of a new Kingdom in power. The monastics gave up the dark world as hopeless and escaped to little islands of light, enclosed and secluded from worldly intrusion. Our forebears of the sects that developed into many of the denominations in America adopted the principle of "Come out and be ye separate." They formed little communities of support to give themselves mutual protection against the outer community of the world. Their chief failure manifested itself in a tendency to abandon responsibility for those outside and to underestimate the continuing penetration of the influences of the larger society even into their tight little communities.

Some modern Christians have attempted to turn their backs on the world entirely and live under the illusion that they are already living in the kingdom of heaven. Thus, the world is described as a "burning ship" and the task of the church is to get a few souls called of Christ onto the life rafts. Since even this view does not advocate immediate suicide, the man on the raft is still obliged to face the stormy voyage ahead with the waves of the world beating upon him.

The basic Protestant view has usually been stated under that well-worn phrase, "in the world but not of it." As Christians who continue to live in the world, we know it is both hopeless and sinful to try to closet ourselves away from our fellows. To do so would be to abandon our responsibility to serve "even the least of these" and to run away from the struggle for righteousness to which we are called. Furthermore, as long as we attempt to serve the Lord on the crowded ways of life we must inevitably continue to live in our families, work in our vocations with our fellowmen, and be citizens of the communities and nations in which we exist. If we hope to influence, we must submit ourselves to the counter pull; dive in and get wet.

The great opposite temptation has always been to "embrace the world"; that is, to adjust uncritically to the compulsions of the environment, join the band wagons, drift with the prevailing winds and abandon the struggle for influence. Then, for creatures of social environment, religious piety becomes a delusion and cloak by which the pressures of injustice are baptized with divine sanction.

The powerful influence of the world is not just a dark abstract cloud of evil that hovers over us. The world is the real and particular situation in which we live. It is the arena in which we conduct our lives, make our decisions, and face our temptations. It is made up of the family, neighborhood, and situation in which we work. It consists of the patterns of life in which we move and all of the influences that press upon us.

The Influence of Silent Social Conditioning

Although they are often hard to distinguish, there are two kinds of social influence. First, there is the silent conditioning in which we grow up so gradually and unconsciously that we are never aware of it. The things we learn at our mother's knee, the taken-for-granted values that we accept in daily conversation and example, seem so true that they become "common sense." They seem as self-evident as the ground we walk on, yet there is prejudice and bias and pride woven into these "moral certainties." For our most objective views are slanted and our broadest perspectives are provincial. "All have sinned and fall short of the glory of God," said St. Paul (Romans 3:23, RSV).

We believe that our family and its attitudes are right. We believe that our own nation is the most trustworthy, the most righteous, and the most democratic. Anthropologists call this universal bias, "ethnocentrism." Most of us are Baptists or Presbyterians or Roman Catholics because we were born into families of that persuasion. You can even tell what a minister will emphasize by the seminary he attended. Like fish, human beings run in "schools." We are very much "what we have belonged to." We believe passionately in what we already are, and we are what our intimate associations have made us. As Professor John C. Bennett warned in his Ayer Lectures,[1] this basic fact of life should worry us and keep us from having too much confidence in ourselves. It ought to induce the mood of searching humility. We are in truth the product of vast influences, past and present. This is part of what the Calvinists have called predestination.

The Deliberate Organized Attempts to Influence Men

The other type of social influence is that which is deliberately organized to change opinions and alter the moral climate. This

[1] John C. Bennett, "The Rediscovery of the Church in Protestantism," Ayer Lecture delivered at Colgate Rochester Divinity School, 1950.

type of influence has increased enormously in our society with new types of mass communication: radio, television, centralized press, and modern advertising. Men and groups have always tried to persuade others of the rightness of their views, but now we live in a world that is a gigantic battleground of organized influence. This has been called the struggle for men's souls. In our own time, we have witnessed the surprisingly successful attempts of Nazi Germany and Communist Russia to change the basic moral views of a whole nation by repetition, bombardment, and intimidation. These demonstrations have been terrifying examples before our eyes of the sinister possibilities of organized influence when monopolized.

We can be thankful that in America, so far, we have escaped such a complete monopoly of organized persuasion and have kept alive the freedom to influence, although even here access to the organs of appeal is far from equal. It takes money and control and organization to put on a nationwide campaign in an attempt to change the habits and the moral outlook of a nation. Efforts have been made in our generation to break down the moral sensibilities of the American people in regard to smoking by women and the smartness of social drinking. The promoters have apparently been highly satisfied with the results, as registered in the gigantic sales increases registered by these products.

We have now moved into an age in which small groups of people, equipped with outlets into almost every home in the land, can set up a campaign to sway attitudes and morals in their own special interests. So sweeping in significance is this change in the centralization of influence that it has produced one of the grave new dangers of our time.

SOLITARY INDIVIDUALS ARE NOT HUMAN BEINGS

The official report of the Oxford Conference declared:

> The church discovers each person, never as an isolated individual, but always enmeshed in a web of organic corporate relationships which surround his life in concentric circles of ever

widening radius—his family, his neighborhood, his race, his people, his nation, all humanity.[2]

One of the most important things for us to understand about the processes of influence is that human beings are not things or objects. They are not airtight little compartments existing unto themselves. As one social psychologist put it, persons do not just live "inside their own skins." Emil Brunner, the prominent Continental theologian, says we are "persons-in-community." This means that our lives are developed in an interplay of responses with other human beings. We respond to others and they respond to us. We influence each other; we share experience and, to some degree, we get over into each other's lives in the give-and-take of association. Our lives become a conversation not only of words but also of feelings and meanings. Our attitudes and our beliefs and the things we cherish are not created by ourselves, but come out of the community and are given to us in the process of sharing. Our relationships, what others do to us and what we do to others, provide the fabric out of which our personalities are woven.

This is why it is not strange that we take into ourselves as our own the loves and beliefs and biases of those with whom we share. This is the miracle and the uniqueness of men who are the children of God. We are creatures who do not live by bread alone, but by responses to others and a continual response to God's action upon us. This sensitivity, this living in the eyes of others, this limited capacity for sharing is the glory and the genius as well as the danger and the vulnerability of men.

For better or for worse, we are created, we grow, and we live in fellowship. Community is the soil and support of our careers. Community is not an option that we can take or leave. No man can deny or escape his community or the powerful influences that are part of his life. The Christian must recognize them and, by belonging to a higher community of Grace in Christ, must learn to criticize the very things of which he is made. And from

[2] *The Oxford Conference Official Report,* J. H. Oldham (editor) (Chicago: Willett, Clark, 1937), p. 201.

the higher fellowship he must strive valiantly to bring the judgment and influence of God to bear in his relations to the communities of the world. He must not submit meekly to family and community but be the leaven that improves even these.

THE FAMILY AS SOCIAL INFLUENCE

The family is the first great social influence in our lives. Beginning when we are almost totally helpless and the world is just buzzing confusion, our parents, step by step, lead us into the world of objects, words, and meanings. In the context of the family, we learn the first painful lessons of restraint and discover who we are and how we stand in the affections, approvals, and disapprovals of this new little world. By continuous guidance and imitation we build up the habits, the ways of doing things, and the early attitudes that establish the foundations of our personalities. These early patterns, developed in response to others, become so deeply and indelibly dyed into our dispositions that they tend to form enduring traits that affect our behavior the rest of our lives.

In these critical early years within the family, we also encounter the shocks, the fears, the insecurities, and resentments that often burn into our lives so deeply that later they haunt us and rise up to intrude into our conduct. Many of these anxieties and neurotic patterns that make us aggressive or timid originate in the early failures or maladjustments in the family. The relation of the parents to one another, the experiences of conflict or mutual trust, the attitudes toward others, the prejudices, and the anxieties—all register their powerful impressions.

This significance of family influence, now emphasized so greatly by students of human personality, has long been recognized by Christian leaders. We cast our influence into the lives of our children, and our failures rise to haunt us in their sins and inadequacies. How dare we face so grave a responsibility except under the aid of grace in forgiveness and guidance in the nurture of the fellowship of Christ?

But, the Family Lives in a Community

The family, then, is the first primary group in which we must translate the faith of our lives into Christian action. But in facing this responsibility, the first thing that confronts one is the impossibility of making "the home" a secluded castle surrounded with an unfordable moat. The family exists in a sea of other influences within a larger community. The family occupies a position in this community that is on the right side or the wrong side of the tracks. It is wealthy or poor or somewhere in between —well-known or obscure—a janitor's family or a banker's family—educated or uneducated—old timers or newcomers. This position will determine a great many things. It will tend to limit the range of friendships, the things to which one will be invited, even the courtship possibilities of the children, and what is most important—the attitudes and moral patterns that are considered respectable.

A great deal of careful research has been conducted in the last few years on the influence of economic and social status on attitudes and moral patterns. It seems clear that many of our attitudes and prejudices are conditioned by "who we are" in the eyes of our community. Even the virtues we cherish and the vices we abhor are influenced by the class perspectives with which we identify ourselves.

Professor Richard Niebuhr has pointed out that the vices and virtues emphasized by religious groups vary according to their basic class affiliation. The sects, working with impoverished and disinherited people, tend to stress the class virtues of fellowship, equality, mutual help in times of trouble, vigorous honesty, humility, and meekness. They especially abhor sophistication and hypocrisy.[3] The middle class emphasizes the more self-centered virtues of personal honesty, industry, sobriety, thrift, and prudence while they neglect the virtues of sympathy and fellowship.[4]

[3] H. Richard Niebuhr, *The Social Sources of Denominationalism* (New York: Henry Holt & Company, Inc., 1929), p. 32.
[4] *Ibid.,* p. 86.

As has been pointed out so frequently in the last few years, complacency about social responsibility and blindness to the significance of community are biases of the middle-class outlook. They are so deeply ingrained that they seem like gospel truth.

Our purpose here is not to describe all of the community and class influences that silently tincture our minds and consciences, but to remind us how deeply immersed we are in the culture around us. The family reacts toward its neighbors and the outer events and pressures about it. In turn, a hundred outer influences impinge upon the family and its members. Each member has his own friends, belongs to his own groups, and may develop attitudes and behavior that run into conflict with the family.

Besides these influences, there is the pressure of the vocational situations in which we carry on our work, and there is the whole area of governmental decision and influence in a massive organized world. The role of refereeing conflicts among the giants has pushed the government into more and more activity. We have added highways and air lanes and wave lengths that need policing and a gigantic defense establishment to defend us in the world struggle. All of these things necessitate employing more of our citizens. Defense requires good morale and surveillance against subversives, and so the state becomes a direct operator in the field of mass persuasion and propaganda, in addition to being a powerful silent influence.

Each aspect of our lives is institutionalized and has its patterns in which we make some adjustment to exist. Since all of our decisions must be made in situations that arise within the patterns of institutional life, it is essential that Christians be concerned with these patterns. Howard Bowen has reviewed our tradition when he says, "Protestant thinkers are . . . definite in their contention that the form of social organization at any given time and place is a matter of great importance. Christianity can be practiced only if the prevailing institutions are reasonably suitable."[5]

[5] Howard Bowen, *Social Responsibilities of Business Men* (New York: Harper and Brothers, 1953), pp. 32-33.

In the modern city, there are so many counter pulls and such a spread of personal interests and contacts that the family may literally be pulled apart. The members may do so little in common that the home becomes a mere assembling place for sleep or a short-order cafeteria. The social and financial pressures are often strong for the mother to work, and she may develop her own contacts and interests. Thus the forces of city life have a tendency to dissolve the cohesive bonds of the family and to exert a greater influence on the members than the family itself. The gang or the drug store crowd may become the primary association of the children, displacing the family and providing the persons whom they most want to please and emulate. For adults, the lodge, the vocational group, or the gang at the corner tavern or even the church circle may become primary.

One of the great problems of the modern urban world is that so many separate aspects of our lives are institutionalized; each has its organization and makes its demands upon us. Most of us belong to several groups that conflict in their goals and moral standards. If one man tries to be a Baptist deacon on Sunday, an Elk on Monday, a typical high-pressure salesman on Tuesday, he is a high priority candidate for a split personality. Personal integrity means consistency, staying in character and having a unified view of oneself. We live in a world that exposes us to powerful cross-purposes and contradictions, and when we belong to both sides of a conflict we become a human tug-of-war. Yet this is precisely where millions of people find themselves today. Sometimes we can resign from the things of which we disapprove, but very often we belong to them for better or worse and there is no escape. We can't resign from the human race or from our nation, or from the workaday world, or from our citizenship in the community, or from our families. Instead, we must learn how to live in a world of cross-fire and tension; we must learn to live under the real pressures of the world, yet call upon the grace of God to keep us from abdicating our position as his children.

The Revolution in Mass Persuasion

A new factor has been added in human life so radical in nature that the world can never quite be the same again: it has been called the revolution in communication. Most of the people in the United States read news selected and sent out by the three major press associations. Radio is piped into most of the homes in the country by the four major networks, which harangue listeners in the privacy of their own living rooms. Now television stands upon the hearth with the very presence of the supersalesman. The commentator with the suave voice dins into our ears not just advertisements but also a set of values and a climate of moral opinion. One concern spends 17 million dollars a year to advertise soap, and five advertising agencies buy nearly 75 per cent of the radio time in America.[6] The great danger of this lies in the commercial test of all our values. The truth sometimes becomes subservient to sales promotion, and the methods used appeal to the least common denominator emotions of sex, success, and popularity. Therefore, the indirect product of this barrage of persuasion is to develop a moral atmosphere that places glamour ahead of integrity and sales results ahead of truth. The extent of overclaims for products in press, radio, and television has become so notorious that it is even the jest of children. Nevertheless, advertisers continue to make surveys that they say prove their effectiveness. Either the advertisers are vastly overrating their services or they are providing a kind of persuasion that jeopardizes the basic values for which we struggle as Christians.

Then, there is always the possibility that the control of opinion might become the direct goal rather than the indirect one. Already vast campaigns have been undertaken to "sell the American way of life." This would be a highly laudable goal if it were a presentation that covered the full scale of Christian values that have been implicitly woven into the texture of American life. But this

---

[6] Frederick C. Gruber, "Radio and Television and Ethical Standards," *Annals of the American Academy of Political and Social Science* (March, 1952), p. 118.

has hardly been the case. The great Christian requirement of living under continuous divine judgment and seeking earnestly to discover our sins and defects is strikingly absent. America is depicted as "the best possible society" and the same pride and exaggeration of accomplishment are as recklessly applied to our national moral life as to cigarettes or mouthwash. Even a report from the conservative Brookings Institution deplored "the mass efforts to frighten the public into appreciating our blessings or to sell them a bill of goods by extravagant extolling of the virtues of our traditional system."[7]

Coupled with these channels of communication are all of the psychological techniques of persuasion that have been worked out in experimentations in social control. As Clyde R. Miller describes them, some of the most effective of these techniques play upon fears, prejudices, and desires with trigger words. Miller says that persuasion's first law is self-preservation. If you can convince people that they are in dire peril, they will become more open to suggestion and immediate action.[8] Relying on this device, advertisers, politicians, and professional opinion influencers work under the continuous temptation to scare their constituencies by exaggerations of perils that do exist and by bogus crises from which they can save us. Even where the dangers are very real, as in the case of communist aggression, the hysteria and fear that is fomented can scarcely help sane citizens and leaders to face the problem constructively. The introduction of fear and panic as weapons to sell products or to get elected to office or to undermine a competitor has brought a new and dangerous type of influence into our world of mass communication.

Four simple devices, says Miller, cover the basic techniques of persuasion: "the virtue device," creating acceptance by association with something good, honored, or esteemed; "the poison device," smearing with association with something bad or revolting; "the testimonial device," showing support by respectable or

---

[7] National Council of Churches, *Information Service* (October 6, 1951).

[8] Clyde R. Miller, *The Process of Persuasion* (New York: Crown Publishers, 1946), p. 139. Used by permission of the publisher.

successful people; and "the together or band wagon device," showing that everyone is doing it.

Human beings come to be thought of as "targets" or even as "suckers." Often morality is a weapon cynically used as sheep's clothing to dress up all sorts of expediencies with an aura of righteousness. In fact, the best of men unwittingly use moral claims as instruments to gain personal ends.

In fairness, it must be pointed out that modern communication does provide marvelous new methods for spreading information and bringing leaders into closer contact with people. But a microphone or a television camera is a one-way circuit, and the audience has little direct opportunity to talk back. As Everett Parker has shown, churches and educational institutions can afford little time or space; they cannot charge up the cost to the price of toothpaste or beer.

The late Professor Louis Wirth pointed out that the revolution in techniques of mass influence has produced a dramatic shift in the type of leaders who occupy the positions of greatest influence in our society. No longer are the educators and ministers in the most advantageous position to wield the symbols and develop the interpretations that capture the will and the imaginations of our people. Today the influential are more likely to be the radio commentators, the script writers, the blue-penciling editors, or even the comic-strip creators. These are now the intellectual and spiritual leaders who have contact with the broad masses of Americans, provide the subjects of conversation and debate, and shape basic attitudes.

If the mantle of effective influence has fallen upon a new set of men, it means that a new moral responsibility now falls upon these people. But as one top public relations director said recently, "Our job is not to improve morals but to sell a product; someone else will have to shoulder the morals job." This means that a tremendous task of counterinfluence falls upon Christian leaders. As a group of Christian laymen who work in this field declared at the Buffalo Laymen's conference, "We recognize that . . . every decision must be made under the acute consciousness of our personal responsibility under God. We accept our responsibility as Christians for doing everything in our power to improve the taste, standards, and sense of values of those we influence by the media we use."[9]

We need Christian writers, editors, public relations men, and advertisers who recognize that you can't separate selling from moral influence; men who understand that their basic Christian responsibility lies not merely in worshiping God on Sunday but will also fight to bring their Christian convictions into their work. And here again the lone eagle working within the framework of prevailing patterns will almost surely be overruled. He needs to belong to an organization of fellow Christians attempting to stand together to face these dilemmas.

In addition to this, the churches need a voice that is their own and that they can direct. That is why the decline in religious journalism needs to be reversed. Seventy-five years ago the most influential journals of public opinion were religious; today religious journals are "like house organs."[10] reaching only church leaders and with little leadership. They deal with narrow ecclesiastical concerns and fail miserably in giving critical interpretation of the great ethical issues that confront our nation and our world. We are told that we have few competent religious journalists who can write with color and courage and that there would be little demand among church members if we had them. It is assumed that Christians would rather look at the lurid pictures in the picture magazines and read the sophisticated filler between the colorful advertising spreads in the mass circulation weeklies. Perhaps this is true. But is it not at least remotely possible that if enough Christians understood the meaning of Christian influence, religious journalism might be revived?

Roman Catholics and the smaller Protestant sects have seized upon the instrument of radio as a means for exerting influence.

[9] *Report on North American Lay Conference on The Christian and His Daily Work* (Buffalo, February 21-24, 1952) (New York: National Council of Churches of Christ, n.d.) p. 41.

[10] Kenneth Underwood, "Problems Protestantism Faces in Contemporary Society," *Christianity and Society,* 17:2 (Spring, 1952), p. 13.

Now this is being extended into television. But main-line Protestantism (representing the major Protestant bodies) was slow in its use of this field. There are now several nationally broadcast programs, but some of these represent the minority opinion of marginal Protestantism and are highly accommodative and secular in their message. It would seem that we have not taken the revolution in influence seriously. While other voices thunder on the networks, becoming increasingly the authentic domestic voice of America, we are either misrepresented or we whisper our timid comments among ourselves. Even in the closed company of our churches our attempts to face up to the pressures that encroach upon us are not suitably vigorous to match either our gospel or the situation. Various analyses of contemporary Protestant preaching and teaching do not reveal either a depth of religious power or a relevancy of application that is likely to overcome our lag unless we can be reawakened to our task.

THE ORGANIZATIONAL REVOLUTION

Another aspect of what the late editor of *Harper's Magazine* called "the big change" is the revolution in the size and effectiveness of organizations, especially in industry and economic activity. Kenneth Boulding has described this as "the organizational revolution,"[11] in his book written in the series on Ethics and Economic Life, under the National Council of Churches. Professor Boulding traces the rise in the power and scale of economic organizations; in industry, in the form of the gigantic corporations; in labor, in the national and industry wide unions; in the great farmers' organizations; and in the national organizations of the professions, such as the American Medical Association. He analyzes the economic, political, psychological, and ethical effects of these new combinations of pressure in our society. All of these groups are organized primarily to promote and defend the interests of their members and to influence their environment favorably.

[11] Kenneth Boulding, *The Organizational Revolution* (New York: Harper and Brothers, 1953).

The methods of one usually enlists a similar response from its competitors. For example, as Boulding illustrates, "racketeering unions and racketeering employers usually go together." Therefore, in the fight for survival, each organization feels it must exert the pressure and use the methods of its competitors to survive. In international relations, this results in an armament race; in advertising, a race in intensity and luridness of appeal; in the struggle for political advantage, increased lobbying and cultivation of favorable relations with public officials through campaign gifts or even personal favors.

In brief, the result is what has come to be called "a pressure group society." Each group exists to exert influence toward increasing its power and its advantages. Since there is never a limit to what seems a satisfactory position, the struggle continues and tends to spiral upward. The eternal temptation is for every group to press on to a point that produces injustice and to use methods of intimidation and coercion, or bribery and other corrupt practices. When such patterns become widespread, individuals can justify it with that oldest and most prevalent of all defenses, "everyone has to do it to survive." "It's part of the game." Professor Boulding says of this "power struggle" of organizations: ". . . the most important problem facing mankind today is how to prevent the defense of each from becoming the destruction of all."[12]

One of the most serious problems to arise in the organizational revolution is that more and more human beings must work under the employ of others. A hundred years ago the overwhelming majority of Americans were their own bosses in their own free enterprises. They assumed responsibility for their own activities and were not dependent for their livelihood upon others. They were free farmers who sold their products on a fairly impersonal market. Or they were small merchants or craftsmen who did not worry about offending a few people if they wanted to be outspoken in their view or "strict" in their dealings.

Today, 81 per cent of American workers work for someone

12 *Ibid.*, Part I, p. 55.

else in business, industry, or government;[13] what is more important, they work in vast organizations where the majority labor under orders and make very few decisions. If their instructions are to speed up work, take ethical short cuts, or misrepresent their product, they are compelled to do so or lose their jobs. Fear of losing one's livelihood is one of the most powerful kinds of coercion in the world. There may be other jobs; but if one has a wife and children, roots in the community, seniority in his job, and has worked up the ladder a notch or two, the risks of beginning again seem overwhelming. Furthermore, it is not just a matter of meeting the requirements on the job; there is the problem of personally pleasing and standing in favor with one's superiors. Having the right attitudes, political affiliations, and meekness in keeping one's mouth shut on moral scruples or even religious beliefs may determine one's future. Therefore, there is an overpowering tendency for workers in large organizations of any kind to become affable "yes-men"—to be overwhelmingly influenced, but never influencing in return.

This is a standard ethical dilemma in a bureaucratic world. Bureaucracy is the name for any graded, large-scale organization whether it be in government, business, or other types of large-scale systems of relations. Everyone has someone over him. Everyone must please his superior. Activity has to be standardized by rules. In a case where the rules don't apply, the man above has to decide, and there is always someone else "to pass the buck to." As someone has put it, only the man at the top is responsible and he is too far removed to understand the problem or sense its ethical implications. Thus, the world of mass organizations is a world that really belongs to no one, where no one really shoulders moral responsibility or blame. Everyone is "over the barrel" or beholden to someone else and the sheer momentum of "how we do things here" determines the ethical practices that surround him.[14]

In summarizing the ethical problems created by the organiza-

13 Stuart A. Queen and David Carpenter, *The American City* (New York: McGraw-Hill Book Company, Inc., 1953), p. 210.
14 C .Wright Mills, *White Collar* (New York: Oxford University Press, 1951).

tional revolution, Professor Boulding states some "iron laws."[15] The larger the organization the more coercive it is likely to be upon its members, the less room there is for personal moral decision, and the more ineffective it becomes in righting wrongs. Another "iron law" is that the larger the organization the greater spread there will be between the power and prestige of those at the top compared with those at the bottom, with a loss of real communication and understanding. Another "iron law" is that the fewer there are of powerful organizations the more conflict and instability there will be. The fourth law is that people in large organizations fit into roles or positions which circumscribe them. Then, when you throw one set of rascals out and get a new set, they tend to behave much like the old ones. The organization and situation itself determines behavior to a great extent. If a person objects, he can only resign and let someone else with fewer scruples carry on. One last important observation that the same writer makes is that in dealing with large organizations, attempts to reform are very difficult and "the results . . . are often totally unexpected."[16]

KEY QUESTIONS FOR DISCUSSION

1. Why are the great silent working influences around us so difficult to detect?
2. Discuss the major fact of social psychology that modern religious leaders are taking so seriously: "personality is social, and only in social relationships can man be a person." Consult T. T. Swearingen, *The Community and Christian Education* (St. Louis: Bethany Press, 1950).
3. If the family is losing its primary influence in our society, how does this make us more vulnerable to mass influence?
4. To what degree do we participate in groups that are at cross-purposes and how does this place strain upon our integrity?

[15] Kenneth E. Boulding, *op. cit.*, p. 78.
[16] *Ibid.*, p. 79.

5. What is the revolution in methods of persuasion? Since mass persuasion has changed the climate of opinion toward women's smoking, do you think it influences our other attitudes?
6. How do big organizations of our society influence our church people in ways that undermine ethical responsibility?
7. How does the world of large organizations threaten individual moral responsibility?
8. In what way does our class position affect the virtues we honor and the vices we abhor?
9. Discuss Professor Bowen's statement that "Christianity can be practiced only if the prevailing institutions are reasonably suitable."
10. Discuss the moral implications of Miller's "four devices" for persuasion.

RECOMMENDED READINGS

Amsterdam Assembly Series, *Man's Disorder and God's Design,* Vol. III (World Council of Churches). New York: Harper and Brothers, n.d. Article by Joseph H. Oldham, "Technics and Civilization," pp. 29-49.

Boulding, Kenneth, *The Organizational Revolution,* Part I, pp. 3-86. New York: Harper and Brothers, 1953.

Lee, Alfred McClung, *How to Understand Propaganda.* New York: Rinehart & Company, Inc., 1952.

Meadows, Paul, *The Culture of Industrial Man.* Lincoln: University of Nebraska Press, 1950.

Mills, C. Wright, *White Collar.* New York: Oxford University Press, 1951.

Swearingen, T. T., *The Community and Christian Education.* St. Louis: Bethany Press, 1950.

"The Christian Faith and Public Opinion," *Social Action,* XVIII:4 (February, 1952).

Underwood, Kenneth, "Problems Protestantism Faces in Contemporary Society," *Christianity and Society* (Spring, 1952).

CHAPTER • 3

Our Oppressive Moral Climate

Vice is a monster of so frightful mien,
As, to be hated, needs to be seen,
Yet seen too oft, familiar with her face
We first endure, then pity, then embrace.

(Alexander Pope, *Essay on Man*, Epistle
II, Line 217).

Do not be conformed to this world but be transformed by the
renewal of your mind, that you may prove what is the will of
God, what is good and acceptable and perfect (Romans 12:2,
RSV).

We have seen that human beings live in a sea of influence that
inevitably permeates their lives, even when they are on guard;
that it is impossible to live at all unless we make some adjustment
to the patterns of behavior that regulate our fellows; that no one
is immune from the values of the "spirit of the times." Secondly,
we have reviewed the basic Christian recognition of this fact in
the historic suspicion and opposition to the world. We added the
great Calvinistic understanding of the fact that even the saved
continue to sin and to be influenced by the world.

Since we cannot escape the social world, it is imperative that
we be realistic about the prevailing atmosphere of our times so

that we may be critically responsible as Christians. We can make no comprehensive analysis of this moral climate in the brief space possible here, but we can look at a few of the more negative indications in our culture.

DEFENSIVENESS RATHER THAN HUMBLE CONFESSION

Many Americans succumb to the eternal human temptation to defend themselves without continuous Christian self-criticism under God. They brag that we live in the best possible world and try to suppress honest confession of our corporate sins and weaknesses. In our times, so blatant is this secular defensiveness that many of our contemporaries claim that Christian criticism is unpatriotic. In this spirit, we defend our sins rather than attempt to fight them. This view may be quite fitting in a dictatorship, but it has no place in the American democracy that has built the method of constructive self-criticism into its very government and institutions. But to Christians, especially, this view is intolerable. Realistic searching and the admission of how far short of the Glory of God we fall is the cardinal spirit of our faith. Nothing short of this can be considered "Christian citizenship." As F. Ernest Johnson, until his retirement Director of Research and Education for the National Council of Churches, has declared: "When the Christian gospel loses its quality of searching, disturbing criticism of accepted ways of living, it is nothing but the ashes of a fire that has burned out."[1]

In this spirit, we turn to a few of the general aspects of our moral culture and practices within which we must live.

THE SCANDAL OF CORRUPTION

Within the last few years, the public has been scandalized by the degree of corruption and blatant dishonesty revealed in government and politics. The Kefauver Committee investigations re-

[1] F. Ernest Johnson, "Neither Hot nor Cold," *Christianity and Crisis* (April 14, 1952), p. 41.

vealed a tie up between organized crime and many local governments. The exposés of favors and gifts, of deep freezes and mink coats, given and received as bribes to obtain special privileges, have shocked us. Tax collectors have been caught accepting bribes for tax reductions. Members of Congress have received handsome gifts and interests in economic enterprises for delivering special favors to their constituents.[2] Still others have been convicted of receiving kickbacks in salary from employees, and have placed friends and relatives on the payroll without their contributing work.[3] Testimony from reliable witnesses has pointed to widespread frauds and grafts. These things have been alarming to morally sensitive citizens everywhere, and indicate a lack of ethical tone among men who administer and legislate our national affairs.

Of even greater significance is that the public attitude toward investigations of corruption in government has shown a general complacency about this state of affairs.[4] Only in a political campaign was much concern generated, and then it was used as a political weapon and was not viewed as a general problem, tincturing our whole political life in both parties. After the shouting of the campaign was over, the issue dropped almost completely out of public discussion. Many naive partisans even supposed that a change of the party in power was a cure. But since the change of parties, the new administration has been harassed by exposés concerning the culpability of some of its leaders who have appeared to have used their public offices for personal gain. There has also been a striking failure in recent decades in the Congress in disciplining its members from both parties who have been involved in corrupt practices.[5] In a number of cases, convicted Congressmen have been re-elected by large majorities.

[2] H. H. Wilson, *Congress: Corruption and Compromise* (New York: Rinehart & Company, Inc., 1951).

[3] Report of the Subcommittee of Labor and Public Welfare of the United States Senate, *Ethical Standards in Government* (Washington, D.C.: Government Printing Office, 1951), p. 14.

[4] *Ibid.*

[5] H. H. Wilson, *op. cit.*

INFLUENCE PEDDLERS NOT CONFINED TO GOVERNMENT

The most important fact of all that has been highlighted by the investigations of corruption in government is that it also reflects the prevailing modes of behavior among business and professional leaders and in the general public. As the Senate subcommittee reported, after listening to testimony from hundreds of top leaders, "Ethical standards of public officials are probably higher than those prevailing in business and other walks of life."[6] More is expected of public employees than of businessmen and others. When businessmen become government officials and do what they had done regularly among their associates, it becomes graft and influence. As the committee found, "the exchanging of gifts and favors is reported to be rather general in the business community."[7] Professor George A. Graham of Princeton University says that "influence peddling . . . makes the front pages when it involves government, while in purely inter-business transactions it is seldom given a line on the financial page."[8] There seems to be little public disapproval of those who offer the bribes that government officials accept. The receivers are crooks; the givers are often thought to be smart operators.

There is a broad gap in our society between our traditional ideals of honesty and personal integrity and the basic patterns of conduct that we both practice and condone. "There is a tolerance in America for unscrupulous methods" and "acclaim for those who can make a fast buck."[9] This has been revealed in many studies in recent years. The *Reader's Digest* reported a study in 1941 in which hundreds of garages were visited by a trained mechanic who brought his car in with artificially produced breakdowns. It was discovered that 63 per cent of the garages would misrepresent the defect or charge exorbitant prices for work not

[6] Report of the Subcommittee, *op. cit.*, p. 11.

[7] *Ibid.*, p. 23.

[8] George A. Graham, *Morality in American Politics* (New York: Random House, 1952), p. 20.

[9] Report of the Subcommittee, *op. cit.*, p. 9.

done or work not needed.[10] The same widespread practice of dishonesty was discovered in radio repairing, watch repairing, and typewriter repairing.[11] A Chicago bank subjected fifty-four of its employees to a lie detector test in 1941, and 20 per cent of the employees admitted to stealing bank funds. Seventy-six per cent of the employees of a chain store confessed to stealing money or merchandise.[12]

In the dignified and honored profession of medicine, which has one of the strictest codes of ethics in the professional world, distinguished physicians have recently declared publicly that the condemned practice of fee-splitting is widespread. This practice is illegal by state law in many states and is a cause in the profession for the loss of the right to practice. The Los Angeles Better Business Bureau, in a careful study in 1948, found that 70 per cent of physicians were accepting kickbacks from drug companies. This was reported in *Time* Magazine, January 19, 1948. In an article in *The New York Times*, Dr. Louis H. Bauer, the president of the American Medical Association, at the annual meeting of the American College of Physicians, was quoted as describing the "indifference to economic and social aspects of practicing medicine."[13]

Judge Elijah Adlow of Boston in a recent magazine article traces the tremendous rise in our courts of personal injury claims, many of which are highly exaggerated. He concludes that we live in an atmosphere in which people are looking for every available excuse to get something out of the other fellow. He calls it "our something-for-nothing age."[14] At an annual meeting of the National Bar Association, one of the prominent members made a

[10] Roger William Riis, "The Repair Man Will Gyp You If You Don't Watch Out," *Reader's Digest* (July, 1941), p. 6.

[11] Roger W. Riis and John Patric, *The Repairman Will Get You If You Don't Look Out* (New York: Doubleday & Company, Inc., 1952).

[12] F. P. McAvoy, "The Lie Detector Goes Into Business," *Reader's Digest*, February, 1941, pp. 69-70. Copyright 1941, B. C. Forbes Publishing Co., Inc., New York, N. Y.

[13] *The New York Times*, April 18, 1953.

[14] Judge Elijah Adlow, "Our Something-for-Nothing Age," *The Atlantic Monthly* (May, 1953), p. 44.

speech calling for a greater enforcement of the canons of ethics of lawyers "because we have lost the confidence of the public." Testimonials before the Senate Subcommittee led the committee to report that "even the most professional practice of bona fide law firms in Washington tends to be tinged with the influence idea."[15]

Even college athletics have been tainted with bribery and "game throwing." A whole series of scandals made the headlines not too long ago. One of the accused is reported to have given as his alibi the most universal of all excuses, "everyone does it."

HONESTY NEEDS A NEW LOOK

Professor Edwin H. Sutherland and others have opened up the largely overlooked field of white-collar crime. Professor Sutherland has pointed out that the losses in crimes committed by people of reputation and prestige through the modern methods of fraud and manipulation is probably many times the losses through the recognized types of crime.[16] He found that 60 per cent of the seventy largest corporations were convicted in criminal courts of criminal behavior. Out of a total of 980 recorded decisions, between 1900 and 1944, 60 per cent of the adverse decisions occurred between 1934 and 1945.[17] But the officers of these corporations were in no way punished or even considered as criminal. No public stigma came to them, and they continued to enjoy their highly respected positions.

False advertising, in which claims for a product are falsified, is one of these crimes. This seems to be a widespread practice in our society, yet few trials are conducted and few convictions handed down. Despite this, many of the largest corporations have been convicted for such practices. There were ninety-six court decisions against twenty-eight corporations in Sutherland's

15 Report of the Subcommittee, *op. cit.*, p. 12.
16 E. H. Sutherland, *White Collar Crime* (New York: Dryden Press, 1947), pp. 12-13.
17 *Ibid.*, pp. 20 and 25.

study.[18] Even then, the criminality of the behavior is "blurred and concealed."[19] There seems to be a kind of immunity and condonement for unsocial behavior for those of "high social status."

A legal precedent has grown up that corporations cannot commit crimes. When found guilty, fines are imposed but the officers who committed them are not held responsible. This produces a kind of institutional escape for leaders in big organizations. Professor Sutherland says his research does not produce evidence that members of the upper socioeconomic class are more or less criminal.[20] It does show, however, a state of public opinion in which dishonesty is more obscured or overlooked among persons of high prestige. In our ethical climate, we have not become sensitive to the manipulative and organizational crimes that are probably far more serious to our social stability and morale than the clear-cut individual crimes of force and violence. This is whimsically illustrated by the old English verse cited in the Senate Subcommittee Report:

> The law locks up both man and woman
> Who steals the goose from off the common
> But lets the greater felon loose
> Who steals the common from the goose.[21]

MAMMON STANDS HIGH IN POPULARITY

St. Augustine in *The City of God* tells us that to determine the quality of a nation you must discover what the people cherish. It has been said that in a free economy the ways in which people spend their money is a good index of the prevailing climate of values. Every financial purchase or contribution is a revealing decision, concerning how we rank the importance of things. Since the average person only has so much money to spend, he has to select the thing that seems indispensable and leave out the

18 *Ibid.*, p. 115.
19 *Ibid.*, p. 42.
20 *Ibid.*, p. 266.
21 Report of the Subcommittee, *op. cit.*, p. 10.

things that are lower in his scale of values. Thus, every expenditure is a vote of evaluation. How we spend our money is a clue to the things we cherish most.

In this light, it is interesting to analyze how the American consumer spends his money in order to discern what the popular values of the times are. Using one of the most reliable studies,[22] conducted by a group of outstanding economists under the Twentieth Century Fund, it is illuminating to note a few significant comparisons. These figures are for the 1940's, but it is doubtful if any radical shifts have taken place. We spend three times as much money for tobacco as for the entire religious enterprise in America; six times as much for liquor; nine times as much for automobiles; and one and one-tenth times as much for movies. Our liquor bill runs higher than all we spend as consumers for religion, education, reading, and welfare and all our social service enterprises combined. The lowest estimates on what we spend on gambling run at least one and one-half times what we spend for all of our religious, educational, and social welfare purposes.[23] For all the combined attempts to enlighten and prepare our people to face life courageously and responsibly, we spend far less than for the methods of escape. We spend more to attempt to get something for nothing in the way of worldly goods than to sensitize and educate our lives to cultural and spiritual values.

Even the virtue of cleanliness seems to be losing out in the struggle of values. A recent study in the city of Cleveland showed that there are now more television sets in that city than bath tubs.[24] The people of Cleveland are better prepared to look at the soap operas than to use the soap.

Materialism or mammonism has, since New Testament days, been considered one of the principle enemies of the Christian faith. This has often been misunderstood as a belief that a Chris-

[22] J. Frederick Dewhurst and Associates, *America's Needs and Resources* (New York: Twentieth Century Fund, Inc., 1947).

[23] Foreword by the editors, *The Annals of the American Academy of Political and Social Science* (May, 1950), p. vii.

[24] *The New York Times* (July, 1953).

tian despises the basic physical means of existence. Christianity has always taken the physical instruments of life seriously and thankfully but has insisted that they must be kept under the control of the higher sovereignty of God. Whenever the material goals of life assume command of our existence and become the final ends, then the Christian must protest. Unquestionably, we live in a time when such a danger has shown itself strongly in our culture. F. Ernest Johnson states, and most Christians agree, that "the evidences of 'materialism' in the grosser meaning of the word"[25] are everywhere before us. Among these evidences, he lists "sheer pleasure seeking, [and] pre-occupation with individual gain."[26] J. H. Oldham, the eminent British churchman, says we live "in an environment in which it is taken for granted that God is irrelevant."[27]

We have been called a gadget civilization in which labor-saving and mechanical devices are cherished above moral sensitivities and even above the capacity to appreciate the values we have. "Production" has almost been deified in some of the literature of those who are trying to sell a materialistic America to Americans who are already oversold on materialism. Production is seen as the "salvation" of the moral crisis that we face, as though our moral defects can be overcome by more deep freezes or electric ironers. This fallacy is almost identical with the chief fallacy of communism: that the processes of production are all that matters; that morality is a by-product of economic forces.

So intriguing are the new playthings of our industrial culture and so persuasive is the advertising barrage that has converted most of them into felt necessities that they have become a chief preoccupation of our lives.

No one can be alive and not succumb to some degree to this preoccupation of the times, no matter how much he rebels. If we read the morning papers at breakfast, the full-page advertising spreads hit us in the eye. If we look through the magazine while

[25] F. Ernest Johnson, *op. cit.*
[26] *Ibid.*
[27] J. H. Oldham, *Work in Modern Society* (study book of the World Council of Churches) (New York: Morehouse-Gorham, 1950), p. 35.

waiting in our dentist's office, the advertising pages have the "eye appeal," not the stories. If we go for a pleasure drive in the country, even the barns are painted with billboards. Everything we hear on radio or see on television has its sales blast, delivered with the urgency of an "old time revivalist."

The most coercive aspect of all hits us in the values, the conversations, the interests, the small talk of our friends, the fashions, fads, and styles that charge the atmosphere about us with the inescapable pressure "to get one too." Even if we become the intrepid resister, frowning at every advertisement, mumbling opposition to every commercial, we have still not escaped the concentration on that eternal theme, "Material things that you can't live without." Advertisers say a negative reaction often gets better results than a positive one. Getting "mad" at a product impresses us more deeply than being "sold" on it. In the end, the negative reaction sells it. So no matter how much we object, they will get us anyway if we don't watch out.

The premium that our culture places on salesmanship and upon the manipulation and influencing of others has made influence-wielding one of the principle occupations in our society. Instead of being interested in making a better product or improving a situation, there is a tendency to concentrate on making people think it is better by using "ballyhoo" or horn-tooting. It is not surprising that many people believe that all the world is a "racket" and only a "sucker" would let his moral scruples keep him off the "gravy train." The classic statement, presenting this attitude, was given by an underworld character, before the Kefauver Committee: "Everything is a racket today. Everyone has his own racket. The stock market is a racket. Why don't they just make everything legal?"

INTIMIDATION IN THE NAME OF FREEDOM

Even freedom, the Number One virtue of the American tradition, has been running into a cold damp fog in the moral climate of America. Taking advantage of the very grave threat of communism, a number of our compatriots have set in motion a band wagon of fear and intimidation that would establish the very totalitarian way of life they claim to be fighting. The alarming thing about it is that millions of people, including many Protestants, meekly go along. They are willing to settle for a narrow-gauge kind of freedom that pretends to allow us to engage in economic activity but discards the freedom to criticize, freedom of conscience, and the freedom of speech and worship that are so imperative in keeping down all kinds of coercion. Freedom to preach and teach and to declare the judgment of God and His saving Grace is the keystone of Christian freedom in America. This is the life or death issue for Protestants. But the prevailing winds are icy cold, and many a Protestant conscience has been benumbed.

There have even been "trial-balloon" attempts to intimidate some of the outstanding Christian leaders in our land in order to kill confidence in the church and to paralyze its influence. The "big lie," which Adolph Hitler adopted as his chief weapon to undermine the opposition, is not as unpopular in the land of the free as we would hope.

Great social movements in times of unrest, fear, and confusion can gather momentum and sweep up masses of frustrated and fearful people in support of goals that they basically detest. Professor Boulding reminds us that chain reactions work among people as well as among atoms and that these reactions can get out of hand.[28] The Christian should have an anchorage before the storms that blow to keep him less tempest-tossed; and, at the same time, he should live under a divine call that ought never to allow him to be complacent about the way things are or have always been.

WE ARE ALL INFLUENCED

The first crucial lesson in freedom is to understand the forces that mold us and coerce us. Man, a child of God, has a capacity

[28] Kenneth E. Boulding, *The Organizational Revolution* (New York: Harper and Brothers, 1953).

for a limited freedom, but this is always being pressed upon and limited. An uninfluenced man has never lived—he is an illusion. To believe that one is totally free is the most enslaving illusion in the world, for we then live in unknowing conformity to our habitual compulsions, to the moral values of our cultures, and the movements of the times. We often think we are free because we merely choose what already is, in ourselves and in our community. It is illuminating to read some of the sentimental "freedom literature" that is being circulated, apparently to obscure a realistic appraisal of the heavy limitations that a massive interdependent society imposes upon its citizens.

> For 160 years, during the greatest demonstration of progress that the world has ever known, each American has been free to decide for himself how to earn money and whether to save or spend it—whether to go to school or go to work—whether to stick to his job or leave it and get another, or go into business on his own—whether to plant cotton or corn, whether to rent or build a house—how much he would (or would not) pay for a shirt or car—and what he would take for the Jersey calf or the old jalopy.[29]

The truth is that we are all highly restricted in nearly all the kinds of choices enumerated in this quotation. Great masses of people have little open choice in many of these decisions. The basic necessity of more urgent primary needs blocks the choice of saving money and of going to college and controls how much can be paid for a car.

In addition to being limited by material necessity, we are "slaves to sin," in Paul's words, and we need to be set free. We are slaves to selfish biases and passions rooted in our nature. We are culture bound; we are victims and pawns unless we can rise above our times and belong to a fellowship of grace in Christ. The first great lesson in Christian influence is to understand the pressures and restrictions of the world that weigh upon us. The position of one dependent man against the massive tides of life is hopeless.

[29] Henry Grady Weaver, *Mainspring: The Story of Human Progress and How Not to Prevent It* (Detroit: Talbot Books, 1947), p. 46.

We do not know whether the world is getting better or worse. Perhaps the best answer is to say that the possibilities for good and evil have both been vastly multiplied. We can say with greater confidence that the pressures of influence that play upon men have greatly increased. Robinson Crusoe lived in a morally less coercive world and so did our grandfathers. We are the most interdependent people in history. Evil deeds radiate consequences further. Selfishness in massive organized form endangers the equilibrium of our society far more.

Increasingly, it is being recognized that the climate of values in which people move has a very serious effect upon their responses to our efforts in Christian evangelism. People who are saturated in the kind of atmosphere that is cynical and materialistic are particularly resistant to the appeals of the Gospel. It seems to them absurd. Therefore, some climates provide very thin soil indeed for the seed of Christian commitment to take root. How men carry their preoccupations with them when they enter the churches will be discussed later. This is the reason why we must be interested in the transformation of our moral climate as well as in redemption for individual men.

THE CHRISTIAN RESPONSE TOWARD CORRUPT PATTERNS

We have reviewed some of the evidences that many fraudulent and intimidative practices are not isolated instances of deviant behavior but form rather widely prevalent patterns in our society. What is even more important is that many of these patterns are so commonplace and so accepted that they are widely condoned as legitimate and respectable. In other words, they are moralized and exonerated and no longer viewed as antisocial behavior.

Our people are so preoccupied with material pursuits and success goals, measured in wealth and possessions, that the higher loyalty of commitment to God is obscured and overshadowed. "Getting" assumes primacy over self-giving. This is not just a matter of individual values but the very ethos of the

times. Christian sensitivity demands that we be realistic in ac-
knowledging these things.

Of even greater importance, however, is the attitude and perspective with which we confront these darker aspects of our
cultural patterns and the ways in which we react toward them.
Such revelations, about the facts of the mixed state of existence,
should come as no startling surprise to Christians who are
grounded in the realistic view of human nature and the belief
that unless we are continuously subjected to restraining and
transforming actions from beyond ourselves we cannot rise far
above dominant self-seeking and uncritical conformity.

The Approach of Righteous Indignation

In confronting our defects, there are two opposite types of
response that the Christian faith should help us to avoid. The
first of these is the reaction of the shocked innocent who is always freshly aghast at each new revelation of the extent of human culpability. Often such people seem to be gleeful alarmists
reveling in the exposures of the turpitude of others. This enables
them to exonerate themselves and with self-righteous indignation
cast blame upon a set of scapegoats who by bearing punishment
or ostracism can be made to carry our corporate sins back into
the wilderness of forgetfulness. Then, too, the innocence of the
vast majority of good people can be defended—and very few
people can resist the temptation to enroll themselves in this
blameless company.

Such a view separates all men into two exclusive classes—the
good and the bad, the black and the white, the trustworthy and
the untrustworthy. The popular notion is that the overwhelming
majority of human beings, at least in our own society, are to be
trusted if given adequate freedom and economic opportunity. It
fails to recognize that all, including the best of us, are mixtures
of good and bad. It suppresses the somber truth that much of the
injustice in the world is perpetrated and supported by good-
hearted conventional men who love their children, are kind to

dogs, contribute to good causes, and even go to church. In fact, those who have the most power over the lives of others and belong to the prestige classes are usually the ones who most scrupulously adhere to the conventions of respectability. But, for the Christian, respectability—which is conferred upon those who conform to the social codes of etiquette and good taste—can never be equated with righteousness or blamelessness. The Christian, as contrasted to the conventional man, recognizes that he himself is untrustworthy and that even in socially approved conduct he is often the initiator and condoner of injustice and coercion upon others. Many pressures are inevitably created that impose suffering and injustice on others. But the pressures of social interaction are not all evil for they also provide important balancing restraints. An unrestrained freedom in which there are no restraints by laws, regulations by institutions, or the counterpressures of the claims of others would be far too taxing for human endurance and too tempting for human self-control. The Christian acknowledges the ways in which God's activity is working to restrain his selfish propensities through the restraints of community.

The man committed to Christ must first react to unethical patterns with a humble review of his own involvements rather than with an attitude of injured innocence and the blaming of others. He believes that only as he begins with self-examination, criticism, and confession under God is he justified in carrying an active challenge out into the practices of others. Then, this must become a truly participative criticism in which he shares responsibility and guilt. By the sin of omission, we silently fail to help develop moral criticism and organizational restraints and are guilty of failing in our responsibility to both God and neighbor. As participative self-critics we are entitled, indeed obligated, to criticize everything to which we belong: our families, our communities, our economy, our nation, our UN, our world. We are all part of them and they are part of us.

This kind of identification is not fully possible, and it becomes progressively harder as we move out over the barriers of separation into the more remote organizations. But, in all of the organizations, to which we can refer as our own, there is an implied acceptance of responsibility. It is easy to say: "Their political party is corrupt"; "their professional practices are fraudulent"; but never so easy if we acknowledge it as our own party or our own group. External denunciation of opponents and enemies elicits defensiveness and antagonism, not only from the other side but within ourselves. This further confirms and galvanizes our biases and deepens our alienations.

No perspective of criticism is fully reliable except that which sees the whole human community from the vantage point of all others. However, that is the perspective of infinite love which belongs to God alone. To serve Him is to set this response as the transcendent measure of ourselves.

The Approach of Cynical Complacency

The opposite attitude toward corruption, which the Christian should escape, is that of the cynic who sees himself as the true realist. He sees the fact that exploitation and corruption are always with us as a justification for complacency. He believes that human life is inevitably a hard struggle of wits and power in which the victor deserves the spoils. Righteous indignation is foolish sentimentality. Reforms are all lost causes or, even worse, a troublesome tampering with unreformable processes of existence. Since everyone is compelled to capitulate, the only sensible response is to shed moral tensions and enter the competition of shrewdness and power—"play the game."

Another device often used to support complacency, despite its incongruity with the first, is to compare our society with the worst examples of other societies, in order to find ours very good. As opposed to Nazi Germany or communist-controlled societies, our patterns seem just and our people the most fortunate in the world. From this view, it is claimed that any critic is both a subversive and an ingrate, and so the popular black-and-white fallacy is at work again. Since our society is undoubtedly more just than these others, it must be a model of perfection. In contrast, the Christian does not compare his society with horrible examples to bolster his pride, but with the Kingdom ruled by God which stands in judgment on all earthly societies. This comparison humbles him and leads him to more responsible citizenship under God.

Many nominal Christians fall into this cynical and conformist view by adding a religious justification. This is the compensatory hope that in eternity this unfortunate state will be reversed for those who meditate upon the love of God even though their practices are adjusted uncritically to the corrupt practices of the world. The struggle for righteousness is abandoned in the hope that God in his mercy forgives all who passively love him. Forgotten is the other aspect of God's activity in which He judges and chastens all for their sinful self-seeking and disloyalty. This view might be summarized in a basic creed and pretext for the "Christian Cynic": "Be not anxious, sin joyfully for your deeds will be forgiven if your sentiments are right."

In this split, between deeds and sentiments, lies the betraying fallacy of this view. Persons are whole and indivisible. There is no waterproof compartment in the human heart, undampened by the habitual loves and values we build up in daily choices. Our sentiments cannot be protected from our deeds, and our deeds are directed by the goals that really dominate our hearts. It is our accumulating decisions that become decisive in molding us, not our compensatory ideals that are relegated to moments of wishful thinking. Our ideals easily become alibis by which we salve our consciences into believing that ultimately we are seekers after these higher things. What men really love is what they choose, not what they claim they ought to love but reject.

We must conclude that neither self-righteous indignation nor cynical complacency are appropriate Christian responses to the glaring imperfections in our patterns of behavior. The humility of contrition and shame is more Christian than the aggressive anger of accusation. The mood of sorrow is more befitting than that of disdain.

However, the passive sentimentality of shame and sorrow are impotent unless carried into resolute action. Wrathful indignation against those whose behavior threatens our values is perhaps the most powerful of all motivations in mobilizing movements for reform, but it is one of the hardest to maintain, which perhaps accounts for the early collapse of many such movements. Even more dangerous is the fact that such movements cannot avoid being directed by selfish goals rather than those that represent the good of others. It is said that the Christian must hate sin but never sinners. But this view sees sin as individual acts rather than as a state of alienation from God and men. Sins and sinners cannot be separated. Divine love is directed toward sinners in spite of their sins. To say that Christians should seek such a response is a counsel of perfection, but it stands in judgment upon all of our attempts to fight injustice without becoming misanthropic. Resolute actions that can endure the cooling of anger and cut through the pretentious innocence of indignation is the response that the Christian seeks. It cannot depend merely upon wooing men individually to mend their ways. Many will not see the light. None will be perfected, but it must use the full force of its divine ministries to cultivate corporate Christian opinion among churchmen, penetrating into general public opinion. This is the attitude that loves mercy and seeks justice as the way of God for men. The Christian and Christians-in-fellowship must not hesitate to participate in the promotion of those balancing restraints, developed through consensus and formulated into law, and those provided by the strengthening of weaker centers of power. The only kinds of laws that the Christians can never support are the types that curtail free discussion, free criticism, free worship, and free social agitation through persuasion or any regulative law that is unchangeable.

The Protestant tradition supports no law, no economic system, no group, no nation, and no church as infallible or immune from criticism and the need of transformation in the hands of God. This principle has been enunciated repeatedly by Christian leaders. Said the Report of the Assembly of the World Council of

Churches at Evanston: "There can be for the Christian no ultimate authority but very God."[30] "Man and all the powers of this
world are under the sovereignty of their Maker who calls men in
families, societies and nations, and all human groups to responsibility to Him."[31]

This carries us into the social responsibilities that Christians
profess, which will be elaborated upon in the next chapter.

KEY QUESTIONS FOR DISCUSSION

1. Who is the true American patriot: the man who uncritically defends our corporate sins and weaknesses, or the one who courageously applies the disturbing criticisms of the Gospel to our
   moral climate?
2. How deeply does corruption and dishonesty in our social patterns
   affect our lives? Do you personally run into the pressures of corrupt patterns?
3. Discuss the finding of the Senate Subcommittee Report on *Ethical
   Standards in Government* that "ethical standards of public officials are probably higher than those prevailing in other walks of
   life."
4. How deeply has "tolerance for unscrupulous methods" penetrated
   our American attitudes?
5. Discuss Professor Sutherland's findings that dishonesty among
   people of higher status is more often "blurred and concealed."
6. How is it possible for the church to attempt to counteract the unethical social influences that are ingrained into the habits and attitudes of its members and accepted and defended by them?
7. Does what the Apostle Paul calls the freedom that we find in
   Christ have anything to do with freeing us from slavery to the
   social forces that influence us?
8. In what ways are the effects of evil multiplied in modern society?
9. What evidences are there that people who are saturated in a
   heavily materialistic culture are particularly resistant to the
   Gospel?

[30] Reports of the Second Assembly of the World Council of Churches, *Evanston Speaks* (New York: World Council of Churches, 1954), p. 28.
[31] *Ibid.,* p. 26.

10. What are the dangers that the response of righteous indignation toward corrupt practices become self-righteous defensiveness that can subvert our efforts toward improvement?

RECOMMENDED READINGS

Barth, Alan, *The Loyalty of Free Men.* New York: Pocket Books, 1952.

"Civil Rights in America," *Annals of the American Academy of Political and Social Science* (May, 1951).

Davis, Elmer, *But We Were Born Free.* Indianapolis: Bobbs-Merrill, 1954.

"Ethical Standards in American Public Life," *Annals of the American Academy of Political and Social Science* (March, 1952).

"Gambling in America," *Information Service* (December 2, 1950).

"Gambling," *Annals of the American Academy of Political and Social Science* (May, 1950).

Graham, George A., *Morality in American Politics.* New York: Random House, Inc., 1952.

Report of the Subcommittee of the Committee on Labor and Public Welfare, United States Senate, *Ethical Standards in Government.* Washington, D.C., United States Government Printing Office, 1951.

Rorty, James, and Moshe Decter, *McCarthy and the Communists.* Boston: Beacon Press, 1954.

Sutherland, Edwin H., *White Collar Crime.* New York: Dryden Press, 1949.

Wilcox, Clair (editor), *Civil Liberties Under Attack.* Philadelphia: University of Pennsylvania Press, 1952.

CHAPTER · 4

The Responsibility That We Profess

What then are the concerns of evangelism? One is surely so to proclaim the gospel that it will transform the groupings and patterns of society in which men and women are involved, to the end that human institutions and structures may more deeply conform to the divine intention, and respect the limiting prerogative of God. We who think ourselves converted to the Christian gospel, and who have indeed entered into its many blessings, should beware lest whole areas of our thought and outlook remain unregenerate, so that it is after all not the whole gospel to which we have been converted (Reports of the Second Assembly of the World Council of Churches, *Evanston Speaks,* pp. 19-20).

> *To the pure all things are pure, but to the corrupt and unbelieving, nothing is pure; their very minds and consciences are corrupted. They profess to know God, but they deny him by their deeds; they are detestable, disobedient, unfit for any good deed* (Titus 1:15-16, RSV).
>
> *Because when they knew God they gloried him not as God, neither were they thankful; but became vain in their imaginations, and their foolish heart was darkened. Professing themselves to be wise they became fools* (Rom. 1:21-22).

NOT THE PRIVATE GOSPEL OR THE SOCIAL GOSPEL— BUT THE FULL GOSPEL

In the early part of this century, when Washington Gladden and Walter Rauschenbusch were proclaiming a new ethical emphasis for Christians that was called the social gospel, many assumed that this was something new and added to the original personal gospel. For a number of years there was a running debate between those who claimed to represent the old-fashioned personal gospel and those who represented the new social emphasis of salvation. This debate has all but disappeared today. We now know that the basic Biblical Gospel is both intensely personal in its call to the new life and that, at the same time, it calls men into a life of Christian fellowship and responsibility in all of their relations. It brings men forgiveness and the power to be made new in Christ, but it demands the rigorous life of responsiveness in love to God and to neighbor. The teaching of Jesus went so far as to demand of us that we love our enemies and lose ourselves totally in others, if we would find God.

It was not the emphasis of living for others or of joining in a fellowship of grace that was new and untrue to the basic faith of New Testament and Protestant Christianity. It was the narrow selfish individualism of a transitional age that had penetrated several generations of Christians and corrupted their faith. This transitional age was the period in which old social patterns were breaking and men were casting aside old "inhibitions" and forming new patterns of freedom.

The early Western hope of freedom had shattered feudalism and released feverish effort in commerce and technology, and had cradled the pattern of democratic government. But the founding fathers of American democracy did not believe that men are to be trusted in an anarchistic freedom. They took the rugged Puritan view of sin seriously and thought that no man was good enough to lord it over his fellows. They set up laws for the maintenance of order and human welfare, and they established a constitution of checks and balances so that men in government could be kept under the pressure of satisfying the majority of its people. Laws were established for equity and justice to save minorities from enslavement by the majority.

This revolution of responsible freedom had a strong tendency to turn into an irresponsible individualism in Western culture that was romantic and sentimental. Many extremists talked about self-made men and imagined that human beings could be Robinson Crusoes or lone frontiersmen living unto themselves forever. Men talked about "private lives" and neglected personal responsibility to others, which is always an indispensable social requirement if a society is to endure. This rampant individual isolationism now seems to have been a relatively short and passing secular phase of Western thought. It was the freedom of democracy and the important Christian emphasis on the individual worth of human beings perverted and carried to fanciful extremes that forgot entirely our creatureliness and the social context of our lives and experiences. This is an interesting chapter in our history that is now reviewed by many of our leading historians and scholars, but the point we must emphasize is that a corrupted idea of freedom carried selfishness and irresponsibility into an extreme secular faith that has been able to distort the basic Christian views of our Protestant heritage.

This view invaded Protestantism and produced a distorted gospel. Many Protestants, forgetting the Biblical faith and their own great Protestant tradition, came to think of their religious experience as totally private and selfish. The requirement of living under the sovereignty of God as a call of total self-giving commitment to be expressed in daily living was all but forgotten. This corruption of the Christian faith was the reflection of a particular cultural era. It was a new and partial emphasis just as the extreme "social reform" kind of gospel was new, short-lived, and partial.

Today we face no such debate about the personal and the social faith. The main stream of Protestant thinking has returned to the full gospel. We now recognize that "no degree of depth in theology and no degree of warmth in piety can compensate for . . .

social insensitivity."[1] In fact, we now understand that lack of this sensitivity reveals the shallowness of our spiritual life and the hypocrisy of our piety. This broad trend toward new responsibility is shown in almost every phase of our theology and our denominational and ecumenical emphases today. There are disagreements in interpretation, but, on the whole, we profess again our responsibility for social influence in the world. However, old momentums linger on and there are still many who are shocked by the old and basic Christian tradition now revived. Some people are still so saturated in a faith that worships secular freedom, instead of God, that they mistake their own consciences for the eternal Lord of creation and redemption.

CHRISTIANITY IS NOT A MORALITY: IT IS A FAITH

Another perversion of the Christian faith that has taken place in accommodation to modern culture is the tendency to view it as a morality rather than a religion. There have been many attempts to lift out the Christian ethic as the imperishable kernel of Christianity while discarding as the chaff of an outmoded mythology its theology, its view of God's revelation in Christ, its understanding of human sin, and its faith in the creating and redeeming activities of God.

Under the impetus of rationalistic interpretations, the Christian ethic has been abstracted from its historical context and from the community of faith, which produced it, into the form of principles, ideals, or commandments that are seen as universally valid rules by which to guide human conduct. In popular secular culture, these principles are considered the great Christian contribution to our modern heritage. What is retained of Christianity is the Golden Rule and the Sermon on the Mount and the second of the two great commandments "to love thy neighbor as thyself." Even to masses of church members these noble thoughts represent the ex-

[1] John Bennett, *Christian Ethics and Social Policy* (New York: Charles Scribner's Sons, 1946), p. 3.

tent of Christian teaching. It is believed that the task of the church is to teach the moral life and that a Christian is one who attempts to lead a good life by conventional standards.

Christian theology has itself not escaped these attempts at abstraction and reformulation of a gospel and a faith into a morality. This was shown in the efforts to distill an ethic from the sayings of Jesus into normative ethical principles, or to lift out the model of the good society from the expectancy of the coming Kingdom of God as presented by Jesus. In this process of boiling out the "permanent aspects" of Biblical truth, the model of the good society often came to look strongly like the "American dream" and the ethical principles suspiciously like the code of behavior of a modern service club. It soon appeared that much of this abstract morality was a projection of modern ideals back into the context of the Bible, which distorted its message as related to its own living situation. In reaction has come the rediscovery that Christianity is primarily a religious faith and not a set of principles or norms at all. If we are careful not to fall into the moralistic meaning that has often been attributed to it, we can say that Christianity is a way of life and not a set of moral axioms or truths. However this "way" is a radical departure from the conventional avenue of decent and kindly living. It is a total way of life that is lived in response to God on the road of decision. It is not a simple directory of proscribed sins—the avoidance of which will assure goodness—nor is it a set of imperatives that will assure loyalty. We are not to be obedient to an abstract ethical demand but to the living God.

For this reason, the Christian moral life is inseparably and totally dependent upon the religious life. The interpretation of the Christian ethic depends upon our understanding of God and how He reveals himself and acts upon the world, our view of human nature, our relationship to the community of faith in the church of Christ, and the way in which we are called upon to participate in the context of personal relations and organizational responsibilities. Therefore, the Christian life is one of dynamic responsiveness to God as revealed in Christ. It is a life of commitment, of submission, of absolute loyalty. As Alexander Miller says of Christian ethics, ". . . the absolute is an absolute loyalty and not an absolute principle."[2] It is a readiness to respond to the will of God in the confronting of changing and unpredictable situations. It is an openness of heart and mind in which we submit our motives and our goals to the "no" of God's judgment and the "yes" of His transforming action upon us.

This submitting of ourselves does not take place merely in a private mystic transaction with God but within a covenant community of faith through the activity of intercommunion with one another in common relationship to Christ. It takes place as we respond to the needs of others and the restraints imposed upon our egocentric selves by their God-given right of existence. It takes place as we confront our decisions amidst the pressures and claims of men and groups in the whole context of life in which we interact. The Christian ethic is not an ethic at all in a philosophic or moralistic sense. It is "an ethic to end ethics" and all logical pursuits of abstract verbal definitions of good or right. It is a faith that asks not for specified deeds but for the self-surrender of man to a total new active orientation of his whole self toward God and the consequent relation of outgoing concern toward his neighbors. Then his responses to his fellow men and toward his ethical decisions begin to take on a new quality of openness to the needs of neighbor and to the continuous transformation under God. The ethical response of the Christian is faith standing in decision in the context of community. It is recognition of responsibility to God in every ethical situation within its limitation and possibilities. Also, it is an alertness in faith to what God is doing in every decisional situation, so that we may act under the possibilities that He opens and the restraints that He imposes. Since Christian ethics issues from a faith, it is necessary to review the basic meanings and interpretations of that faith to understand the responsibilities that we profess as Christians.

In so short a space, it is impossible to even outline the Biblical origins and the basic Protestant tradition concerning our faith and

---

[2] From *The Renewal of Man*, by Alexander Miller. Copyright 1955 by Alexander Miller, reprinted by permission of Doubleday & Company, Inc., p. 94.

our social responsibility, but it seems necessary to review several basic concepts upon which we stand.

MAN'S PREDICAMENT

The first fundamental Christian belief is that man is lost; he is enslaved and is unable to free himself. He is enslaved to his own past, which has formed and limited his personality in his own experiences, tragedies, and relations with his fellow men. His life is short and beset with fears and frustrations. He knows that he must die and learns to fight for position, for popularity, and for worldly goods. So, the more anxious he becomes, the more he struggles to get ahead and the more he excuses himself for his lack of concern for others. Facing criticism is his most painful experience and he resists it in himself and contradicts it from others.

Furthermore, he lives in a vast world of external influences. These shape and condition his temperament, his habits, his role in life, and even his thinking. There is a strong and inevitable tendency to use his mind to excuse his conduct and justify the groups with which he is identified.

Thus, a human being tends to be enslaved to his own past and his human limitations and imprisoned in his social surroundings. Nevertheless, he has a conscience that makes him dissatisfied with himself, and he knows enough in the midst of his enslavements to sense his plight. Therefore, he is not a mere thing, although he is a child of the earth; he is not a free being, though he is a child of God. He is a being suspended between the two, not fully at home in a vegetative or herd existence, and not at home with the God of love who has shown himself in the mighty revelation in Christ. His sinfulness lies not in his particular deeds, which are always partly exploitive and oppressive of others, but in his state of alienation from God and his fellows in which he has broken his covenant and lives unto himself. In this state of estrangement, defensiveness and aggressiveness tend to dominate his life as he anxiously seeks to provide his own flimsy security and define his own ends in a struggle against his God and his fellows on whom his very existence depends. The more he fights for his own security the deeper becomes his alienation and the more his focus is turned in on himself. Life in full responsiveness to God requires the surrender of self, and this is what he cannot accomplish. As Alexander Miller says, "The human dilemma . . . calls not for a resolve but for a rescue."[3] Man needs "renovation and redemption" and this requires "divine intervention."[4]

This is what we mean when we say that all men are sinners. Sin is the slavery from which we need emancipation in what Paul calls the freedom of Christ. This is why we are lost without salvation. This human predicament is true of all men. There is a secular view that some men are bad or criminal and need rehabilitation while others are decent respectable men and can be trusted to take care of themselves. Even some Christians seem to be strongly tainted with this conventional view of morality. They think that if a person does not steal or kill or commit adultery, he is a decent, upstanding man and does not need continuous grace and forgiveness. But this has never been a Biblical nor Protestant view. The fundamental Christian view is that all men are estranged from God and from fellows and need salvation to be freed from sin and bias and from pride and selfishness. All Christians believe this, in one form or another, or salvation would be an unnecessary "frill" and not the fundamental basis of our faith. As Reinhold Niebuhr has declared so often, "It is not just our worst deeds that are sinful, but our very best deeds" that are tinged with selfishness and motivated by personal bias and circumscribed by social pressure. Our best acts fall far short of the glory of God and the life of love that Christ revealed.

There is another great Protestant belief that has been basic, especially to all groups influenced by Luther and Calvin. This is the understanding that even the saved continue to sin, that they continue to blunder, and that all of their selfishness and prejudice

---

[3] From *The Renewal of Man,* by Alexander Miller. Copyright 1955 by Alexander Miller, reprinted by permission of Doubleday & Company, Inc., p. 59.
[4] *Ibid.*

has not been wiped out. Furthermore, they must continue to live under the external pressures and the internalized influences of worldly institutions and climates of opinion. This is the historic doctrine of the "continuing sinfulness of the redeemed."

It is very important to understand this great Christian belief in connection with the problem of Christian influence. Christians do not suddenly begin to radiate perfect Christian love at conversion or face all their temptations with a new iron will and perfection of attitude. They continue to be caught in baffling dilemmas and temptations, and they still are harassed with institutional pressures. One great decision does not save them from all future decisions; one great commitment does not save them from the never-ending struggle to recommit and to find new power within the fellowship of Christ for every new temptation. The Christian does not become privately trustworthy without continuously submitting himself to both restraint and transformation in meeting the claims of others and in responding to God anew in every situation.

The Call

When men come to feel their own inadequacies and enslavements, they feel the need of emancipation and rescue that can bring a newness of life. They are prepared to listen and respond to the Call of Christ. This call of God through His mighty revelation in Christ, through the events of his life, his suffering, his self-giving love, his sacrifice and his victory over death is one of Christianity's cardinal views. It is a call to rebirth, to a transformation of life, to a new centering of one's hopes and purposes. In answering this call, the individual breaks from "the prison of self love, of preoccupation with the self, its interests and securities . . . [so] as to enter creatively into the lives of others."[5] He becomes one who begins to understand that perplexing passage of Scripture, "Whosoever will lose his life for my sake, the same shall save it" (Luke 9:24). He is "the kind of man who no longer asks, 'What do I ex-

[5] Reinhold Niebuhr, "The Christian Witness in a Secular Age," *The Christian Century* (July 22, 1953), p. 840.

pect to get out of religion?' "[6] As long as a man is preoccupied with his own salvation, he has not broken from the prison of self. The old Calvinists used to put the question in its most shocking form, "Are you willing to be damned for the glory of God?"

Answering this call has often been seen as a momentary sentimental experience in which the person is released from his anxieties into a life of complacent self-righteousness—it is in reality the extreme opposite of this. It is a call to live under the sovereignty of God as a new pivotal center of our lives. Professor Robert L. Calhoun says that God's call "does not come in one loud shout."[7] It comes as we stand in need, as we face critical decisions, as we call upon Him in our temptations and dilemmas. It comes "now here, now there."

In the historic interpretation of the Reformation, it is a call to "full time Christian witnessing for all believers" that includes "the whole human person . . . demanding a total devotion involving minds, hearts and hands."[8] This call is a call to all Christians to an active expression of a new outlook and power in all aspects of their daily lives.[9] Even Martin Luther, who is sometimes accused of lacking a social emphasis concerning responsibility in the world in his great emphasis on the call, saw it as a life of ministry in daily relations. Said Luther:

> For man lives not for himself alone in the works which he does in this mortal life, but for all men on earth, yea he lives only for others and not for himself. . . . It is not possible, therefore, to take his ease in this life and abstain from works toward his neighbor. For, it has been said, he must perforce live and have converse with men. . . . To this end the Christian must have a care for his own body and strive . . . to help those who are in need, so that the strong may serve the weak and we may be the sons of God, caring and labouring the one for the other, mutually bear-

[6] From *The Renewal of Man*, by Alexander Miller. Copyright 1955 by Alexander Miller, reprinted by permission of Doubleday & Company, Inc., p. 44.

[7] Robert L. Calhoun, *God and the Day's Work* (New York: Association Press, 1943), p. 8.

[8] Robert L. Calhoun, speech at North American Laymen's Conference, "The Christian Meaning of Work and Its Relevance Today" (February, 1952).

[9] Robert L. Calhoun, *God and the Day's Work.*

ing each others' burdens and so fulfilling the law of Christ. Behold this is truly Christian life.[10]

This "call" of the Christian is not something laid only upon professional clergymen, but is a call to all believers into a life of ministry and influence in the daily round of life. In fact, this is one of the chief distinctions between the Catholic and the Protestant views carried in the historic doctrine of the "priesthood of all believers."

The second important thing about the call of the Biblical and Protestant faith is that it is a call into a divine fellowship of believers. John Calvin, another great initiator of Protestantism, also emphasized the Christian call of vocation. According to John T. McNeill, the church historian, this call as seen by Calvin is "of the individual; but it is of individuals who, normally, have been exposed to grace through the communion of saints in the church."[11] The Christian then "become[s] at once cooperatively active in that divine society, the church of God, and in the social order."[12]

THE NEW COVENANT WITH THE CHRISTIAN COMMUNITY

The call of Christ, then, is a call into a new life of fellowship in the community of Christ. It is no mere personal experience that leaves man adrift in a hostile sea of influence. The Christian "joins" a fellowship of believers, which surrounds him with fellow pilgrims among whom there is mutual support in meeting the burdens and temptations of the world. But, most important of all, this fellowship is a called community with which God has made a covenant. The chief theme of the Old Testament is that God had entered into a special relationship with the whole people of Israel.[13]

[10] Quoted by James Mackinnon, *Luther and the Reformation,* II (London: Longmans, Green & Co., Ltd., 1925), p. 269.

[11] John T. McNeill, "Reformation Sources," *Foundations of Democracy,* F. Ernest Johnson (editor) (New York: Harper and Brothers, 1947), p. 49.

[12] *Ibid.*

[13] Bernhard Anderson, *Rediscovering the Bible* (New York: Association Press, 1951), p. 72.

It was a mutual promise and decision entered into at Sinai after the act of deliverance from the Egyptians.

The great theme of the New Testament concerns a new and renewed Covenant in Christ sealed in the act of God in revealing Himself in a supreme act of love in Christ. The New Covenant with those called in Christ now continues and supersedes the old Covenant with Israel. Jesus himself spoke of the New Covenant at the last supper (Mark 14:24; Luke 22:20), and St. Paul saw the new fellowship as the New Covenant in Christ (I Corinthians 11:25; Galatians 3:15-17).

Jesus "regarded his disciples as a covenant-community."[14] Paul emphasizes this new community as the Body of Christ in which Christians are parts one of another. C. H. Dodd calls this "a community of persons who bear one another's burdens, who seek to build up one another in love and have the same thoughts in relation to one another as they have in their communion with Christ."[15] Belonging to this partnership or communion in Christ is one of the most significant aspects of the Christian faith. It is "a partnership in divine power and enthusiasm."[16]

Therefore, the Christian lives the Christian life in the church, and it is within it that the sustaining power of the Holy Spirit works. John Knox says that the "fresh activity of God" is present whenever there is genuine Christian fellowship. Emil Brunner asserts that the "original Christian church was before all a living community, [and] that the Holy Spirit worked primarily by means of communal life."[17]

We must conclude that the fellowship of the church is completely essential for the Christian life. If we are careful to make clear what we mean, we can even say that there is no salvation outside the covenant and participation in the Christian fellowship.

[14] C. H. Dodd, *The Meaning of Paul for Today* (London: George Allen & Associates, Ltd., 1922), p. 144.

[15] *Ibid.*

[16] William Temple, *Essays in Christian Politics* (New York: Longmans, Green & Company, 1927), p. 3.

[17] Emil Brunner, *Christianity and Civilization* (New York: Charles Scribner's Sons, 1949), II, p. 48.

Of course, we do not mean any specific institutionalized body. Emil Brunner in his new book describes "the misunderstanding of the Church." He says that the early church was not an administrative legalistic institution at all, but that the New Testament church was "a pure communion of persons." Furthermore, it was not an "invisible church" of all true believers, for this is a fundamentally individualistic conception. The real "communion of the fellowship with Christ . . . meant also a communion of the members one with another."[18] He declares that one cannot exist without the other. This fellowship is "the true people of the covenant" and "is nothing else than this people of God dwelling in the Spirit."[19]

This living fellowship is dynamic and loses something when its beliefs are reduced to mere creed, and its teaching reduced to dogma.[20] It assembles a congregation who come together in an "act of vital cooperation . . . a reciprocal giving and taking."[21] It had originally no laity or clergy but an equality of sharing and mutual service. All of its members shared in both the mundane tasks of work and in the renewing tasks of worship. Therefore, it was closely related to the common daily round.

It has often been held that Baptists, Congregationalists, and other free-church believers have individualized the faith, so there is no real place for the Christian fellowship in their tradition. We find that this is far from true. The kind of Christian communion that Professor Brunner outlines is an excellent description of what the early members of these sects thought of themselves and how they lived in closely knit groups of believers.

James H. Nichols in his book, *Democracy and the Churches*,[22] says it was the left-wing Puritans who provided the real basis of democracy in America through their emphasis on the free fellowship of believers in free discussion under the Holy Spirit. They believed in "a gathered church" where every member became a

[18] Emil Brunner, *The Misunderstanding of the Church*, Copyright 1953 by W. L. Jenkins, The Westminster Press, Philadelphia, p. 17.

[19] *Ibid.*, p. 24.

[20] *Ibid.*, pp. 53-54.

[21] *Ibid.*, p. 61.

[22] James H. Nichols, *Democracy and the Churches* (Philadelphia: Westminster Press, 1951).

member by deliberate choice, and where they faced the issues of life in a process of forming consensus in their common decisions.[23] It is the contention of Winthrop Hudson that the free churches in their strong sense of individual decision in binding "themselves under a solemn oath to walk in the ways of the Gospel"[24] were able to form a discipline in fellowship that gave them stronger and more sustained solidarity and influence in society than that of any other tradition.

We conclude that voluntary churches of decisional Christians, in covenant with one another under God, find the church to be the indispensable context for the Christian faith, and that they have suffered less from the great misunderstanding of the "institutionalized" authoritarian church that has affected others so heavily.

There are three great functions of the fellowship in the church that are fundamental in the Christian faith. First, in common worship and in moral discipline, this fellowship sustains and supports the believer in the communion of the Holy Spirit against the heavy intrusion and indoctrination of the world. One cannot be a Christian walking alone through the entanglements of his life and the dangers that confront him. Those who believe that they can be "just as good Christians without the church" do not understand the call of Christ into covenant, nor do they have the faintest notion of the burdens of mutual obligation that Christians take upon themselves to live by love and fellowship.

Secondly, the Christian cannot dare the presumptuous task of entering the struggle for influence in the contentious and confusing arena of life to which he is called, unless he submit his plans and his enthusiasms to the mutual criticisms of his fellow Christians. This does not mean that he should not witness alone, if he finally finds that his own conscience is not supported by his fellows, but it does mean that there is an indispensable chastening and refining that comes in interaction with others in the faith. The Amsterdam Assembly report recommended the practice "of

---

23 *Ibid.*
24 Winthrop Hudson, *The Great Tradition of the American Churches* (New York: Harper and Brothers, 1953).

Christians facing much the same problems in their occupations to pray and to take counsel together in order to find out what they should do as Christians."[25] This is part of what Professor Winthrop Hudson calls the "discipline" of the fellowship.

Thirdly, the Christian fellowship is the divine vehicle of shared influence in the community as a whole. Clarence T. Craig said, ". . . the New Testament Church was pre-eminently a witnessing community, for its members were under obligation to proclaim the word of God and live in obedience to Him."[26] It is true that the church may have become in many ways conventional and tamed in conforming to the world. Its members may be largely untouched by the fires of the Spirit, but it carries "a built in" focus of self-criticism under God. As C. H. Dodd puts it, briefly and to the point: "The Church is also bound to pronounce in Christ's name moral judgments upon human conduct beyond the limits of its own membership."[27] If the church is to be restored to power and influence, this is the kind of role to which it is ordained. Its role is not to withdraw men, not to abdicate to the lures of popularity, but to gird itself humbly to become the vehicle of divine grace for the transformation of both persons and the patterns of injustice and moral restriction under which they live. "The issue for the church is not so simple as the choice between the evangelization of individuals or the transformation of society. It is not either or, but both and."[28]

GRACE

This is one of the most common terms in the Christian vocabulary. We hear it in benedictions and sometimes in everyday conversations when someone says something happened "by the grace

[25] Amsterdam Assembly Series, *The Church and the Disorders of Society* (New York: Harper and Brothers, n.d.), III, p. 196.

[26] Clarence T. Craig, Amsterdam Assembly Series, *The Universal Church in God's Design* (New York: Harper and Brothers, n.d.), I, p. 36.

[27] C. H. Dodd, *Gospel and Law* (New York: Columbia University Press, 1951), p. 81.

[28] George Kelsey, *The Challenge of Our Economic Culture to Our Churches* (New York: Federal Council of Churches) (booklet).

of God." Professor Williams says that sometimes it means forgiveness, but more broadly it applies to the whole activity of God in human existence.[29] It is a fundamental Christian belief that God does make a difference in human affairs. We believe that he does transform human life and he does act in history. Professor Robert L. Calhoun says that He is "a working God." He acts in creation. He acted in a great act of saving grace through Christ, and he acts in history.[30] Creating, destroying evil, and saving are the primary kinds of divine activity. He works through and upon the instruments of men, prophets, and saints who are moved mightily by his grace and through common men who serve him in their daily efforts as they serve their fellows. All called Christians are humble co-workers under God "working together with him" (II Corinthians 6:1, RSV). But God also reproves and chastens men, and his greatest servants are those who are moved most deeply in continuous humble repentance. That is why the "best men" feel that they are the greatest sinners, because they become more sensitive to their selfish and compulsive deeds. As Paul said of himself, "I do not do what I want, but I do the very thing I hate" (Romans 7:15, RSV).

As we have seen, God's Grace works through the "community of grace." There He supports and empowers by the Holy Spirit and also chastens men. "God travels with men along a road . . . [and] revelation is progressive."[31] As we share, we are enlightened. But God works in mysterious ways outside of individuals and the church fellowship. He stands always above and beyond our little efforts and above the church, which so easily settles into conformity with the world. He works in spite of men and often against their well-laid plans. He visits destruction upon the intolerable evils that men accumulate in their works, and He thwarts human schemes when they go awry. He transmutes the evils men do and

[29] Daniel D. Williams, *God's Grace and Man's Hope* (New York: Harper and Brothers, 1949), p. 60.

[30] Leonard Hodgson (editor), *The Second World Conference on Faith and Order* (Edinburgh, 1937) (London: Student Christian Movement Press, 1938), pp. 224-228.

[31] Emil Brunner, *The Misunderstanding of the Church*, p. 22.

sifts the wheat from the chaff. He holds the eternal love revealed in Christ, which forgives and releases from the massive accumulated injustices of the past. This does not mean that God saves us from the consequences of our sins in this world nor allows us to escape the massive catastrophes of judgment that are visited upon us; it does mean that His chastening and redeeming activities are never ceasing and ever transforming. Man's hope lies forever, not in what we may accomplish, but in what God can do with us and with our mistakes and our efforts. We must do everything in our power and then entrust the outcome to Him.

The Life Under Continuous Divine Criticism

This leads us to one of the most often neglected yet indispensable aspects of the Christian Faith. The Christian life is lived under the continuous judgment of God, who seeks a total response of His children—love of the whole heart, the whole mind, and the whole self. Only Christ has revealed such a whole response to the Father. Sinful man cannot attain to such a focus for his life, and all of his acts fall short of such a love and commitment. Therefore, self-criticism and recognition of failure can only represent the continuing mood of the faithful.

All of the declarations or commandments of Jesus about human behavior are concerned, not with prescribed regulations, but with modes of response to God and to our fellow men. "Love your enemies." "Do good to them that hate you" (Matt. 5:44). "Love thy neighbor as thyself" (Matt. 19:19). "Be perfect even as your father in heaven is perfect" (Matt. 5:48). These commandments are a very strange kind of commandment in that they do not tell men what to do but only how to relate themselves in outgoing response to the "other." They call men out of self toward acceptance of God's will in any context of relations. They call for acts that cannot be defined in advance of what love requires in unique sets of relations.

An ethic of love can be at the same time both absolute and flexible, for it is a relating absolute that can discover what ought to be done in faithfulness only when one stands in the concrete situations. For love as an abstraction has no meaning and no content. It is a relational and responsive kind of activity. It is an imperative only in that it asks men to enter dynamically what is happening and throw their weight into every balance of decision toward the good of others in the community of love. Every outcome must be accepted as both failure and victory: failure in that we have failed to be fully responsive to God and to the welfare of others; victory in that God has foiled our biased plans and restrained us all, both weak and strong, in ways we cannot understand. We must recognize in faith that our appraisals of victories or defeats are not God's appraisals; our ways are never His ways.

This means that the Christian faith calls men to a never-ending struggle—a life of tension in which every attempt falls short of the mark and every victory opens new evils to overcome. The end of this struggle the Christian entrusts to God.

In addition to this, the Christian recognizes that his understanding of what love requires will always be faulty, because it is colored by his own narrow perspectives. And, in attempts to improve social arrangements and guide social movements, his goals will always be less than adequate. This is why our projects toward social improvement need continuous redefining and reordering in relation to unforeseen factors that corrupt our activities.

Of all the misunderstandings that have invaded Christian thought, probably, the most paralyzing is the notion that the Christian gospel is a kind of sedative that benumbs the conscience and brings an easy peace of mind. This type of peace allows the self-deluded Christian to lie down by the side of suffering and injustice and relax in the enjoyment of his own selfish blessedness.

This callousness is the precise contradiction of the sensitive responsiveness to which Christians are called. There is no escape from the dilemma that the more sensitive we are, the more we suffer; the more closely we identify ourselves with our brothers, the more their fears and pains are ours; the more closely we live in Christ, the more we sense our failures. So the peace of mind that comes to the Christian is peace in the storm, not escape to some retreat beyond the hearing of the cries and needs of men. To hide from the least of these is to hide from Christ.

This rugged life under perpetual judgment is possible because "the judgment of God carries forgiveness within it"[32]—a forgiveness that brings releasing power for new action, not just comfort for the conscience. God's power does transform and make some gains possible, although neither men nor institutions are ever perfected in this world.

FINDING GOD IN FACING DECISIONS

God may touch our lives in many ways and places. But the time we encounter God most surely is when we face dilemmas and problems demanding moral choice and action. When Jesus used the old proverb and said, "A good man out of the good treasure of his heart brings forth that which is good" (Luke 6:45), He had just asserted in the statement before that "every tree is known by his own fruit" (Luke 6:44). "Bring forth" is a primary emphasis here. What we hold passively in our hearts does not constitute the test of the Christian faith, but how we respond in the moments of decision does. And the treasures of our hearts are not our own. They have been gleaned from others and transmitted to us in the fellowship of community. Moths and rust perhaps cannot corrode the treasures of the heart, but they will not be the treasures of God unless shared, expressed, and made decisive as we confront our obligations under God. C. H. Dodd says that most of the parables of Jesus are about "the great moment when the relations between God and man were put on a new footing, when great moral issues could no longer be shirked."[33]

The most important thing about the Christian life is decision and action, not just contemplation.[34] Conversion and every experience of worship is an *act* of acceptance—a genuine response

---

[32] C. H. Dodd, *Gospel and Law,* p. 32.

[33] *Ibid.,* p. 58.

[34] Paraphrased from John A. Hutchison, "Two Decades of Social Christianity," *Christian Faith and Social Action,* John A. Hutchison (editor) (New York: Charles Scribner's Sons, 1953), p. 17.

—in which the personality is shaken and reoriented and begins again in a life of new sensitivity under God. It is not just a vision that floats through the mind. We do not meet our Lord in the easy flow of unobstructed habitual living where everything is settled. True worship is not a quiet relaxation into the torpor of self-content. In genuine worship, there is the element of shock by which our petty plans and contentments are shattered, our conscience is disturbed, and we realize we cannot go on in our well-worn grooves. In confession and humility over the inadequacy of the best that we can do, we meet our God. We are penetrated, and our best laid plans and pious wishes are overruled. We are transformed and redirected, not just in a gentle passive mood, but in confronting the agony of what we must do in response to Him. What does the Lord require of me now as I act and face the world? It may be strongly doubted that men ever fully find God except on the Damascus road of decision when in darkness they cry for the light to illuminate the crossroads. We must beware of meeting only ourselves in the rendezvous of quiet meditation, unless we are ready to decide and to act in faithfulness to God.

Too often Christians have felt that they could live their faith and confront their God in the little circular closet of the inner life, walled off from the world of relations and decisions. Sometimes the text, "as he thinketh in his heart so is he" (Proverbs 23:7) is misconstrued to support inner feelings as the substitute for decision.

The Hope That Sustains Us

Nearly all writers who trace the significant changes in the first half of the twentieth century emphasize the remarkable plunge in mood from the heights of glorious hope to the depths of despair. Early in the century the faith in inevitable progress prevailed; now fear of catastrophe and the end of an age are in the ascendency. Liston Pope warns us that probably both should be discounted. We have learned that the "forms and vitalities of social injustice are . . . more intransigent and perennial than had been assumed."[35] Corruption and selfishness are permanent aspects of the human situation, and no tinkering with social institutions will wipe them out. The hope of either perfect men or a perfect community, supporting love and justice, has been abandoned by most Christians as impossible in a finite world of selfish rivalries and limitations.

There is, of course, great danger that we be thrown into a kind of cynicism that abandons Christian responsibility. As Daniel D. Williams and Nels Ferré have insisted, there is a positive transformation by God in history or we are "shorn Samsons" indeed. Unless we hold that "real and dominant change"[36] can come, we are not Christian. Williams reminds us that hope is a "powerful and constructive force" in history, but he says we must base our hope not upon man alone but upon God's grace working "creatively and redemptively."[37]

John C. Bennett discusses what we may hope for in society. He says, "we must reject the idea that progress is inevitable."[38] He also asserts that gains that are made against the sources of evil can never be secure, but he declares that "every act of social justice, every corporate encouragement to the spiritual freedom of men, every achievement of true community is a gain."[39] He assures us that "to work for . . . institutional embodiments of justice and fraternity is to serve the Kingdom of God," and while we cannot expect the perfect society to come, the "powers of the Kingdom of God are present and working in history."[40]

Liston Pope asks whether individual social problems can be solved. This, he says, is a very different question from whether or not the Kingdom will come on earth. He states with convincing argument that they can and have been solved. This does not guar-

[35] Liston Pope, "Can Social Problems Be Solved?" *Christian Faith and Social Action*, p. 220.
[36] Nels F. S. Ferré, *Christianity and Society* (New York: Harper and Brothers, 1950), p. 136.
[37] Daniel D. Williams, *God's Grace and Man's Hope*, p. 11.
[38] John C. Bennett, "What May We Hope for in Society?" *Christianity and Crisis* (January 5, 1953), p. 179.
[39] *Ibid.*, p. 181.
[40] *Ibid.*, p. 182.

antee that fresh problems will not break out in a world of sinful men. He sees no support for the hope that all social problems will ultimately be solved.[41] He warns us not to be defeatist; transformation of many of the great injustices is a solid hope, if we confront them with vigor and persistence.

We believe with C. H. Dodd that it is a "ding dong battle all the way," but we believe that the Christian faith in the power of God's activity calls us to greater effort in the battle for justice. This is the eternal task of every Christian. We must overcome both the easy optimism that reduces effort and encourages the sin of complacency and the hopelessness of cynical pessimism. Our faithfulness in effort is more important than the specific outcomes, which we can never predict. These with our own destiny we must place in the hands of God.

THE GREAT REVIVAL OF SOCIAL RESPONSIBILITY

Every evidence seems to support the belief that in the last twenty-five years Christian social responsibility has attained a great resurgence throughout Protestantism in both Europe and America.[42] There is now a much stronger Biblical emphasis and a much more realistic view of the stubbornness of injustice in our society than was true in the period just past. Social action is not seen as simply an attempt to reform society, but as the fruits of the basic Christian faith in action. It has become clearer that concern about the institutional and moral climate surrounding the church is not something new and added, but is founded in the basic Biblical faith and is fundamental in the Protestant tradition.

Professors Dillenberger and Welch, in their historical review of the enduring and defining principles of Protestantism that run through its many periods and divisions as a distinguishing thread, find a peculiar relation of this tradition to culture. They observe that "Protestantism is, on principle," concerned with "relating its message directly to the concerns and problems of men in particu-

---

[41] Liston Pope, "Can Social Problems Be Solved?" *op. cit.,* p. 223.
[42] John C. Bennett, *Christian Ethics and Social Policy.*

lar historical periods."[43] In its principle of "protest," it acknowledges the judgment of God upon all social structures including
itself. It believes that there is no area of life exempt from criticism.
On the "positive side of the principle of protest—is the Protestant
impulse to maintain the vitality of connection between the witness
of the faith and a changing culture."[44]

Social Responsibility Shown in Theology

The great movements of theological thought, as represented by
the leading scholars in the Protestant life of America, show a
powerful impetus toward invigorated responsibility, toward bringing our Christian influence to bear upon our cultural and institutional life. Daniel D. Williams, in analyzing what present theologians are thinking, says that all four of the great Protestant ethical
traditions: The Anglican, the Lutheran, the Liberal Protestant,
and the Calvinist Puritan tradition are converging in their emphasis on the Christian judgment on society.[45] Even some of the most
conservative sects are awakening to the impossibility of promoting
the Christian life without facing social pressures and developing
decisional Christians in response to ethical issues.

Perhaps the most interesting though dangerous sign of the times
is that even disgruntled leaders who deplore Christian social action on the part of the major religious bodies have thrown their
own criticism to the winds and have become active Christian actionists. They, however, fight on the opposite side of the fence.
They want Christian action to fight strongly against attempts to
bring our injustices under Christian criticism. In other words, they
have entered the arena of influence on the side of gross materialism and the forces that spread intimidation and hysteria against
our basic social liberties. So here again, actions speak louder than
words and some of the loudest social actionists today are fighting,

[43] John Dillenberger and Claude Welch, *Protestant Christianity* (New York:
Charles Scribners' Sons, 1954), pp. 1-2.

[44] *Ibid.,* p. 324.

[45] Daniel D. Williams, *What Present Day Theologians Are Thinking* (New
York: Harper and Brothers, 1952), p. 39.

through all cooperative means possible, for America just the way it is—corruption and all.[46]

Social Responsibility Shown in Our
Seminary Training

The second major indication of the recognition of our responsibility for social influence is shown in the type of courses taught in the accredited theological seminaries in the country. This shows the weight given to social influence and action in the training of ministers. In 1948, there were seventy-eight professors teaching courses in Christian Social Ethics in the accredited seminaries. Thirty-two of these men were full-time in the field, while the rest also taught other courses. The Methodist schools led the list with the highest number of courses taught. Next, were two of the Presbyterian schools and two interdenominational schools, and then the schools affiliated with the Congregational Christian Churches. In several of the best-known seminaries, as high as 20 per cent of all courses relate to the church's responsibility to community and to social issues. In several schools, only Biblical courses were given more time.[47]

Of the seven seminaries connected with the American Baptist Convention, four stood very high in the number and variety of courses offered in Christian Social Ethics and the other three rather low. But all Baptist seminaries offered courses including Christian ethical teachings concerning social responsibility.

We must draw the conclusion that most of the major training schools for ministers of the ten largest Protestant denominations give a significant part of their teaching effort to preparing men for understanding community and social forces and to the application of the Christian faith to responsibility in these areas. It is true that some schools may still be dominated by a self-centered interpretation of the gospel and show a weakness in this field, but general

[46] John A. Hutchison, "Two Decades of Social Christianity," *op. cit.*, p. 7.
[47] Albert T. Rasmussen, "The Relation of Social Ethics to the Practical Field" (Report to the Association of Seminary Professors in the Practical Field, June 10-12, 1950).

evidence indicates that offering courses in social ethics is the basic trend.

Social Responsibility as Shown in Our Denominational Councils

A third indication is shown in the official denominational commissions or departments that have the responsibility for developing Christian social influence in their denominations. The Congregationalists have the Council for Social Action, which has provided vigorous leadership and excellent and widely used literature. This council publishes *Social Action,* one of the best journals in the field, which is used widely by other denominations. In the last few years, there has been a vigorous organized attack on this council, but it has been led by a very small minority, apparently aided by outside individuals or groups who were not even Congregationalists. A special board of review studied the work of the council and recommended a greater emphasis on grass-roots education rather than pronouncement. However, it strongly supported the right and Christian purpose of social action. Most important of all, the last two official General Councils have resolutely and overwhelmingly refused to abolish or censure the council and have commended its purposes, expressed confidence in its leaders, and reaffirmed the responsibility of Christian social action with near unanimity. Thus the Congregationalists, even under fire, in a period of special reaction, have vigorously supported the influential and judgmental role of the church and its official organization founded to promote it.

The Presbyterians have their Department of Christian Social Education and Action, which publishes the monthly journal, *Social Progress.* The American Baptist Council for Social Progress is the official arm elected by the American Baptist Convention. It was organized in 1941, and has a secretary and assistant. It has the task of promotion and education under the mandate of resolutions passed by the annual conventions. It also has carried a representative in Washington to keep a window on what is

happening in legislation in our capitol and also to interpret denominational resolutions on great issues. The Methodists have
undergone a transition. The Methodist Federation for Social Service was an independent organization, which for several years was
under fire largely because of criticisms levelled at a few leaders.
But the official Methodist response has been to organize a new
official Board of Social and Economic Relations, which will work
more responsibly and have greater access through all the official
channels of the church. Here criticism of a few individuals has
not been allowed to undermine the responsibility of Christian
social influence and has been met with greater official denominational support. The Disciples of Christ, the Evangelical and Reformed Church, and the Protestant Episcopal Church have departments and secretaries. These groups are also vigorously
carrying the ministry of social witness to their constituencies.

A period of attack on Protestant social action has served constructively to force honest rethinking of theological and Biblical
bases and of organizational responsibility. In many ways, it has
reinvigorated the determination to confront with new devotion
the intimidations of those who wish to paralyze the social influence of the church.

Social Responsibility as Shown in Our
Denominational Resolutions

A fourth indication of Protestant social and political concern
is shown in the resolutions and proclamations passed by the
national conventions, assemblies, and councils of the major denominations.

At the 1955 American Baptist Convention, resolutions on
thirty-one subjects were passed by that body. One of these was
a routine resolution of appreciation to the hosts; one was a
resolution to have more discussion and study in order to make
resolutions more meaningful, together with a general call to the
churches to positive action and expression of convictions to
legislators; eight concerned denominational affairs; one concerned

interdenominational relations; and all of the rest, twenty of them, made declarations about social, political, and international issues and responsibilities of various kinds. These touched problems all the way from Indian affairs to support of the United Nations.

One of the resolutions declared that "the gospel applies to all areas of life, including the political," and it urged that "our people participate actively in political life." Other resolutions declared against the imposition of loyalty oaths on churches under the threat of withdrawing tax exemption; against "the legalizing of the manufacture, sale, and use of beverage alcohol"; against "a permanent peacetime system of military conscription"; and against gambling in any form. It urged vigorous support of the UN and its Atoms for Peace, Technical Assistance, and International Children's Emergencies Fund programs. It urged our government to revise the McCarran-Walter Act on immigration as being too restrictive. It supported the principle of "coexistence" with other nations, urging that we refrain from "malicious criticism of one another," and endorsed negotiation with Communist China on a cease fire in the Formosa Strait. Other resolutions covered other aspects of social and governmental policy.

Other issues covered in the 1953 and 1954 Baptist resolutions were civil liberties, labor-management relations, housing, racial segregation, and stewardship of natural resources.

In continuity with Assemblies of prior years, the 167th General Assembly of the Presbyterian Church in the United States of America passed a long and comprehensive list of pronouncements, as recommended by the Department of Social Education and Action of the Board of Christian Education.[48] These social deliverances declared the responsibility of both the church as a corporate body and individual Christians to "take sides in the struggle between light and darkness." In this inspiring document, which is worthy of study by all Protestants, Christians were called upon "to relate faith to fact" and "to seek to be an influence in political life."

[48] Adopted at the 167th General Assembly at Los Angeles, May 24, 1955, reported in *Social Progress* (July, 1955).

It called upon our nation in international affairs to go beyond "coexistence" toward "peaceful competition with growing cooperation."[49] It called for reaffirmed and renewed support of the United Nations, of negotiation as a method of settling international problems, and of "elimination and prohibition of all weapons of mass destruction . . . under adequate arrangements for international inspection and control." It supported foreign aid, the Expanded Program of Technical Assistance and the UN International Children's Fund. It opposed "peacetime conscription and universal military training" and reaffirmed "the widely acclaimed *Letter to Presbyterians,* adopted by the 166th General Assembly," on the rights and freedoms of our religious and political heritage.

It called for "operation desegregation" to remove racial segregation from the churches. It emphasized the importance "for churches to join with other institutions and agencies . . . in community planning and in serving various community needs." Many other areas urgently requiring Christian influence and witness are enumerated in these deliverances. In addition, it is stated that all of the social deliverances of the General Assembly in recent years "are commended to the churches . . . for study and action." Specially listed are "those dealing with international affairs, foreign aid, colonialism, immigration, refugee resettlement, freedom and civil liberties, Indian affairs, agricultural surpluses, migratory farm labor, farm price policies, conservation and development of natural resources, industrial relations, problems of alcohol, gambling, housing, education, and other community problems."[50]

A memorable resolution on civil liberties and one in condemnation of the contemporary attacks on religious and political freedoms was passed by the 165th General Assembly in July, 1953, at a time when hysteria and the atmosphere of intimidation were at a peak. George Dugan reported that it was "regarded by observers here as one of the most forthright statements on

[49] *Ibid.,* p. 7.
[50] *Ibid.,* p. 5.

civil liberties ever issued by a national Protestant Church body."[51]

The Congregational Christian denomination at its last General Council meeting covered much the same territory in its resolutions as the Baptists and Presbyterians and vigorously maintain its traditional concern for the witness of the Christian Church in all the significant affairs of our society. Out of twenty-two resolutions, eleven directly concerned specific issues or a call to vigorous political and social responsibility.[52] Laymen were charged with a definite responsibility "to make our churches better instruments of Jesus Christ, the better to serve the community in which they are located and the world community." It was also "resolved that we urge our lay members and ministers to become active in the political parties of their individual persuasion, that the Christian ethic may be more completely expressed in all affairs of state and on all levels of political life." The support of UN was reaffirmed. "Political demagoguery that confuses dissent with disloyalty" was repudiated and a warning issued "against the false witness of innuendo and insinuation of the . . . concealed informer." Another resolution called for the development of public support and "timely and tolerant implementation of the Supreme Court decision" against segregation in the public schools. Still other resolutions called for support of technical assistance, "the use of surplus commodities to alleviate human suffering," "adequate housing," and the preservation of Indian rights.

The immediately prior General Council meeting in June, 1952, had voted "that every economic order must be evaluated and its practices judged in the light of the Gospel; and that it is our Christian responsibility not only to bring Christ to the individual, but also to bring his teachings to bear upon the corporate problems of our society."[53]

Lack of space prevents continuing a brief analysis of official

---

[51] George Dugan, *The New York Times* (July 2, 1953).

[52] Resolutions of the General Council of the Congregational Christian Churches at New Haven, Connecticut (June, 1954).

[53] Official Resolutions adopted by the General Council of the Congregational Christian Churches at Claremont, California (June, 1952).

pronouncements of other major Protestant bodies. But the same general spirit of determination to assume responsibility under God to cast the Christian influence into the formation of policy in our corporate life is professed with equal clarity by most of them.

One can only conclude that if these great church bodies really mean half of what they officially declare they have taken upon themselves in no uncertain terms the task of Christian social influence as a sacred commitment to their Lord. Whether or not these statements really express the convictions, upon which the Protestants whom they represent are willing to act, is another matter that we shall discuss in a following chapter.

Social Responsibility as Emphasized in National and World Councils and Conferences

In addition to these great social emphases in denominations, the National Council of Churches (formerly the Federal Council) and its various departments and the great ecumenical conferences and world missionary meetings have affirmed the Christian responsibility toward the culture and institutions of our world.

The International Missionary Conference, held in Jerusalem in 1928, acknowledged with "shame and regret" that Christians have not been sensitive enough "to mitigate the evils which . . . industrialism has brought in its train."[54] A later meeting, held in Madras in 1938, with representatives from major groups around the world, recognized that converting individuals is not enough unless "you organize those changed individuals into collective action in a wide scale frontal attack upon those corporate evils."[55] It was also declared that "it is a half truth to say that changed individuals will necessarily change the social order, it

[54] Jerusalem Meeting, International Missionary Conference of 1928, *Ecumenical Documents of Church and Society* (Geneva: World Council of Churches, 1954), p. 10.

[55] Finding and Recommendations, Madras Meeting of 1938, *The World Mission of the Church* (New York: International Missionary Council, 1938), p. 127.

is also a half truth to say that social change will necessarily produce individual change."[56]

Several great world conferences of Christian leaders (which
were the origin of the World Council of Churches) were nurtured
in a revived sense of responsibility for Christian influence. The
Universal Conference on Life and Work, held in Stockholm in
1925, said in these vigorous words: "Responding to His call
'Follow me,' we have in the presence of the Cross accepted the
urgent duty of applying His gospel in all realms of human life—
industrial, social, political and international."[57] And again at
the now-famed World Conference on Church, Community, and
State (held in Oxford, England in 1937) came the same kind
of growing conviction among Christian leaders: "Christianity
becomes socially futile if it does not recognize . . . that the
Christian is under an obligation to secure the best possible social
and economic structure, insofar as such structure is determined
by human decisions."[58] Just after the founding of the World
Council at Amsterdam in 1948, which had so much to say upon
the imperative of Christian influence, its Study Department said:
"The recognition that the churches do have responsibility for the
common life, for political and economic institutions, is now a
part of real ecumenical consensus."[59] The Reports of the Evanston Assembly gave new confirmation to the strength of this trend.
In the Report of Section III, it is asserted, "From Christ men
receive the direction for their service, the obligation to share
heartily in the world's work and daily tasks, and the responsibility
to seek a better social and political life." It also declared, "The
churches have come to realize more fully that they have a duty
to society as part of their mission in the world."[60]

[56] *Ibid.*
[57] The Message of the Universal Christian Conference on Life and Work,
Stockholm (August, 1925), *Ecumenical Documents on Church and Society,
op. cit.,* p. 3.
[58] *The Oxford Conference, Official Report* (Chicago: Willett, Clark, 1937),
p. 78.
[59] *Christian Action in Society* (New York: World Council of Churches,
1949), p. 11.
[60] Reports of the Second Assembly of the World Council of Churches, *Evanston Speaks* (New York: World Council of Churches, 1954), p. 26.

The Federal Council of Churches of Christ was founded on the principle that the denominations could cooperate in registering influence upon our society, even though they had disagreements in doctrinal matters.[61] Among its primary objectives, as stated in its statement of organization, was this one: "To secure a larger combined influence for the churches of Christ in all matters affecting the moral and social conditions of the people, so as to promote the application of the law of Christ in every relation of human life."[62] In 1908, the Federal Council adopted *The Social Creed of the Churches,* which took a stand on fourteen great ethical problems of our society. In 1932, there was a revision into *The Social Ideals of the Churches.*

By the time the Federal Council had joined the National Council of Churches in 1950, there had been some shifts in the theological basis for cooperative influence; but the statements of the new council continued to express the same moral demand and urgency for common action.

In a statement issued by the Department of Life and Work of the new Council, it reviewed "the Christian's community responsibility" and stated:

> The dedicated Christian has responsibilities as a citizen of a secular state and as a member of the community . . . it is not enough for the Christian to reaffirm his faith. He needs to make choices on the basis of his faith in areas which he may not have been in the habit of relating to his religious convictions.[63]

In 1954, after several years of painstaking discussion and revision, another great statement was adopted by the General Board of the National Council of Churches. This was entitled *Christian Principles and Assumptions for Economic Life.*[64] Although it is

[61] John A. Hutchison, *We Are Not Divided* (New York: Round Table Press, Inc., 1941), chap. II.

[62] *Ibid.,* p. 36.

[63] *The National Council of Churches Views Its Tasks in Christian Life and Work* (pamphlet of the National Council of Churches, 1951), statement of the Division of Christian Life and Work of the National Council of Churches of Christ in the United States of America and approved by the General Board of the Council.
pamphlet form, Department of Church and Economic Life, National Council of Churches) (New York: 297 Fourth Avenue). $.10.

[64] *Christian Principles and Assumptions for Economic Life* (available in

directed mainly to our economic life, which has always been one of the most controversial areas, it has many general implications for broad social influence. This statement has been regarded as another milestone in continuity with *The Social Creed of the Churches* (1908) and *The Social Ideals of the Churches* (1932).

The statement on Christian principles and assumptions reveals changes that have taken place in Christian ethical thought and a recognition of new dangers to responsible freedom that have shown themselves in the last twenty-five years.[65] But again, and with relevancy to the conditions of our times, it declares that "the churches dare not abandon the prophetic role," which it sees as "the churches' mandatory responsibility under the Gospel." It states that "the church is under a divine imperative to call all men—and especially its own members—to recognize the meaning of God's Lordship over their economic activities."

In the last few years, various departments of the Council have had a number of significant meetings which have assembled representatives from the clergy and laity of all the participating denominations. The Department of the Church and Economic Life has held three great national meetings, at Pittsburgh in 1948 under the Federal Council, in Detroit in 1950, and in Buffalo in 1952. These meetings have attempted to help us find guidance from our faith for the great economic problems of our times.

The Pittsburgh conference report said:

> The ethical doctrines [of Christianity] . . . are of unlimited scope, and relevant to all areas of human relations. . . . The principles of the Christian Gospel are applicable to the structure of social relations and to the organization of society, as well as to the personal relations of human beings.[66]

We can only conclude that from our Biblical and historical foundations and from the great Protestant convictions of our

[65] An excellent discussion on this statement can be found in Robert T. Handy, "From 'Social Ideals' to 'Norms for Guidance,' " *Christianity and Crisis*, XIV:24 (January 24, 1955).

[66] *Report of the National Study Conference on the Church and Economic Life* (Pittsburgh, Pennsylvania) (New York: Federal Council of Churches, February 1948), p. 8.

generation that we profess a faith in Christ that demands that we share in a cooperative impact upon our society and our world.

The degree to which we are faithful to our Gospel and this commitment that Protestants so strongly profess is the topic of the next chapter.

KEY QUESTIONS FOR DISCUSSION

1. Why is the "private" version of the gospel, which emphasizes an intensely selfish experience, unfaithful to the Biblical gospel?
2. In what ways are all men enslaved—no matter how good they are—and, therefore, in need of emancipation?
3. Discuss the declaration: "It is not just our worst deeds that are sinful, but our very best deeds."
4. What is the full meaning of the "Call in Christ"? Is it a call to continuous decision and influence through daily living?
5. Discuss the great Christian principle that the Christian life can be lived only in Christian fellowship.
6. What are the basic functions of the Christian church?
7. What does the term "grace" mean to you? How does the church help to bring divine grace?
8. In what ways do you believe that the Christian view of "living under continuous divine criticism" is often neglected?
9. May Christians hope to build a perfect society? What sustains their efforts toward social justice?
10. What are the reasons for believing that a great revival is taking place in our understanding of our Christian social responsibility?

RECOMMENDED READINGS

Amsterdam Assembly Series, *Man's Disorder and God's Design* (Reports on Four Sections of the Amsterdam Assembly of the World Council of Churches). New York: Harper and Brothers, n.d.

Anderson, Bernhard W., *Rediscovering the Bible*. New York: Association Press, 1951.

Brunner, Emil, *The Misunderstanding of the Church*. Philadelphia: Westminster Press, 1953.

Christian Action in Society (an ecumenical inquiry published by the Study Department of the World Council of Churches, 297 Fourth Ave., New York 10, New York, 1949).

Dillenberger, John, and Claude Welch, *Protestant Christianity.* New York: Charles Scribner's Sons, 1954.

Dodd, C. H., *Gospel and Law.* New York: Columbia University Press, 1951.

Ecumenical Documents on Church and Society, 1925-1953. Geneva, Switzerland: World Council of Churches, 1954.

Evanston Speaks. New York: World Council of Churches, 156 Fifth Ave., 1954.

Hutchison, John A. (editor), *Christian Faith and Social Action.* New York: Charles Scribner's Sons, 1953.

Richardson, Alan, and Wolfgang Schweitzer, *Biblical Authority for Today* (A World Council of Churches' Symposium on the Biblical Authority for the Church's Social and Political Message Today). Philadelphia: Westminster Press, 1951.

Williams, Daniel Day, *What Present Day Theologians Are Thinking* (especially chap. III). New York: Harper and Brothers, 1952.

CHAPTER 5

Weakness of the Churches' Influence

. . . the evils of the world have so deeply penetrated our churches
. . . that amongst us too there are worldly standards of success, class
division, economic rivalry, a secular mind (Report on Section I, The
Universal Church in God's Design, *Man's Disorder and God's De-*
sign [Amsterdam Assembly Series] [New York: Harper and Brothers,
n.d.], p. 208).

. . . I will find out not the talk of these arrogant people but
their power. For the Kingdom of God does not consist in talk
but in power (I Corinthians 4:19-20, RSV).

WEAKNESS DESPITE SIZE

We began the first chapter with a question: Why is there such a
disturbing discrepancy between the numerical size of the church
and its influence in our nation? In 1953 this headline appeared in the morning paper: "Church Membership Soars to
Record High." The story beneath this headline began: "Churches
in the United States have been adding new members at the fastest
rate in history, the National Council of Churches said yesterday."[1]

[1] *Rochester Democrat and Chronicle* (August 24, 1953).

This release went on to say that this was a 4.1 per cent increase and was a growth two and a half times as fast as the population. At that time 59 per cent of the population were members of churches; there were over fifty-four million Protestants in America.

Recently, the release of the latest *Yearbook of the American Churches* compiled by the National Council of Churches shows that there are now over fifty-seven million Protestants, and that 60.3 per cent of Americans belong to churches or Jewish temples. The opening sentence of the article in *The New York Times* reporting these figures says, "Interest in religion, as measured by church and temple membership, has reached new heights."[2] The rate of growth of church membership continues to exceed the rate of growth of the population.

If we couple this size and growth with the vigorous ethical professions that we declare, this should add up to a powerful transforming influence in our society. Yet, I am sure that most of us would agree that there is no necessary relation between size and influence. It may even be, as Franklin H. Littell has suggested, that "tremendous expansion of membership has been bought at the price of relaxing internal discipline"[3] and the forfeiting of real influence.

The total budget of the religious enterprise in America has also been soaring to an all-time high. *Time* magazine reported that "the U. S. is witnessing the greatest church-building boom in its history."[4] It stated that $3 billion has been spent in the construction of churches in the last decade and that estimates for the next decade are for over $7 billion. Tremendous financial crusades and campaigns have been carried out successfully in the last ten years "to extend the influence of Christ." But here again prosperity does not mean impact. In fact, it may mean just the opposite. Is it possible that the more money that is

[2] *The New York Times* (September 5, 1955).
[3] Franklin H. Littell, "Pastoral Care Under Totalitarianism," *Christianity and Crisis* (April 13, 1953), p. 45.
[4] *Time* (September 19, 1955), p. 76.

raised the more the vigor of the gospel is watered down in its claims upon our lives?

Eugene Carson Blake, the President of the National Council, has recently warned that a religious boom may be a spiritual "bust." He believes that at the very time that church membership is on the upsurge, morality is on the decline. He recites the facts that show how everybody seems to be getting interested in religion. However, he warns that "many people with new religious interest are attempting to turn that interest into magic—to use God for their own purposes rather than to serve God and find his purposes."[5]

Dean James A. Pike, in commenting on the upswing in religious interest in an address to the Triennial General Convention of the Protestant Episcopal Church said, "While trumpeting our religiousness we do not in our personal and corporate action and attitudes sufficiently display that we really mean what we say."[6]

It is not easy to estimate Christian influence in a society; we must always take account of the vast amount of unrecognized influence of religion in our culture in the same way that there is a vast amount of unrecognized influence of society upon religion. But very few honest critics would hold that this is a time of dominant Christian influence. "The churches mirror rather than change" is the lament of churchmen everywhere. The Senate Subcommittee report, *Ethical Standards in Government,* asked whether or not widespread corruption indicates that the moral influence of the church has declined.[7]

F. Ernest Johnson analyzes the impact of the churches on public morality in an excellent article in *The Annals of the American Academy of Political and Social Science.*[8] Dr. John-

---

[5] *Look* (September 20, 1955), p. 29.

[6] George Dugan, *The New York Times* (September 6, 1955).

[7] Subcommittee of the Committee of Labor and Public Welfare, United States Senate, *Ethical Standards in Government* (82nd Congress, 1st session) (Washington, D.C.: U. S. Government Printing Office, 1951), p. 10.

[8] F. Ernest Johnson, "Do the Churches Exert Significant Influence on Public Morality?" *The Annals of the American Academy of Political and Social Science* (March, 1952), p. 125.

son, one of the most realistic spokesmen for American Protestantism, gives a very straightforward and candid answer. Says he: ". . . it is probably safe to say that beyond enforcing standards of common decency, the churches have on the whole played relatively little direct part in the continued building of social-moral standards." He confesses that "the churches tend to remain aloof" and concludes that the churches' ministry has been "socially conservative rather than regenerative." He believes that the church helps to enforce the moral sanctions of our society, "but they have not . . . conspicuously influenced the sanctions themselves."[9]

Various studies of the topics covered in preaching and teaching in the churches have shown a disturbing lack of either education or action in the great moral tension areas of our times. The Metropolitan Pittsburgh Church Survey, completed in 1948, showed that out of the 504 churches reporting, only a small number seemed to be relating their work and message to the issues that are providing the great temptations that surround us. In religious education only 20 per cent of the Sunday Schools dealt with race prejudices as a Christian issue, 19 per cent with international relations, 17 per cent with economic and social conditions. Only 19 per cent of the churches had social education or action committees despite the fact that most of the churches belonged to denominations urging such committees in all their churches. The women's societies were the one phase of the churches' effort that seemed to be doing the most, 60 per cent having direct dealings with such issues in their programs.[10]

When *The Christian Century* conducted a poll of its subscribers on the "greatest churches" of the country, it was forced to conclude that none of "the twelve great churches" seemed to be able to resist "the temptation to subordinate the prophetic to the pastoral claims of the calling."[11] The summary of the results

9 *Ibid.*, p. 126.
10 Metropolitan Pittsburgh Church Study, 1948.
11 "Twelve Great Churches," *The Christian Century* (January 3, 1951), p. 8.

said: "the church is more likely to take on the social character of its membership . . . none . . . seriously attempts the Christianization of industrial labor . . . none can honestly be called interracial."[12] So *The Christian Century* concluded that these great churches in "the social expression of the gospel [are] generally timid and [are] circumscribed by the economic and social character of their peoples' lives."[13] Some people might assert that readers of *The Christian Century* are a special lot and are more likely to be liberal than other representative Protestants, but it is doubtful if more conservative church people would have picked churches any less timid in their social responsibilities.

Perhaps Professor Hudson is right when he says that the churches have embraced the world.[14] The most individually pious groups have often tended to embrace the world most completely because their faith has not put them on guard but, instead, has given them the illusion of escape. Thus, they support all sorts of secular causes uncritically and unknowingly.

The most pointed summary that can be made is a statement from the World Council Study Booklet, *Christian Action in Society:*

> All discussion of the Church's action must begin with the admission that the Church has been relatively ineffective in the sphere of social action. It has allowed secular groups and agencies to take the initiative and these rather than the Church have, in the modern period, "given form to life."[15]

All these things comprise the "shame of the churches," for which they must seek divine forgiveness and call upon God for revival and reformation that they may return in contrition to a greater faithfulness to their Lord.

[12] *Ibid.*
[13] *Ibid.*
[14] Winthrop Hudson, *The Great Tradition of the American Churches* (New York: Harper and Brothers, 1953), chap. IX.
[15] The Study Department of the World Council of Churches, Geneva, Switzerland, *Christian Action in Society* (New York: World Council of Churches, 1949), p. 12.

Reasons Why Christian Influence Is Low

There are probably a hundred reasons why the influence of the vast Christian enterprise is weak in our society. We do not pretend to understand them all or to be able to treat them here, but we do hope that our brief analysis will draw out a lively discussion concerning this problem. The various causes are interrelated, and it is probably a combination of all of these and many more. Some of these causes are rooted in the churches' failure; some are rooted in the new social environment; but most of them are combinations of both. The great problem has already been stated: the inability of the churches to resist the pressures of the outer world. Let us look at eleven great causes of impotency.

The Cooling Off of the Protestant Dynamic

Most Christian denominations and Protestantism as a whole started as powerful movements of protest and reawakening. A small group is restless and alarmed at the complacency of the major religious bodies that have settled into conformity to the arrangement of the world around them. The members are drawn together in support and inspiration and feel that they are bearers and restorers of the original vigor and power of the gospel. Most of the new Christian groups have rallied people who were disinherited or left out of the regular church or churches. Such people are less involved in the controlling activities and benefits of the society and have "fewer hostages to fortune." Therefore, they are not overpowered by the influences of the world, and can cut themselves off for a more vigorous acceptance of the radical requirements that a total commitment demands.

Thus, new movements produce an intensity and spiritual contagion that capture the loyalties of men and fire their enthusiasms. Other restless and dissatisfied souls are challenged, and join. To enter such a movement requires burning bridges and stepping out from the accepted patterns of things. So the members are selected by their willingness to go further and do more than conventional faith has required. When many such men join forces, the spirit of the group is charged with an intensity and a single-mindedness that create a dynamism others lack. Of course, it must be pointed out that many of these movements have tended to separate themselves from responsibility to the larger society. In fact, the most intense groups in the sect pattern tend to withdraw from rather than participate in culture. Nevertheless, they do develop a vigor and a loyalty that make religion a dominant focus in all the activities of members.

There seems to be an overwhelming tendency for vigorous movements to begin settling down. As they grow and new generations enter the ranks, the movement begins to formalize and institutionalize its life. The rank and file begin to depend on professional leaders to carry the load of winning others and discharging the responsibilities of the group. The dynamic faith that begins with such urgency and enthusiasm is crystallized into rules or formally accepted creeds. There is a strong tendency for active convictions to become beliefs and beliefs to become conventional acceptances.

If such a movement flourishes and prospers, it may win people of greater wealth and prestige who cannot be as devoted to the fellowship and its work because of their heavier duties and interests in the secular world. And if the prestige becomes greater, it may begin to attract people who are less interested in the religious convictions and more interested in the other benefits that the association offers: the respectability gained from association with good respected people, the opportunities for the prestige of leadership, better association for one's children or even good professional or business contacts.

Many people join conventional churches for many of these reasons with little understanding of the life-centering commitment or rigorous moral claims of the Christian faith. The more of these people that come into the group the less emphasis on religious matters there will be in conversation and interests. As this development progresses, the lower will be the demands and the intensity of conviction in the general atmosphere of the whole group. The tension between the religious fellowship and the patterns of the world will disappear. The church may become a Sunday club of contented people who gather to celebrate their high opinion of themselves rather than to confess their grievous sins and submit themselves to Divine transformation. They may even go so far as to object when their minister preaches the rugged truths of an interfering Christ.

Many of the American denominations began as radical, self-disciplined movements, protesting the quiet conformities of the great churches and finding a new intensity in the spiritual and moral demands of a dynamic and less accommodative Biblical faith. But it seems to be almost an ironclad law among the movements of the world that time and success produce conformity and loss of vigor. The church is no exception. Unless it can undergo continuous reformation and a new dynamic self-discipline under the grace of God, it too becomes complacent, conformist, and saturated with the standards and practices of its social surroundings. Such a church can have little influence except to support existing conventions with pious ceremonials. Such a church can hardly be relied upon to transform men or be the fire to burn away the injustices in which its members participate.

How far this development has gone among the churches of America is hard to determine, but it is safe to say that we have traveled along this road. Our dynamism has cooled, and with this cooling we have lost our tension with the world and also much of our influence.

Dean Willard Sperry reminds us that great religious institutions have often lost their original purposes, even though they have continued to exist in empty motions and routines from which all the real meaning has gone. Anthropologists used to call such institutions "survivals." Dr. Sperry asks whether the churches of America are becoming survivals rather than powerful instruments of God.[16]

An influential scholar who studied the Shinto religious insti-

16 Willard L. Sperry, *Religion in America* (Cambridge, England: Cambridge University Press, 1946), p. 17.

tutions of Japan discovered a remarkable example of religious survivals. The Shinto priests went through intricate ceremonials on all the religious holidays and great social occasions. When the people were asked about their meanings, they shrugged their shoulders—they didn't know. But even more surprising, when the priests were asked the meaning of some of the liturgies, they didn't have the slightest notion. They said, "It is the great tradition. We have always done it this way for the good of the people."[17]

Our Religious Illiteracy

Coupled with the loss of dynamism has come a loss of interest in the meanings of our faith. Educators tell us that interest is essential as a requirement for learning. Lack of enthusiasm and a sense of urgency means that our people are neither excited nor moved by the things of religion. We have discovered among masses of our church members an amazing illiteracy and misunderstanding about the Bible and the great meanings of our tradition. As one layman put it, "We try to be good Christians, but we simply don't know what we believe." Can a Christian have any defense against the powerful influences of the world, if he does not understand the divine claims upon his life or the sources of renewal by which he attempts to live? How many of our people have conviction about the basic things that we discussed in the last chapter: the call to witnessing for Christ in daily living; the life of rigorous self-criticism under God; the significance of the Christian fellowship to give support, criticism, and witness in action; and the Biblical understanding of decisional living under the sovereignty of God?

Our Misunderstanding of the Gospel

What we do believe about our faith is an amalgam of Christian meanings, cultural prejudices, and of attitudes derived from the

[17] Paraphrased from John F. Embree, *Suye-Mura: A Japanese Village* (Chicago: University of Chicago Press, 1939), p. 236.

influences of our society. We have already discussed how a particular pendulum swing of selfish independency in Western thought has penetrated our faith to the point that, for many Christians, a narrow brand of moral isolationism has been elevated into a substitute for the responsive Christian faith. A few people in our time, caught up in the atmosphere of Marxism, have even converted this God-denying doctrine into a psuedo-Christianity. The spirit of the times always tinctures our faith and colors our attitudes. If our religious faith does not prepare us to understand this, and confront it, we are bound to be victims rather than ethical leaders.

One of the greatest problems in our attempt to register a Christian influence is that masses of our people have no understanding of the divine obligation to act together in Christ. The full Gospel has been strained through a sieve of self-serving anxiety, and the milk of Christian obligation to God and community has been thrown away while the cream of selfish reward is retained. We have seen that anxiety for one's own good and one's own salvation is the root source of sin. "He who seeks his life shall lose it." He who stands aloof from community inevitably finds his life focus turning in upon himself.

Misunderstanding Freedom of Conscience

One of the important misunderstandings that has undermined Christian social responsibility has been a perversion of the great belief of freedom of conscience. Some people believe that this means "letting every man believe as he pleases," with the result that any attempt to influence other men or to act together in common faith is an intrusion into the private spiritual rights of the other person. Very few people actually believe this, although it receives considerable homage to this day. It means that all attempts at evangelism and missionary effort are wrong. It also abandons the Protestant faith that the Scriptures carry the essential revelation and focus of the Christian faith. If you believe the Biblical gospel, you cannot believe anything you please.

The first misunderstanding about freedom of conscience overrates the individual human conscience and substitutes it for God. This belief that our own inner voice is the final authority of right and wrong if taken seriously would make every man his own deity. Aimee Semple McPherson once wrote a book titled: *Give Me My Own God.* If this means literally what it says, it is the rankest kind of secular humanism. Each Christian cannot have his own independent idea of God or his own peculiar faith. He worships his Creator and Redeemer as revealed in historic acts, not his own unconscious.

Every man's conscience is filled with expectancies drawn out of the common pool of meanings of the intimate groups in which he has lived. People reared in families and cultures where everyone practices racial discrimination or gambles do not find that their consciences bother them about these things. A person who has been reared to believe that Negroes are inferior gets no guidance from his conscience against social discrimination. He may even quote Scripture to justify his view.

It was long ago discovered that the conscience carries all the blindnesses and prejudices that have influenced our lives. The only conscience that is a Christian guide is one that is constantly enlightened and criticized by demands and relations beyond the individual. It is doubtful that any serious Christian can actually believe that his own naked conscience is a divine guide to action. What freedom of conscience does mean is that every man must make his own decision in response to God, must freely join the community of Christ, and must face the issues of life with decision rather than by drifting in the social tide. Every Christian needs a running criticism of his own conscience. It needs to be challenged and re-challenged.

This is a requirement because the norms or standards that individual conscience applies are subjective. This is the reason the Evanston Assembly of the World Council of Churches warned of the danger to the Christian "of limiting the gospel to his own understanding of it."[18]

---

[18] Reports of the Second Assembly of the World Council of Churches, *Evanston Speaks* (New York: World Council of Churches, 1954), p. 24.

The Christian has several objective ways in which to submit these narrow demands of conscience to challenge and correction. The first is by responding, in the light of the responsive love revealed in Christ, to the particular claims and needs of others as encountered in actual situations requiring decision. These claims and needs of others must be accepted as both restraints upon our selfish perspectives and objective forces of divine transformation in which our consciences undergo creative enlargement. As Professor Richard Niebuhr[19] has pointed out, God's activity works upon and through this process of submitting and relating to others to restrain and transform the selfhood of man. The response to these activities must be a response of humble faith or they will be viewed merely as frustrations to ourselves.

Another way in which conscience is tested and re-created is by recognizing and responding to the claims that the whole inclusive community, in which all men live interdependently, presses upon human responsibility. The Christian cannot act toward individuals or select groups as though they alone were to be the recipients of his outgoing concern in Christian love. Love cannot serve the special advantage of only those with whom we happen to come into direct contact to the disadvantage of outsiders, but must seek and serve the balanced requirements of all men in the community of life. As Emil Brunner says, "Love can only do more, it can never do less than justice requires."[20]

Another way in which the Christian is called upon to submit the subjective self-demands of his conscience to objective correction is through interaction in the worship and discipline of the Christian community of faith. As we found in a prior section, the Christian ethic is not a scheme of human conduct regulated by abstract rules or ideals but is a community ethic of loyalty and interactive fellowship in Christ. The idiosyncrasies of individual conscience concerning the will of God need to be mutually tested and reoriented in this fellowship of the church. The church's

---

[19] Richard Niebuhr, class lectures, Yale Divinity School.
[20] Emil Brunner, *Justice and the Social Order* (New York: Harper and Brothers, 1945), p. 129.

common focus of commitment to Christ, Her promise of the Holy Spirit to renew its members and lead them into unity as they prayerfully confront their decisions, and Her common worship, all provide the transmitting, chastening, and sustaining context in which the Christian conscience is re-created and sensitized.

Since the conscience is not a mirror or receptacle of divine laws or an infallible organ of divine intuition but the tension within a man of a higher loyalty over against himself, this loyalty requires constant cultivation and invigoration. Then, and only then, does the Christian dare to feel any humble assurance of guidance in his moral choice. Then he must personally decide and take the risk and blame upon himself before his God. When he fails—and there will be some error and prejudice in all his decisions—he must humbly turn to God in confession for forgiveness and new insight.

There is nothing in the authentic Protestant doctrine of freedom of conscience that says that a Christian must confront his burdens and temptations alone without mutual judgment and discussion in the Christian fellowship. In fact, our forebears, the early Puritans and dissenters, were those Christians who practiced fellowship and group discipline against the world most fully and most faithfully (as James H. Nichols and Winthrop Hudson have shown in their historical analyses).

Free Christians are not men so puffed up with self-piety and prideful independence that they insist on confronting the pressures of the world alone. They need personal divine help, and they need the help of their fellow Christians in the church as they stand together in a mutual witness of personal conviction and decision.

Because of the false independence that many free-conscience Christians have shown toward one another, they have at times almost taken pride in dissent for dissent's sake. Therefore, they have produced a curious excuse for social irresponsibility. They say Christians can't act to influence social problems because they can't agree. Surely, there is something in the Biblical Protestant faith that draws Christians toward a fundamental agreement on what the Lord requires of them; and, surely, there is a process of fellowship that enables them to work out many disagreements in the grace of guided discussion. This does not mean that they can form a convincing consensus under which to act in all matters, but it does mean that a togetherness in Christ is the basis for facing the world—not a divided dissension. It does mean that many issues can be faced, after a mutual process of persuasion, with the power of unity and general conviction. The Evanston Assembly of the World Council of Churches said of itself, "We of the World Council of Churches are committed to a fellowship in which we are ready to bring our convictions under scrutiny in the presence of our fellow-Christians and in the presence of the living Christ."[21] This should characterize all Christians and churches who belong to the communion of Christ.

The practical problem of social action in the churches is to find channels to form Christian consensus for building great moral agreements under which to act.

Lack of Methods of Forming Consensus

Since consensus-under-the-Spirit is the authority upon which the free Christians act in concert, it is imperative to have organized ways for the churches and their members to develop Christian opinion and to coordinate action. This lack is one of the chief reasons why denominational pronouncements have insufficient backing and why official councils for the promotion of responsibility do not have grass-roots impetus behind their work. One Baptist minister says: "The American Baptist Convention is formally committed to a policy of social action." But, he continues: "Whether they can be said to believe in it is another matter. A majority are not well enough informed."[22] There is real truth in this observation, and it would be applicable to other denominations. The staff and resources for the promotion of broad discussion of great moral issues has been alarmingly small and far too few churches have entered the process of developing moral sensi-

---

[21] Report of the Second Assembly of the World Council of Churches, *op. cit.*, p. 15.
[22] David P. Gaines, *Beliefs of Baptists* (New York: R. R. Smith, 1952), p. 154.

tivity and informed opinion. Denominational pronouncements should express a ground swell of Christian concern and not just the will of a few leaders "who put something over on tired ecclesiastical gatherings."

Misunderstanding Separation of Church and State

Another great American doctrine that is often misconstrued to oppose Christian social responsibility is the historic doctrine of separation of church and state. This is especially applied to the area of influencing political decision but often is used to cover the whole gamut of social influence. This negative view seems to "throw the baby out with the bath" and to overlook the very reason why this doctrine is so indispensable.

Separation of church from state was originated to free the church from state dominance, so it could teach and preach the gospel without interference or control of any sort. The purpose was to keep the various groups free to persuade any man to their convictions without favoritism in prestige and without any financial or other special backing whatsoever from government. The state is always armed with legal coercion, and could use legal force to put down some groups and favor others, unless prevented by custom and law. Under the separation view, the state cannot use legal means to coerce or intimidate the religious and moral teaching of any religious body. At the same time, the church has no legal force whatever and is dependent entirely on its persuasive influence and leadership in society.

The fundamental basis of this view is to keep the church free and unbeholden to government in order that it may be unintimidated in its God-ordained role of continuous criticism of institutions and practices of all men and of the very state itself. Even Martin Luther, who believed in a state church, felt that it was the duty of Christians to criticize kings and princes and the authority of the state when they fall away from the ways of justice. In the Old Testament the prophets dared to criticize their kings in the name of God.

Professor Nichols in his splendid analysis of the doctrines of the relation of church and state says that there are three basic views. The first is the view under which the church claims authority in moral matters over the state; this is the Roman Catholic position. The second view places the church under the state and administers it as a branch of government; this is the Lutheran position in several of the countries of Europe. The third method is separation as practiced in America.[23]

This American view of separation means that the church is neither officially under or over the state. The two coexist in a kind of tension in which neither can coerce the other. It does *not* mean that the churches should not mobilize all the moral influence at their command, through their members and the promotion of their basic convictions, to keep a continuous moral reminder and criticism focused upon the authorities in government. In fact, this is precisely why the church has insisted on being free; so it can register influence without the danger of coercion or reprisals. Its task is to act through the moral consensus of its people as the free conscience of the society.

If the basic purpose of separation is not to keep Christians free to exercise the right of ethical criticism and persuasion, it is hard to see that it would make any difference at all if the churches were not free. If, as some people seem to argue, the church is to keep in its place and teach and preach only about subjects that have no bearing on justice and corruption—and upon righteousness in government decisions that influence the lives of all our citizens— then there is little reason to support freedom. That kind of freedom already enslaves the church and controls and restricts its message. If religious beliefs and morals have nothing whatever to do with how governments treat men, then the whole issue is of no consequence.

The purpose behind separation of church and state is not to deprive the churches of general social influence, but to preserve it and safeguard it in the very structure of our life and to make

---

[23] James H. Nichols, *Democracy and the Churches* (Philadelphia: The Westminster Press, 1951) (copyright by W. L. Jenkins), p. 26.

sure that its influence be restricted to the realm of persuasion and moral pressure through its members acting as citizens, both independently and in groups. The great religious freedom of our society is the right to congregate, to organize, and to express our moral demands in free consensus as long as we use orderly and peaceful means.

Christians are not disfranchised citizens who forego their right to influence their society because they have joined a church. On the contrary, they become citizens who carry a new kind of critical social and civic responsibility under God.

The Growing Gap Between Clergy and Laity

Another great difficulty in the way of the church's influence is the growing gap in understanding between the clergy and the layman. We say the gap is growing because one of the great principles of the reformation was the "priesthood of all believers." Among many of the denominations, in the earlier period, there were few professional clergymen. Laymen who could preach served their fellows on Sunday and worked in ordinary pursuits during the week. These men were not trained in a special discipline concerning the traditions and intricacies of the faith, nor did they lose the outlook of men who toil and confront the hard realities of the work-a-day world. They were doubtless more swayed by immediate currents of opinion and less informed about the background of their faith, but they did preach from the common perspective of their fellows.

Today, we have a heavily professionalized type of leadership in our churches. We send our ministers to school to search and interpret the Bible, to trace our history and tradition, to learn about the great ethical issues, and to study the principles and methods of leadership. The minister is saturated in the doctrines and moral and spiritual urgencies that have come to be central in his life. This has tremendous advantages, and we do not argue against it, but it does create a spread between ministers and laymen. The laymen are heavily preoccupied with their struggle in the world.

All they know about their faith is what they have learned from their parents in childhood, from their Sunday School lessons, and from the sermons and other discourses of ministers. It is surprising how many laymen who have gone to church all their lives think that to be a Christian simply demands going to church and obeying the golden rule.

Two significant problems arise from this gap. First, laymen have increasingly let the minister carry the burden of the spiritual life of the church. He is thought of as the man who is set apart and whose piety, influence, and devotion are adequate to supply the needs of his congregation. Therefore, the minister is hired to carry the Christian influence into the community, do the good deeds, say the prayers, and even to have the great experiences for his people. He is in a sense the stand-in or substitute who assumes all the religious responsibilities while the laymen can go about their more mundane concerns. What leadership the laymen do provide in the church has tended to become less and less religious and more and more administrative and financial. Ushering, keeping up the property, and organizing the financial campaign become the type of functions turned over to the laymen.

The second problem is that laymen see themselves as churchly custodians rather than as active witnesses for Christ and the Christian faith in their own affairs. They have not had the time and opportunity to study and ponder over the awesome meanings of the Christian faith and its difficult demands. Few have developed an understanding of their faith that is prepared for the powerful secular attitudes and influences that they encounter in daily life. Then, too, they are often the victims of the timidity of the clergy who, sensing this gap, reduce the rigors of their message to conform to the secular climate rather than cultivate a patience and persistence that can inform and sensitize their members. Therefore, "the pulpit catches on fire, but the pew fails to ignite."[24]

When laymen do understand the radical claims of a gospel of love, they are often overwhelmed by the difficulties that they face.

[24] Milton Yinger, *Religion in the Struggle for Power* (Durham, N.C.: Duke University Press, 1946), p. 35.

And if the courageous minister calls for absolute faithfulness, without an adequate understanding and interpretation of the fearful dilemmas and limitations in the real world, the embattled layman begins to feel that his minister is good-hearted but visionary and unrealistic. He begins to take the way out of this dilemma that has been so disastrous to the Christian gospel: trying to be religious on Sunday and secular the rest of the week. This is what Professor Nichols calls the "betrayal of the gospel by means of compartmentalization."[25]

The outcome of this gap is that laymen do not understand or feel either the ethical demands of the Christian faith or the seriousness of the intimidations of the world. This is natural, because the minister does live a more separated and cloistered life.

Whenever this gap between clergy and laymen exists, it reduces the effectiveness in the influence of the church. It creates tension in which ministers feel that laymen are cold and complacent, and laymen feel that ministers are trying to stir things up that they ought to leave alone. The result is lay pressure on the minister to "soft pedal," and exasperation on the part of the minister at the apathy of his people.

It seems clear that if laymen do not develop convictions and interests concerning Christian influence, the efforts of the church will be feeble. For, as a basic principle, we must say that the primary Christian influence has to be carried into the world by laymen. They are the people who live and choose—out where decisions are made and opinion is developed. Ministers are in a very real sense secondary leaders, registering their basic influence through the lay people whom they can inspire and encourage. Too few ministers recognize this basic principle and attempt to carry the battle personally, even without lay support. This often increases the gap we have described. Such ministers are not taken very seriously by secular leaders, because they know that they do not have the power to deliver the real moral backing of their congregations or an adequate understanding of the complex context in which decisions are made.

[25] James H. Nichols, *op. cit.,* p. 241.

Naïveté About Power and Influence

Another reason for the failure of Christians and the church to enter the struggle for influence in the negotiations and pressures of the world lies in the Protestant individualistic bias that overlooks the controls exerted by the organized power structures of society. We touched on this problem in the first chapter.

A society operates and functions under a vast network of power relations.[26] Men are assigned positions, and exert authority according to the offices they hold and the roles they occupy in economic, political, and other social organizations. Power is a very important aspect of social life to understand in analyzing the limitations that surround individuals and the authorities that determine most of the major policies under which we live. Many men and groups do not have the power or authority to carry out many of the things that they believe are morally right simply because they have a subordinate position and work under orders. Only by mobilizing strength in unity and entering the competitive struggle in the formation of policy can individuals and groups fully participate in social action.

Power is armed with latent force. This does not mean brute force, but it means the control of decisions through institutionalized authority. Power operates under sanctions—that is, the authority to enforce demands by penalties or the withholding of rewards or advantages. It is found in all kinds of relations where sanctions are provided or are possible within the structure of relations. Power must never be confused with influence, for the latter works only by persuasion.

A minister has power over his secretary if he can dismiss her, but in congregationally governed churches he has no real power over his congregation or official board. In this last relationship, he has only influence, but the congregation has power over the minister if it can dismiss him. Although a professor can flunk a student, actually he has only influence in society, unless he has been

[26] Robert Bierstedt, "An Analysis of Social Power," *American Sociological Review,* 15:6, pp. 730-737.

delegated other real powers. An employer has, over his employees, a certain amount of power, which may be limited to some degree by a union contract and by standardized grievance machinery. An employer has no direct power, though, over the labor union president elected through constituted union procedures. Even persons who occupy top positions in bureaucratic organizations find themselves in a context of horizontal pressures from competing organizations, independent organizations of employees, public opinion, or governmental controls. There are innumerable direct and subtle pressures playing on everyone, restricting and complicating decision.

Power is a function of organizations and institutions through which authority is assigned to graded offices and those who occupy them. Power is wielded by those in authority within a particular system of relations over those who occupy subordinate positions in that system. Wherever there are formal or legal instruments of authority available, through which sanctions can be applied, there is latent power.

Citizens have latent power available over elected officials in a democratic government. It is only *latent* and cannot be exercised by individuals, unless they combine into political blocks that at least threaten to affect the outcome of elections. As political scientists point out, individual voters have little political power except through organization. In a society in which large-scale organizations form political, economic, and other pressure blocks in the power system, unrelated individuals can have little effect in influencing policy, unless they work in and through such organizations.

Participating in such organizations limits the independent freedom of individuals, since decisions are organizational in character; at the same time, it gives them a channel through which they can influence decision and join with others in throwing some weight into the balances of power. Thus, in a complex society, freedom, as some measure of control over one's own activities, is greatly increased by joining in group effort, while rugged independence subjects the individual to controls without representation.

Power is always compulsive because it has sanctions at its disposal to dismiss men from jobs, block vocational advancement, withdraw advantages, or punish in various ways. Coercive power is far from being monopolized by government, as many people try to make themselves believe. Power is involved in all but the most intimate primary relations. Even parents have power over their children. One can sentimentally deplore the existence of power relations that control and limit so many activities and decisions of men, but this does not abolish the fact that organized authority and power are indispensable in the functioning of even a free social order.[27] Social organization operates through a complex network of power relations that exert pressure and limitations on everyone in many ways. It provides the only way that human activity can be coordinated. The more complex a society becomes the more indispensable is a formal structure of authority.

Those who have only influence can enter into formal policy decisions in two ways: They can attempt to educate and persuade those who are in positions of power to govern their actions under the moral perspective or way of action that is taught, or they can unite to create a climate of public opinion that enters the common value systems and that exerts moral pressure both internally within individuals and externally on what is commonly expected of them.

Christians and churches are not excluded from these social facts. A church has no power, unless it can enter power relations with unified strength. And it has little influence, unless its moral perspectives are carried by its members out into the organizational decisions in which they participate, or unless it makes a unified impact on public opinion through effective channels of communication. Church people tend to have great confidence in moral force. However, they fail to see that it is not a force at all, unless cooperatively carried out into the organizations where decisions are made or vigorously proclaimed so that people on a

---

[27] Talcott Parsons and Edward A. Shills (editors), *Toward a General Theory of Action* (Cambridge: Harvard University Press, 1952), pp. 190-233.

wide scale will know what the shared moral convictions of church people are, and the justice for which they are willing to struggle.

Individual moral influence is effective in social control in intimate groups, such as the family, or in a small community where there is a strong sympathetic identification with others. However, in the impersonal relations in a mass type of society, personal sensitivities do not operate effectively, and individuals tend to control their activities more by formal expectancies and the meeting of practical pressures in the power system. As long as they are discharging their assigned responsibilities effectively in their offices in the interest of their organization, they are considered to be meeting their obligations. In fact, they are likely to be considered as exceeding their authority if they challenge or go beyond these formal responsibilities.

It is generally agreed that in our society individualized moral influence is extremely limited, since basic policy decisions are made by organizations in terms of pressures and possibilities that are confronted. Of course, personal moral convictions guide the ways in which individuals participate in such decisions, but these convictions tend to be considered personal eccentricities unless there is strong support from others and powerful backing from commonly held values and expectancies.

Therefore, if churches are to carry weight in public opinion, they must unite to proclaim their convictions vigorously through channels that can give them a hearing. If they are going to enter the pressure struggles, they must act corporately to press for just policies, and they must send their members into their offices to use this authority in negotiating decisions with the backing of strong Christian consensus.

The failure of Christians and church groups to understand these facts of life has left them largely isolated outside the processes of power and influence.

The Ambiguous Role of the Minister

Another reason for the weakness of the influence of the church is the confusion concerning who the minister is, what his office requires, and the authority under which he works. This is closely related to the problem of the gap between clergy and laity, which has been discussed.

The role of a minister consists of the position he holds and the functions he is expected to discharge. Social roles are not created by individuals themselves, but are assigned to them by the organizations in which they work and by the basic traditions and expectancies of the people whom they serve and among whom they live. A person who assumes a role is under compulsion to conduct himself in a way befitting these expectancies, or he is considered a failure and is likely to be removed from office if he does not meet them.

Therefore, the traditional authority and institutional structure in which he works will define and limit what he can do. The Christian church operates in society as a social organization, and the minister serves under assigned authority, as do all other occupants of institutional offices.

The office of the minister suffers particular ambiguity, because there are several dimensions or sets of relations under which he views himself and under which he is subjected to controls. These often come into conflict within his own focus of loyalty and also in the eyes of the people whom he serves. There are four levels of authority under which the role of the minister can be viewed.

The first of these is the authority of God in Christ. The minister believes that he is ordained in Christ to serve God rather than man. If this is taken as the primary authority under which he must act, he will often feel himself obligated to challenge the other authorities that assign his role. Since what the authority of God actually requires from a minister must be determined in his own conscience at the very same time that he is attempting to win his people to an acceptance of that authority, he is always involved in a double focus. Unless he can convince his members to agree on what God requires, he has lost his leadership. Interpreting the ways of God to man always involves a translation into the vernacular of their own understanding, and herein lies the risk of lowering the divine claims.

The second focus of authority lies in the larger denomination or body to which the minister belongs. It has both an organized structure of authority (polity) and a set of practices and beliefs (traditions) that provide a common discipline to which the members adhere in accepting membership. The religious body, in spite of its transcendent commitment to Christ, cannot escape being a social institution with a structure of formal controls and a pattern of authority under which its clergy and lay leadership function. Ministers are ordained, assigned churches, carry out their prescribed functions, and are disciplined under constituted denominational procedures and patterns, whether this be under a structure of organizational authority or under informal traditions.

Among Protestant denominations there is a considerable range in the types of polity and in the degree of adherence to established tradition. There are three major types of polity: The first type is the hierarchic form of organization in which authority is vested in those officers of the denominational organization who have control over property and leadership in local churches. The second is the presbyterial organization in which authority is vested in the organized association of churches that has the power of approval and veto over the selection of ministers, the defining of beliefs, and the property of local churches. The third type is the congregational polity in which local churches are entirely independent units and are free in the choice of ministers, theological interpretations, control of property, and all other matters.

The polity under which a minister works has a great deal to do with determining which of the role-defining contexts will be primary in outlining his role as a local minister. There is a dilemma involved in the problem of polity—the problem that asks to whom the minister is responsible and who should call and dismiss him. While he may feel ultimately responsible to God, those who control his call or assignment to the church and those who hold the purse strings maintain powerful sanctions over him. In the hierarchic structure, the minister is less vulnerable to the pressures of the local church, but is less likely to work in close responsibility to his people. He is under greater denominational control of the whole communion but more free and protected from the pressures to accommodate to the ideologies and biases of the local church. In a congregational type of church, he is extremely vulnerable to local church pressures, because his position depends on pleasing the local people and conforming to their wishes and expectancies; however, he is more free from restraints and pressures of the larger body of Christians. He can appeal to the traditions and Christian consensus of his denomination, but in actuality the local congregation decides and he has no defense against their idiosyncrasies. For this reason, it is often more difficult for a clergyman under congregational polity to carry a prophetic ministry of serving Christ rather than the wishes of local parishioners. It is much easier for a local congregation that has all practical authority vested in itself to come to think of its minister as an administrator. It thinks of him as one hired to preach what the people want to hear and one to carry out its wishes and errands, rather than as an ordained servant of Christ, proclaiming the authority of the gospel over all of life and performing the historic ministries of the church.

So the third set of relations that assigns to the minister his role and defines his functions is that of the local church. The expectancies of the local congregation circumscribe in powerful ways what is welcomed and what is resented in the activities and message of its minister. Loyalty to Christ and the Biblical gospel and faithfulness to the larger Christian community may call for a prophetic ministry, but if the local church rejects it because of its own more narrow tradition, or its more accommodative orientation to secular culture, it can dismiss its minister or at least prevail upon him to accommodate his ministry to the expectancies of his people.

Under local church domination, the particular class of people that predominates in that church, or a few dominant leaders with a shallow understanding of the function of the church, or an eccentric or noncooperative local tradition established by past clergy, can impose restrictions on the minister that do not allow him to perform fully the traditional ministries to which his denomination has ordained him, and which he believes his loyalty to God requires of him.

Where there is no denominational authority or established pattern to which a minister may appeal for judgment and support, his influence can be greatly restricted. He is, therefore, compelled to be cautious and is more likely to place popularity with his congregation ahead of faithfulness to his higher mission. This can then easily become a vicious circle in which he is afraid to pursue a vigorous policy—afraid to lead his people to a higher expectancy concerning the role of the minister because of the lower view that they already hold.

The structure of organizational authority or polity is only one side of church authority, although a powerful one because it is armed with the power of calling and dismissing ministers. The other side is the power of accepted tradition in the church, concerning the Christian message and the role of the minister. This, too, varies in denominations and churches. It is the one factor in the free churches that can offset the vulnerability of ministers to the pressure of secularized expectancies. The local church must want and appreciate a minister who leads them into the focus of serving God rather than man. They must expect and demand a prophetic leader who preaches the personal and corporate sins of man and the salvation of Christ, and who assumes the task of joining with them in relating their daily decisions to the claims of God upon them. If they do not hold to such a tradition, the minister will have to spend most of his time in what has been called the "glamour market," trying to lure his people into a greater confidence in him through being "an affable guy," "a good sport," or a "handy errand-runner."

As James Gustafson has pointed out, this produces "an excessive personalization of the ministry," which places much of the responsibility for the success of the mission of the gospel on the minister's personality.[28] In other words, he will have to spend his effort

---

[28] James M. Gustafson, "An Analysis of the Problem of the Role of the Minister," *Journal of Religion,* XXXIV:3 (1954), pp. 187-196.

in doing that which is foreign to the basic role of a minister of the Church of Christ. Such a minister will have very little real influence, and he will be serving a church that can make little use of the leadership to which he was ordained. He will lose his status as a professional man and the legitimacy of his authority as a man of God called of Christ to serve his people.

Therefore, in the congregationally governed church, the role of the minister is likely to fluctuate and not form a stable pattern, unless it has a strong theological tradition, a well-defined understanding of the church, and an awareness of the full range of its personal and social ministries.

It should be abundantly clear from our discussion that we are not saying that a minister is under no obligation to win the support of his people and establish their confidence in him. His task is to live so closely to them and the genuine problems and conflicts of their lives that he can "interpret their organized and unorganized relationships with one another in the dimension of the relation of life to God."[29] Unless both ministers and people hold to a common belief concerning what the minister's function is, he will labor under the strain of anxiety and under a lack of assurance as to what his people expect. If his very functions are in controversy, he cannot discharge them.

The fourth set of expectancies that help to formulate the role of the minister are those of the general culture in which both the minister and the church live. This is the general social stereotype of the minister in the folklore of our society. He is often depicted in novels, motion pictures, and television plays as a pious, kindly, and unrealistic character who spends most of his time straightening out small congregational squabbles and keeping big givers from walking out of his church. His work is usually almost totally unrelated to policy decisions of social consequence or to ethical guidance in the world of practical affairs.

This stereotype always penetrates the perspectives of church members to some degree, helping to reinforce a very narrow con-

---

[29] *Ibid.*

cept of the role of the minister and restricting his prestige and influence. Of course, the view of the typical minister seems to vary in the different classes of a society. To the laboring classes, he is often a stern austere man, intent on keeping people from enjoying small pleasures and trying to get people into heaven by avoiding these. One graduate student, working in various departments in an automobile plant for a summer, interviewed hundreds of men informally. Ministers to them were "pious women's home companions, who maybe did some good improving the character of the kids." To upper middle class people, he is an affable tea drinker and golf player who reminds us of our high ideals of neighborliness and honesty: "A good Joe to go fishing with."

College students seem to be acutely aware of these "representations" of the clergy, and they do not generally appeal to them as roles that they might choose to fill. Unless a person, seriously considering the ministry, has been influenced by a particular minister who attracts him, he rarely elects it as a vocation through which to live "an influential life."

The members of the clergy are extremely conscious of these rather unfavorable stereotypes and react toward them in various defensive ways. They are tempted constantly to demonstrate that they are normal, urbane, sports-loving men of the world, seeking to interpret the faith in practical terms of the advantages and benefits that religion offers. This is the way to enhance prestige and win friends in the secular world, but it tends to accentuate accommodation rather than strengthen the vigorous role of religious leadership.

The four levels of role expectation come into continuous conflict, and the minister is at a loss to know what his position is and what the reception of his people toward his ministry will be. Under this ambiguity, his leadership is likely to be timid with too much preoccupation in defending and justifying himself to himself, to his congregation, and to the community in general. No simple solution can be formulated, but from the vantage point of sociological analysis it seems clear that only in a consensus of the larger fellowship of the denominations can a role expectancy be developed that will support and keep clearly defined the historic ministries of reconciliation and judgment under which Christian leaders can enter into the channels of influence.

The minister must be a servant of God through a better defined role assigned to him within the structure of a prophetic church. Laity and clergy must interact intimately in a mutually sustained loyalty in Christ, if the church is to have unity and power in its social witness.

Disillusionment about Social Reform

Another important reason for the low ebb of the social impact of the church is the disillusionment that has come to those who believe in it, but who have tried and failed. Lost causes have discouraged Christian actionists. In the last generation, the churches have mobilized vigorous campaigns for Prohibition and against war, and despite massive efforts have failed in both causes. It is easy to join the "tired reformers" and conclude that the opposition is too strong and that constructive changes are hopeless.

What is needed to confront this problem is not defeatism but a more realistic understanding of social forces and of the need for divine redemption. In a world of human sinfulness and continuous social tension, there are no final victories that solve all problems and set things aright. The struggle for righteousness will endure as long as the present world. Every achievement opens up new conflicts and injustices, but as Liston Pope showed us in a prior quotation, this does not mean that particular discriminations and injustices cannot be overcome in many specific situations. Above all it does not excuse the Christian from responsibility to join the struggle for righteousness. The Kingdom of God is not a perfect order, soon to arrive by the efforts of men; it is already in action, for God has been revealed in Christ and His mighty Spirit works. But the final perfect Kingdom is no simple goal of human effort. It is in God's hands. Our Christian duty is to spare no effort in fair weather or foul to attempt to live in response to God within the actual situations that confront us and to advance our community toward justice. Archie Hargraves, formerly of the East Harlem parish and now doing the same type of work in Chicago, puts it well: "It means preaching the gospel of hope with two dimensions—the hope of God's final redemption of the world, and the assurance of what God can do and is doing now in this situation."[30]

Too Much Emphasis on Success

Another reason for the lack of real influence on the part of our American churches is that the secular success goals of "bigness" and "growth" have invaded the spirit of our churches without adequate counterbalances. As we have seen, we are apt to believe that the "great churches" are the big going-concerns that "pack 'em in" on Sundays, that raise big budgets, and run an all-week three-ring-circus of activities. The actual machinery of the church can become so important that furious activity and the successful attraction of large numbers emerge as the marks of success, rather than the power to change men and radiate a powerful influence into the community. This is the "administrative church" as against the "transforming and saving church." Instead of calling men to vigorous devotion in faith and deed, it stacks its success on what Professor Hudson calls the "added attraction."[31]

The lure of success is perhaps the most fatal temptation in undermining the churches' spiritual and ethical faithfulness. The church wants crowds and strong financial support, so it broadens its appeal and makes it easier to join. It talks about the glorious benefits and excellent advantages of belonging to an active church. It offers bowling and baseball and dinners and entertainments, picnics and prizes, contests and style shows. Sometimes it goes out after members house-to-house with the same flip superficiality of a minor charity fund visitation. "Sign the card and join the fellowship." (We favor visitation, but not shallow sign-up campaigns.)

[30] Beverly W. Dean, "Trail Blazing in City Jungles," *City Church* (May-June, 1953), p. 4.
[31] Winthrop Hudson, *op. cit.*, p. 216.

The result is that the church is loaded with people who have been "recruited" under false pretenses. Many of them would be horrified, if they were told that they had joined a pilgrimage of self-giving sacrifice in which they struggle to live not for self but for Christ and neighbors within the new community of grace. And when the minister preaches to this motley congregation, what can he say? Should he proclaim the gospel to the remnant of the faithful and jeopardize his successful church and its magnificent budget? Should the men's club discuss "serving Christ in my daily work" or play shuffleboard?

Nearly all studies of church attendance, covering hundreds of thousands of people all over the country, show the same results.[32] Roughly one-third of our people who claim Protestant membership attend church with some regularity; approximately one-third are casual goers on "big days" or when the weather is good. From 20 to 33 per cent are lapsed members. They are often carried on church books but never go. They feel that the church is a splendid influence, and they are willing to contribute five dollars a year if you can catch them at home on Canvass Sunday.

Obviously, such a loose amalgam of people will not produce a prophetic church. The Protestant church has been willing to accept millions of people who have neither been really won nor educated to the cause of Christ. Is it any wonder that we have had such difficulty in producing what Justin Wroe Nixon calls "responsible Christianity"?[33]

We must hasten to add that we in no way want to slander the many decisional Christians in our churches, nor cast aspersions upon our hard-pressed ministry. This is a complex problem with many causes, not the least of which is the flood of secular interests that so easily dominate our lives. Nor is it an easy problem to face. This dilemma of "success versus influence" is a permanent problem of the church in the world.[34] We must be fully aware of it and

---

[32] Surveys conducted by Albert T. Rasmussen in Illinois, California, New York, and Washington, D.C.

[33] Justin Wroe Nixon, *Responsible Christianity* (New York: Harper and Brothers, 1950).

[34] Milton Yinger, *op. cit.,* p. 18.

face it as the most critical and perennial problem of all Christian leadership.

KEY QUESTIONS FOR DISCUSSION

1. Discuss Dr. Johnson's statement that the churches enforce the commonly accepted standards of decency in our society, but do little toward raising these standards, which are often alarmingly low as judged under the Christian perspective.
2. In what ways has the church defaulted its leadership in social influence and allowed secular agencies to take the lead (as the World Council of Churches Study Book declares)?
3. In what ways have materialistic goals invaded our interpretation of the gospel?
4. How seriously do the people in your church attempt to face the Christian imperative to act together in Christ against the intimidations of the world?
5. Do you agree that one of the main reasons why we fail to cooperate in moral action is that we no longer have regular opportunities to talk things through to a consensus?
6. Do you believe that we have exaggerated the misunderstanding of (a) the belief in freedom of conscience, and (b) the separation of church and state as contributory to our weakness in Christian influence?
7. What is meant by "power" and how does it differ from "influence"?
8. What is the problem of authority for a minister in a congregationally controlled church?
9. Why are laymen the key to Christian influence in society?
10. Discuss the danger of the institutional goal of success in making churches weak in genuine influence.

RECOMMENDED READINGS

Bendix, Reinhard, and Seymour Martin Lipset, *Class, Status and Power: A Reader in Social Stratification.* Glencoe, Illinois: The Free Press, 1953. (Recommended: the introduction and articles by Max Weber, Pitirim Sorokin, and Talcott Parsons).

Christian Action in Society (A study booklet). New York: World Council of Churches, 297 Fourth Ave., 1949.

Douglass, Truman B., *Mission to America*. New York: Friendship Press, 1951.

Hartt, Julian N., *Toward a Theology of Evangelism*. New York: Abingdon Press, 1955.

Hudson, Winthrop S., *The Great Tradition of the American Churches*. New York: Harper and Brothers, 1953. (Chapter IX: "The Churches Embrace the World").

Johnson, F. Ernest, "Do the Churches Exert Significant Influence in Public Morality?" *The Annals of the American Academy of Political and Social Science* (March, 1952), p. 125.

Nichols, James H., *Democracy and the Churches*. Philadelphia: The Westminster Press, 1951.

Yinger, Milton, *Religion in the Struggle for Power*. Durham, N.C.: Duke University Press, 1946.

CHAPTER • 6

Relating Faith to Social Action

A valid Christian decision is a compound always of both faith *and* facts. *It is likely to be valid in the degree to which the faith is rightly apprehended and the facts are rightly measured. It is the product, that is to say, of an absolute loyalty related to a pragmatic choice* (From *The Renewal of Man,* by Alexander Miller. Copyright 1955 by Alexander Miller, reprinted by permission of Doubleday & Company, Inc., p. 94).

Do not be conformed to this world but be transformed by the renewal of your mind, that you may prove what is the will of God, what is good and acceptable and perfect (Romans 12:2, RSV).

We have now considered the inescapable ways in which we are socially conditioned and the powerful forces that press upon us in our social existence. We have also reviewed the historic Protestant awareness of these conditions and the Protestant call to the decisional life in all our activities and relations. We have observed the contemporary renewal of the belief that they can be confronted faithfully only within the fellowship of the church and through its corporate witness and action.

In an attempt at realistic honesty we have looked at the weakness and failure of the church to be a vital witness for Christ and a transformative influence in our society despite its size and growth.

Our performances fall far below our professions. We have already discussed the basic reasons why this gap cannot be fully closed. Total faithfulness to God is not possible for sinful men living within the boundaries and limitations of social existence. Nevertheless, we believe that a clearer understanding of the difficult problem of relating faith to action can help us to see how we can better enter the processes of decision and discharge more faithfully our social responsibilities. Now we turn to the consideration of the problem of decision in the arena of organized social relationships.

A HEROIC ETHIC IN A PRAGMATIC WORLD

"Stooping to conquer," adjusting conduct to fit expediency, "settling for less than the best" are phrases that describe conduct that is shocking and repugnant to the American conscience. We have been schooled to despise compromise, to honor heroic goals such as "liberty or death" and "justice for all." If we are also Christians, we elevate the cross that symbolizes the revelation of the love of God in the sacrificial death of Christ on the cross. As the supreme law of our lives, we emblazon the two great commandments: "Love the Lord thy God with all thy heart, and all thy soul, and all thy mind . . . and . . . love thy neighbor as thyself" (Matt. 22:37, 39). We admonish ourselves with the great Biblical injunctions "be not conformed to this world" (Romans 12:2); "Seek ye first the Kingdom of God" (Matthew 6:33); "Blessed is the man that endureth temptation" (James 1:12).

These are the lofty flags that we fly over our lives even as we negotiate, bargain, conform to social pressures, choose among limited alternatives, and pick our way through the inevitable maze of blockages and ambiguities through which our lives lead us. Flying these flags and doing obeisance to these noble sentiments warm our hearts and sometimes galvanize us to choose the high road in simple situations that offer fairly clear alternatives. But they have little contact with our practical lives wherever compromise and adjustment are required. We have a strong tendency to view the practical life as either a kind of neutral necessity or even a field of evil that can be escaped only by living in ivory towers of noble thought, retreating to cloistered sanctuaries, and meditating on the good, the true, and the beautiful that shimmer high above us only to be revered. Our God is one whom we worship in the beauty of silence but whom we lose sight of almost entirely in the world of daily decision.

There is no doubt that we belong to the heroic tradition in our dreams and meditations, but at the same time we live in a society that demands concentration on practical action and pragmatic results as no other in human history. So we sentimentalize our noble ideals and ritualize our love of them on rare occasions while we are almost totally preoccupied with building, producing, selling, and struggling to succeed in the harsh competitive world of material existence. When such successes are attained, the enslaving concentration on their attainment has often so blunted our appreciative sensitivities and ethical distinctions that we are likely to be incapable of finding any higher purpose or meaning even in our meditations. The instrumental has become the end. Satiation and boredom are the result instead of the happy goal of rainbow's end.

If, instead, we seriously turn to these shimmering ideals as policy guides, they almost totally misfit us to live in our real world. If we try to join these two levels of our experience and use the heroic injunctions to guide our negotiated decisions, we develop internal anxieties and meet external obstructions that tear us apart internally and immobilize our efforts practically. The strain of meeting the baffling crosscurrents of practical decision has already driven us to a wistful search for moments of withdrawal that can restore our "peace of mind." So our religion is seized upon as the portal of blessed escape, rather than the generator of more earnest ethical responsibility.

Therefore, as practical people, we have dealt with our dilemma practically. We celebrate our possession of lofty aspirations to pacify our agitated souls and our anxious consciences in order to free ourselves to live less anxiously in the world of adjustment and compromise. We tend to live in a two-story existence with no stairways between. In the upper story we meditate and on the lower story we act and live. Each has its separate philosophy. Upstairs there are absolute and unrelated ideals. Downstairs there is an instrumentalism toward uncriticized and powerful material ends. Vigorous effort is stimulated by the incentives of material gains, but a moral tension and loyalty powerful enough and relevant enough to challenge and guide the powerful organizational engines within which we live is reduced, rather than sharpened, by our religion.

This is an extremely unfortunate and un-Christian relationship between faith and practical action. And it is contrary to the defining traditions of our Christian faith. When our religious worship and motivations become irrelevant or even escapist in relation to the burdensome and baffling problems of decisional life, conscientious men are deprived of guidance from the one source that focuses their lives above the levels of accommodative self-interest. Even worse, religion itself deteriorates into "religiosity" and becomes idolatry.

Contemporary theologians have been laboring to rescue us from this unhappy split in our existence. As Edward L. Long, Jr. declares, "abstract philosophies may be permitted the luxury of contemplating beautiful ideals, but Christian love must find a practical ministry for living men. This requires us to take up burdens in the service of Christ and express love in relationship to the hard and realistic world about us."[1]

An early modern attempt to bridge the gap between faith and action was performed by the social gospel movement. It observed the mounting injustices created by the radical transition into an urbanized, industrial society in which masses of immigrants to cities were poverty stricken, exploited, and powerless. It recoiled in shock at the insensitivities of Christian people and the churches to sense any tragedy, injustice, or responsibility. The sentimental personal piety of the times did not convict its adherents of sinful involvement nor enable them to see how social structures mold

---

[1] Edward Leroy Long, Jr., *Conscience and Compromise* (Philadelphia: The Westminster Press, 1954), p. 20.

and limit men. It made them peacefully quiescent in the assurance of their own salvation without entering the practical struggle for righteousness.

The ethical answer developed by the social gospel to close this gap took the form of a vigorous re-emphasis of the Biblical injunctions to live by love. Christ was viewed not so much as a revelation of God to man as an example of what any man could perform if he conformed to the ideal law of love and called on God's grace for help.

In reaction to self-centered pietism, many believed that Christians had never earnestly tried this ideal ethic of Christ and that such an effort, informed by the gospel, reinforced in worship and prayer, and empowered by the Spirit could bring into being the Kingdom of God on earth. This was reinforced by the faith that God was working continuously through the processes of natural evolution to make men more rational and less barbarous and was transforming social structures into patterns of greater justice.

What is most pertinent to the present discussion is that they presented an ethic of rugged uncompromising love as the law of Christ for man. They believed that this higher law could be met and lived by as a social policy in personal relations and social patterns.

Therefore, they called for the raising of human objectives to the ideal of Christ and a galvanizing of the human will to accept no compromises. Practical life was to be elevated into conformity with the demands of Christ, and society was to become the "community of love" in the Kingdom of God. As Edward Long, Jr., puts it in his book, this view trusted "that Christian love could be translated into social reality without a process of compromise. . . . They took the ultimate norm of Christian love as equivalent to a practical program of action."[2]

This was a heroic call to follow, unconditionally, the sacrifical love of Christ. It produced a great many valiant Christians who attempted to rise to its demands by declaring the condemnation of Christ on our whole self-seeking social order at the very zenith

[2] *Ibid.*, p. 28.

of secular American optimism. It called for the life of love and self-sacrifice at the very peak of confidence in the competitive process to harmonize the drives of self-interest into a just and stable social order. In many respects, it stood resolutely against the whole tide of secular values and practices. This was responsible, in part, for its undoing. For there can never be enough heroism or will power to lift people completely out of the value systems in which they have been reared and have come to accept as the patterns for their existence. And will power cannot remove men from the context of society within which all their decisions must be made—this is true even for Christians who believe they have a higher ground from which to criticize and challenge the value systems that have cradled them. Although self-conscious human beings are not mere pawns, they are culturally conditioned creatures even in their consciences; their whole lives must be lived within the context of existing social patterns, which limit them in many ways.

Social change is always taking place under the influence of competitive and cooperative action within various centers of power and in interplay between these centers of power. But total reversals and revolutions are socially and ideologically impossible. Absolutely fresh starts do not come even under bloody political revolutions. Completely fresh beginnings do not take place for men even in the new birth of Christian conversion. When new men seize political power with new rationalized interpretations and interests, their new order will reflect conditioned reactions to old patterns. The rank and file of people cannot suddenly shed their personalities or their self-centered perspectives. This is why revolutionary leaders know that their people must be coerced and propagandized to accept radical new patterns. This is likely to thwart freedom and impose vast injustices worse than before, as the Marxist revolution in Russia so well exemplifies.

Therefore, the social gospel, in spite of its emphasis on the evils of our social organization, failed to understand adequately the contextual nature of social existence and the associated fact that guidance and influence can be exerted only through and within the limiting processes of this very context. Furthermore, its concept of love was not sufficiently sharpened to show the height of the self-giving responsiveness that love requires. The distinction between self-love and outgoing love was not clarified. Men do acts of kindness for exhibition before men to bolster their self-respect or increase their popularity. Much of our charity seems hardly dominated by love, but by paternalism or a desire not to be "pikers" before our fellows. Therefore, the absolute and uncompromising ethic of love was already somewhat diluted in what it meant, and was rather easily reduceable to the sentimental notion of being kind and expressing genial good will toward others.

The social gospel also failed to sense adequately the universal self-centeredness of creaturely human nature that makes the consistent heroism of self-giving love impossible. It failed also to recognize the indispensability of the fellowship of Christ, as the vehicle of divine grace to both criticize and support the Christian in a community in tension with cultural forms. It also tended to underestimate the need of a corporate Christian witness in a world dominated by organizations with power. Although it was acutely conscious of worldly principalities and powers and their coerciveness on men, it did not recognize how deeply embedded and dependent on those structures is all human activity.

For these reasons, its heroic ethic tended to collapse again into the split between the high ideals of perfect love and practical adjustment to the processes of the world. Those who took it seriously and were compelled to make continuous accommodations in the world were disillusioned. Some longed for a new monasticism in small communities where the social context could be limited and controlled at the cost of giving up the good society on the larger scale. Adjustment for many now became more "uneasy" than for the personal pietists, because an uncompromising demand had entered the consciences of vast numbers of Christians. Perhaps this collapse presaged the swing to the new cult of "peace of mind" for many liberals. This seems to be the return to a new and more sophisticated form of individual pietism, but without the intense eternal hope beyond this world. It promises secularized rewards that are more immediately available in the form of wealth, popularity, and happiness to those who take their frustrations to their benevolent-but-never-chastening God. It has been against the background of these trends and currents that our theologians have launched another attempt to meet the problem of Christian guidance in the limited world of events in which restriction and compromise offer no escape.

Instead of making and sanctioning further concessions to the ideas and values of contemporary culture, there has been a return to the Biblical sources and defining events of our faith. There has been a return to that constant perspective provided in the revelation of God in Christ and that mode of divine action that has maintained the continuity of the community of Christ through the changing cultures of history. It is vigorously insisted again that the Christian faith does not simply provide holy sanctions and blessings for the popular values of shifting cultures, but points continuously beyond to the way that God has revealed Himself and continues to act in judgment and redemption in the passing parade of all cultural change.

It poses again one of the most important questions that the Christian can ask: How do the Christian and the church work within the cultural forms and processes of society in order to cast influence into these and yet not abdicate to cultural values and goals?

Therefore, two fundamental tasks have been undertaken. The first has been an attempt to rediscover the culture-transcending and defining foundations of the Christian faith. The second has been to find the mode in which God has acted and continues to act to illuminate and redeem men and transform cultures, so that the Christian response can be made to God rather than to culturally defined expediency. The nature of this last task has forced the addition of a third basic consideration for Christian ethics. This is the analysis and understanding of the social and political processes within which man lives and acts—how they impinge upon his inner consciousness, set the framework within which decisions are made, and provide the only possible context in which he can become a creative center of influence in response to God. This last pursuit defines the field of sociology of religion and is an indis-; pensable area of consideration for understanding the context of ethical decision.

The adherents of the partial gospel of individual piety and its petty morality, divorced from the practical decisional life, are still numerous and tend to resist attempts at their rescue. It is easier for the clergy to preach a repetition of glorious truths and to repeat descriptions of the crowning act of God in Christ, thus escaping the agonizing task of joining their parishioners in confronting the actual pressures of existence. And it is easier for laymen to live by the pressures of expediency and adore this Christ of the sanctuary from afar.

One of the outstanding leaders in this reformulation of the relation of faith to action has been Reinhold Niebuhr. We cannot survey his extensive theological treatment except to summarize his view of the dilemma of responsible social participation versus an absolute Christian ethical demand. He vigorously reaffirms the obligation of Christian participation in social action, and has been an untiring advocate and example of Christian entrance into the formation of political and social policy. With a bombardment of penetrating criticism, he has challenged the easy conscience of modern man and his trust in material progress, in natural vitalities, and in rational ideals to produce the good society. Even more significantly, he has leveled his criticism at complacency and accommodative tendencies in theology and the church. As Professor Niebuhr himself has summarized this criticism, it was directed against "pietistic individualism," "Christian and secular moralism," and the "Catholic idea of a Christian civilization."

Pietistic individualism "was judged the most indefensible of all allegedly Christian positions because it combined a naturalistic version of society with a highly individualistic version of the Christian faith."[3] Against easy moralism and its faith in the ideals

---

[3] Reinhold Niebuhr, "Christian Faith and Social Action," in *Christian Faith and Social Action,* John A. Hutchison (editor) (New York: Charles Scribner's Sons, 1953), p. 226.

of love to persuade individual men to abandon self-seeking, he has emphasized tension and conflict as permanent aspects of human life. Against notions of Christian civilization, he has emphasized the pretensions of all groups that claim to know the ultimate formula for the just society.

The word that characterizes Niebuhr's thought is judgment. He sees the judgment that Jesus Christ and what he calls "the law of love" lay upon all human striving, all rational goals, and all social structures. He is deeply realistic in analyzing human pride and sinfulness and the inevitable conflicts of power that enter into the formation of organizational policy. He sees these as being perennial, and as never to be overcome within historical events. The elevation to primacy of any organization or any set of ideals as productive of the divine society or the will of God he sees as idolatry. The sovereignty of God stands high, transcendent, and judgmental.

In an age of pretension and sentimentalism, his voice has been both a prophetic warning against ultimate confidence in all our human schemes and vaunted institutions and a penetrating reminder of how human decisions are actually made in the arena of power and negotiation. All our religious accommodations and sanctions of passing cultural and class values are challenged, measured, and found wanting. This Biblical and basically Protestant view has been restored again as an undisputed part of our faith. And for this we are deeply indebted.

However, there seems to remain an almost unbridgeable gap between the action of God together with his claims upon us in Christ and the pragmatic manipulations and conflicts of the world. The Christian ethic is the "final imperative"[4] of the "law of love," which is a staggering indictment on all the pragmatic policies and manipulations of the world. It is "a principle of criticism upon all our political and economic realities."[5] With this judgmental side of our faith, we cannot disagree, but there is an almost complete dualism between the actions of God and the activities of men; between the ethic of love and the world of practical decision. Pro-

[4] *Ibid.*, p. 241.
[5] *Ibid.*, p. 228.

fessor Niebuhr has repeatedly pointed out the direct inapplicability of this principle of love to social realities. Love is seen as sacrificial self-giving, heedless of consequences, and uncalculating. As a realistic social analyst, however, he shows that policy decisions necessitate calculation of consequences, balancing of self-interest and power, and planning in the light of projected goals. Therefore, love can only stand in eternal judgment as "the spirit of contrition." The result is a permanent tension—if not a complete split—between what God demands and what men can do even by God's grace. The Christian ethic is "a law of love" and "an impossible possibility" that has "relevance"; at the same time, it is "an impossibility" as an "ideal." The paramount question of how relevant pure criticism or pure judgment can be in directing our behavior stands over us.

Thus Professor Niebuhr has done us the service of stripping away the soft illusion about the efficacy of sentimental good will, but we cannot feel that he has escaped some of his own criticisms. Are not "the injustices of society . . . placed into such sharp contrast with the absolute moral ideal . . . that the religiously sensitized soul is tempted to despair of society"?[6] And, under this view, is it not true that "religion . . . degenerates into an asocial quest for the absolute" or "draws the bow of life so taut that it . . . snaps the string [defeatism]"?[7]

Is there not here a real carry-over from a rationalist ethics that provides a law, or an absolute commandment, to be laid down as a measure of all human decisions? Does this interpretation of love as a law and principle of criticism do justice to the Biblical view? Is there not another interpretation of love and the Christian ethic that preserves both its judgmental aspect, yet which reveals a transformative activity of God that goes beyond judgment into redemption?

These questions we derive partly from Mr. Niebuhr himself and partly from other critics of idealistic and rationalistic ethics who

---

[6] Reinhold Niebuhr, *Moral Man and Immoral Society* (New York: Charles Scribner's Sons, 1936), p. 70.

[7] *Ibid.,* p. 71.

are returning to Biblical and reformation sources. We fear that this view still does not fully solve the problem that is stated by Professor Lehmann as "how to live constructively in the gap between the will of God, theologically understood, and the concrete human situation, pragmatically understood."[8] The basic Christian recognition of sin and failure is not, in itself, a positive guide to action or a mode of decision. It is humbling but not regenerative.

There are several basic components of the Christian faith that are neglected or left unrelated to decision in this view:

1. Christian behavior is not just criticized under a law; it is transformed, reshaped, and redirected by the transforming grace of God as men stand within the tensions of pragmatic action and negotiate their decisions in relation to others.

2. The Christian response is to the action of God in the restraints, reconciliations, and openings in the sphere of events; as confronted from the perspective of faith and devotion and as criticized and reinforced in the community of Christ.

3. Love is not a principle of disinterestedness, but a gift of grace that comes to those who have felt the impact of love in their own lives and begin to respond spontaneously in self-forgetting acts toward others. Such love is generated and transmitted in that community of grace founded on the response to the love of God revealed in Christ.

This love is never fully possible for sinful men, but this does not mean that it is not partially possible or that it cannot be a directing orientation in our lives. It is the gift of divine grace and action, and it is carried in the Christ-oriented perspectives of men as they confront concrete decisions. It is an ethic of submission to God and a dynamic response to the requirements of others in community, rather than merely one of applied principle. Daniel Williams declares that ". . . all Christian social action depends upon faith in grace."[9] He reminds us that there are new possibil-

[8] Paul L. Lehmann, "The Foundation and Pattern of Christian Behavior" in *Christian Faith and Social Action,* John A. Hutchison (editor) (New York: Charles Scribner's Sons, 1953), p. 101.

[9] Daniel D. Williams, "Christian Faith and Social Action" (unpublished paper for discussion).

ities of reconciliation even in what seem to be the most hopeless situations. "There is a new order of life always ready to come into being. As Christians we act in the light of both our knowledge of sin and our faith in grace."[10]

RELATION OF FAITH TO CULTURE

Professor H. Richard Niebuhr has discussed five different views of the relations of Christ to culture that are found in theological interpretation. On the extreme end of the scale is the radical view that rejects the world as totally evil. The Christian's response can only be one of abandoning the world—"to come out from among them and be separate." Participation in the world can only bring contamination, and all attempts to improve or transform human institutions are futile. This view supports no obligation for Christian social responsibility because it is both hopeless and irrelevant.

On the opposite end of the scale is the position of fundamental agreement between Christ and culture. Jesus is the hero of culture. His teaching is the pinnacle of human achievement. He himself is regarded as part of the social heritage. Under this view Christ affirms culture and is often identified with cultural achievements and democratic institutions. There is no tension or criticism between faith and existing institutions and values. Thus, accommodation not only is justified, but prevailing value systems and social patterns are seen as the fruits of this heritage and are not only pronounced good but given religious sanctification. Religion becomes the emotionalization of cultural values and a fortress of defense for the *status quo*. It operates as an instrument for transmitting these values and of focusing loyalty in uncritical support on them. Religion cannot be distinguished from national or cultural patriotism. Worship merely reinforces the social bonds of a society. Culture, then, easily displaces and becomes the underlying object of devotion in place of Christ. When Christianity is related to the culture within which it exists in this form it becomes what is often called a natural religion. A natural religion is one

10 *Ibid.*

that is both a product of and apologetic for the existing value system. Modern sociologists who have studied the functions of religion in society have tended to see it as performing this function of social integration and the social ritualization of such universal crisis experiences as birth, marriage, and death. This type of religion is socially reflective rather than regenerative.

In this interpretation the Christian faith is culture-bound and has no transcendent reference and no real "formative power,"[11] to use Paul Tillich's term. Christ is seen as a natural product of a past culture and only a retranslated symbol of present cultural values. Religion has no dynamics or activity of its own independent of particular cultures that can influence events, break cultural forms, and create new patterns. In other words, the Christian faith and the activity of God are not creative but merely refer to and sanction what is already happening naturally through social processes. Christ and God are no more than social symbols for the collective representation of society.

The third type of relationship, which Richard Niebuhr calls the *synthetic* type (or Christ above culture) is presented in Thomistic and Roman Catholic doctrine. God works through natural law, forming and fulfilling cultural aspirations and institutions. But God through Christ is also discontinuous with culture, bringing supernatural gifts of salvation and guidance through the means of the Church.

The fourth type of interpretation is dualistic or paradoxical. It represents a view that has been in the ascendency in Continental theology and among many groups in America. It is represented in Lutheranism and its doctrine of two spheres and among those who see God as totally transcendent. In this duality, "the inescapable authority of both Christ and culture is recognized."[12] In being subjected to two authorities in two realms that must both be obeyed, the Christian is subject to two "largely opposed"[13] moral-

[11] Paul Tillich, *The Protestant Era.* Copyright, 1948, by the University of Chicago Press, chap. XIV.

[12] H. Richard Niebuhr, *Christ and Culture* (New York: Harper and Brothers, 1951), p. 42.

[13] *Ibid.,* p. 43.

ities. This means, as Professor Niebuhr puts it, that "In the *polarity* and *tension* of Christ and culture, life must be lived precariously and sinfully in the hope of a justification which lies beyond history."[14]

It emphasizes the gulf between God on one side and man and all his works on the other. In the conflict between man and God has come a great reconciling event in Christ. Grace comes only from God. There is "corruption and degradation in all man's work."[15] All men and all culture are under judgment because of their rebellion against God: their Godlessness. Men are always trying to play God—to be the "judge and ruler of all things." Therefore, all things in culture are in self-contradiction. The lust for power pervades all human relations and institutions, including the church.

The one distinction—between this view and that of the radical opposition of God to culture—lies in the fact that the dualist recognizes that there is no escape and believes that God's grace will sustain him in it. Because of this double status of man in being under grace, yet a sinner living under sin, the concept of paradox has been used to explain this position.

The fifth view, which Professor Niebuhr sets forth as the position that he favors, is from our view the most satisfactory interpretation of the relationship between Christ and culture. He calls it the conversionist or transformationist view. Although he does not find this position consistently advocated in all of the great theologians that he cites, he finds it as a "motif" running through their writings. He finds this motif in the First Letter of John, in the Fourth Gospel, and in many of the writings of Paul, Augustine, Wesley (to some degree), F. N. Maurice, Jonathan Edwards, and many others. Mr. Niebuhr says this view belongs to "the great central tradition of the church"[16] and that it is marked by "a more positive and hopeful attitude toward culture."[17]

Christ is seen more as a Redeemer than a giver of a new law.

[14] *Ibid.*
[15] *Ibid.*, p. 152.
[16] *Ibid.*, p. 190.
[17] *Ibid.*, p. 191.

Whereas God's work in Christ is very different from man's work in culture, it is not isolated from civilization. This Redeemer does not offer "ideas, counsel, and laws"[18] but lives with men contemporaneously. Sin is seen as deeply rooted in man and culture, as with the dualists, but a defining "major theme" is added in "the creative activity of God."[19]

Culture is corrupted, but it is "perverted good, not evil."[20] Therefore, the Christian response to culture is not total rejection but a belief that it needs conversion and that God is acting upon it. History is understood to be "not a course of merely human events but always a dramatic interaction between God and men. . . . history is the story of God's mighty deeds and of man's responses to them."[21]

Professor Niebuhr says that the Christian is not as much preoccupied with what God has done or is going to do as "with divine possibility of a present renewal"[22] in the present situation. He identifies himself as a "social existentialist."[23] He sees the Christian and the Christian community as called from the easy chair "into the middle of a present conflict."[24]

To make decisions in faith is to make them in the context in which they are confronted. To quote Mr. Niebuhr, "They are made . . . on the basis of relative insight and faith, but they are not relativistic. They are individual decisions, but not individualistic. They are made in freedom, but not in independence; they are made in the moment, but are not nonhistorical."[25]

Thus, we must make decisions in our own particular roles with our particular duties and limited perspectives, within the relative situation in which we find ourselves. Our decisions are related to political relations and economic relations, neighborhood relations, family relations, and so forth. We are reminded by Professor Nie-

[18] *Ibid.*
[19] *Ibid.*, p. 192.
[20] *Ibid.*, p. 194.
[21] *Ibid.*, pp. 194-195.
[22] *Ibid.*, p. 195.
[23] *Ibid.*, p. 241.
[24] *Ibid.*, p. 233.
[25] *Ibid.*, p. 234.

buhr of the relational or contextual character of all our values.

In reference to Christian social action, there are several important insights that we derive from this view. First, the Christian must live and make his responses to God within and through cultural activities. In interpreting and quoting Augustine, Mr. Niebuhr writes: "The Christian life can and must make use not only of these cultural activities but of the 'convenient and necessary arrangements of men with men.' "[26]

Secondly, men are intrinsically social in nature and have their very existence as "sons, brothers, and members of community." For men to be truly human they also exist in the universal community of God as it has been revealed in Christ. It is universal, including all living men, and not just converted men who recognize that God's action is always creating and holding community in existence. This leads Mr. Niebuhr to say that "the world of culture—man's achievement—exists within the world of Grace— God's Kingdom."[27] Julian Hartt, who presents somewhat the same view, calls it "that actual community which underlies all societies and all cultures."[28]

Thirdly, sin is a universal fact of human existence emphasized in theology but is not the basis of theology. This basis is more positive in what God does in personal and historical transformation. The church needs "to direct all its interest toward the realization of the divine possibility of universal, willing acceptance of . . . [His] actual rule."[29]

Fourthly, men are always "dealing with God" in every situation and in every decision in their lives. His activity is working upon them and upon the situations which they confront. As Julian Hartt puts it, "in every period of history, God is active, effecting revolution and transformation."[30] To respond and enter into what God is doing is the fundamental basis of Christian social action.

[26] *Ibid.*, p. 215.
[27] *Ibid.*, p. 256.
[28] Julian Hartt, *Toward a Theology of Evangelism* (New York: Abingdon Press, 1955), p. 117.
[29] H. Richard Niebuhr, *Christ and Culture*, p. 225.
[30] Julian Hartt, *op. cit.*, p. 77.

Paul Tillich reminds us that religion is concerned with everyday "things and events in their religious significance,"[31] in their relationship to God. Again he says, "Religious action . . . must create its forms out of the experiences of the daily life and the actual situation."[32] Daniel Jenkins declares that "the spirit of the living God moves in all the affairs of human life."[33] We relate ourselves to God in worshipfully confronting events and decisions in the perspective of faith. The ways and will of God are not discovered in some totally removed heavenly sphere or some mystical sphere of private meditation cut off from events. The data of religion is the data of events that are viewed in faith in their relation to the ruling sovereignty of God as revealed in the event of Jesus Christ. This is why God's action is hidden and easily confused with the sheer flow of cultural history. God is acting upon events not merely within them; therefore, man's response to God is always to what He has done and what He is doing. God's ways are not men's ways, but they are ruling and overruling the events of history. Events are understood and ethical decisions must be made in relation to God who stands above them all.

Fifthly, our decisions are individually made in self-responsibility, but they are never "individualistic."[34] It is never "I" but "we" that are involved in all decisions. They are made in relation to associates, "collaborators," "corroborating witnesses." We cannot confront Christ "apart from a company of witnesses."[35] "It is not in lonely internal debate but in the living dialogue of the self with other selves that we can come to the point where we can make a decision and say, 'Whatever may be the duty of other men this is my duty.' "[36]

Sixthly, the Christian in the midst of his relativities responds to

---

[31] Paul Tillich, *op. cit.* Copyright, 1948, by the University of Chicago Press, p. 217.

[32] *Ibid.,* p. 219.

[33] Daniel Jenkins, *Tradition, Freedom, and the Spirit* (Philadelphia: The Westminster Press, 1951), p. 101.

[34] H. Richard Niebuhr, *Christ and Culture,* p. 243.

[35] *Ibid.,* p. 245.

[36] *Ibid.*

an absolute. Professor Niebuhr says we have three alternatives: We can become "nihilists" and total skeptics; we can choose to make some relative authority absolute, such as a Church, a value, or the self; or we can give our faith to "the infinite Absolute to whom all . . . [our] relative views, values and duties are subject."[37] The living and acting God is the only absolute to whom we must give our absolute loyalty if we are to truly have no other gods before Him.

Christians must make their social responses in obedience to God. They must consider their neighbors in all their "value-relations" in the context of the whole community of relations and in their "value-relation to God."[38] Mr. Niebuhr believes that

> a combination of relative insight and duty with faith in God does not involve compromise . . . among incommensurable interests and values; and an absolute standard cannot be compromised—it can only be broken. . . . We cannot excuse ourselves by saying that we have made the best compromise possible. . . . [We must] recognize our faithlessness, and in faith rely on the grace that will change our minds while . . . it heals the wounds we have inflicted and cannot heal.[39]

To Compromise or Not to Compromise

Those who attempt to serve God in the struggle for righteousness require strength and courage that will enable them to withstand the pressures of influence on every side. They must be prepared to live in permanent tension with the popular tides of opinion and the conventional practices of society. Fortitude and resistance "and the whole armour of God" are needed to stand against the sly wiles and oppressive forces that are ever surrounding and beguiling us.

Unfortunately, high fortitude and resistance are very often coupled with obstinacy and self-righteousness. Resolute men of principle are often so rigid and inflexible that they cannot sense

[37] *Ibid.*, p. 238.
[38] *Ibid.*, p. 240.
[39] *Ibid.*, p. 241.

the deeper demands of love in their relations or let God break through their pride. The Christian is one who is always sensitively responsive to the needs and suffering of his fellows, and ready to be overruled by the action of God. Humility must always be able to say, "I may be wrong and you may be right." Resoluteness is always touched with defensiveness, and moral principles can be used as weapons that pride wields to stave off the claims of others.

How, then, can fortitude and valorous contention for righteousness be coupled with the openness and self-denial that Christ lays upon us? So many of the aggressions and coercions of men and groups are done in the name of principle. How can we carry on the war on evil when we may be the chief sinners?

This brings into focus the perplexing problem of compromise. The valiant Christian warrior against injustice and exploitation ought never to compromise but stand firm in his demands. But the obstinate and prideful man who claims to know what is the absolute good for others ought to give way and adjust to their claims. The perplexity arises when we recognize that these two men are always one and indivisibly the same man. We ought never to compromise with divine justice, but we ought always to compromise our stubborn self-centered views of justice to a higher claim.

The word compromise adds to the ambiguity by having two meanings. Originally, it was derived from the Latin *compromissum* which means "a mutual promise to abide by a decision." As a verb, it means on the one hand, "a settlement by arbitration" and on the other, "a prejudicial concession or a surrender." As a verb it means either to adjust and settle a difference by mutual agreement or to expose to discredit. The more reputable meaning of the term seems to have been somewhat discredited through guilt by association.

Compromise decisions are arbitrated or negotiated decisions. In a negotiated decision, there are two elements involved: first, the interests of those participating and, secondly, their moral principles or sense of what is right. It is usually thought that our self-interests should be modified in compromise but never our principles. Unfortunately, self-interests and moral principles are always intermixed. Compromise is likely to involve both concessions in interests and settling for less than what all the participants believe that their principles require. Principles-in-application are likely to be tainted with "self rightness" and be more closely allied to self-interest than is usually recognized.

Therefore, the notion that principles are easily distinguishable from, or in opposition to, interests is far too simple an analysis. Let us look at two apparently opposite kinds of unfaithfulness that are involved in participation in ethical negotiations: one through refusal to participate in adjustive decisions because of an absolute ethical unwillingness to compromise, and the other from an uncritical willingness to adjust.

THE SIN OF DECISIONAL DEFAULT

There are two types of temptation that the Christian must recognize as he attempts to act responsibly within the framework of human existence. These are often distinguished in our prayers as the sins of "omission" (inaction when decision calls) and "commission" (decisions exploiting others in the interest of self, rather than serving God and neighbor).

The first kind of temptation that confronts the Christian in the practical world is on the side of omission. It is the temptation to use lofty ideals or even the high sense of obligation to God as an excuse for crawling out of responsibility in concrete ethical situations. For sinful men, within limited situations, the full demands of living in the community of Christ and of seeking balanced justice are beyond possibility in most actual decisions. Therefore, one can be an ethical absolutist only at the expense of withdrawal into the realm of private meditation and wishful thinking. To avoid the risk of compromise in the selection of real alternatives, he is tempted to choose none and let the drift of events determine outcomes under the illusion that in this way he can keep himself religiously faithful and simon-pure from moral error. But doing nothing is in itself an effective type of decision. As Richard Niebuhr says, "If I withdraw into weakness in the pressure system and become an atmospheric low instead of an atmospheric high, the weather changes."[40]

Against this view must be laid the simple fact that no decision can be postponed until the propitious time when there are no ambiguities or deterrents in the way of a perfectly just act. Such a time can never come. The Christian like every other responsible actor must do whatever can be done in the pressing situation at hand. It is necessary to begin a course of action from where one is, in the context where one stands.

This is rather neatly illustrated by the old Irish story of the man who was lost in the country and stopped to ask an old man the way to Dublin. The old man answered, "Well, can't say. But faith, if it's to Dublin that you'd be agoin' I wouldn't be startin' from here." The existing situation is the only place to start from, no matter how many adverse factors it contains. The Christian must cast his influence through existing social institutions, for they are the existing patterns of activity in any society.

To wait for better institutions to arise, as a point of departure from which to challenge these same institutions, is to land in a vicious circle. Even revolutionaries who seek a complete overthrow of old institutions find it necessary to begin by "boring from within" in order to participate in subverting them. It is within the process of ongoing activity that the Christian makes his decisions, cooperates with others, and makes his witness for Christ.

In contrast to the revolutionist, who believes he has a neat formula and set of prescriptions that can be followed to produce the just social order, the Christian believes that he must respond to his God in the ongoing context of activity. Christianity is revolutionary, but its transformations are produced by God rather than man.[41] It is the activity of God that opens up new possibilities and uses and redirects human effort. The Christian cannot discover the will of God as an abstract demand but as a concrete response

---

[40] H. Richard Niebuhr, classroom lectures in Christian Ethics, Yale Divinity School, 1954.
[41] Julian Hartt, *op. cit.*, chap. VII.

of faith in a decisional situation. It is not until he begins to act responsively in decisional activity in confronting the claims of others, the actual blockages, and possible alternatives that he is prepared to respond to God or that he begins to really see the factors involved.

The Christian, then, is ever alert to step into every new situation to promote the community of love and the kind of organization that makes responses to the needs of others possible.

Hence, it is morally obligatory to enter the interactive life of the community and to participate in the negotiation of decisions. Compromise is obligatory in the sense of participation in the development and choice of open alternatives rather than defaulting to others or waiting until other men produce a better situation. Consequently, no Christian who interacts at all in the social context can escape participation in corporate acts and arrangements that are far less than just to all concerned.

Those who belong to the "realist" school are rightly impressed by the tendency on the part of those who demand uncompromising adherence to Christian love, or some other absolute principle or ideal, to retreat to the ivory towers of criticism rather than accepting the risk of participative responsibility. When the "perfectionist" does find the nerve to act in a situation in which he believes that he sees the answer clearly, he will be tempted to insist that the solution he offers represents the uncompromising will of God. He then risks the sin of absolutizing his own ideals and playing God.

Other Christians also believe that they have access to divine guidance. Also, nonreligious men with consciences and practical knowledge are confident in their policies. Confronting practical problems always involves working with other Christians and non-Christians. Since others see moral issues from divergent perspectives, they will conscientiously differ on what the will of God or social justice seems to require. Thus, flexibility and the willingness to consider the legitimacy of the moral claims of all others is required, unless policy is to be determined entirely by the unilateral power to coerce the opposition.

In fact, a sensitive response to the claims and moral concerns of others is the distinctive characteristic of an ethic of love. Love cannot work by inflicting my dogmatic views of moral action on others for their own good but by attempting to identify myself with them. It is necessary to understand their needs as they feel them, and then to modify my response in the light of this transformed perspective. Then, a cooperative decision can be made to the newly understood situation.

On the other hand, love is not merely a capitulation to the unmodified interests of others but is entering a relationship with a sensitive willingness to let the higher good of neighbor, in the total community of neighbors, prevail at sacrificial costs to oneself. It must be insisted that love, itself, is a kind of self-compromise in which one's interests and moral certainties are modified in an outgoing identification with the good of others.

The divine love of totally sacrificing one's own claims to those of others (the kind of love revealed in Christ's going to the cross) is never fully possible for men. Since all human perspectives are tainted with the sin of self-interest, the biases of culture, and class and group identifications, the capacity to get over into the perspectives of others is limited. Even more significant is the rather clear fact that sacrificial love, if actually practiced in human relations, would destroy community. It would do this by creating vacuums in power which would unduly tempt all men and would deprive other men of the restraints they need against their claims—just as we need the restraints of others upon our own. These facts make it imperative that all ethical responses must be modified by the claims and restraints imposed by others in every ethical situation. Any community requires this type of adjustive modification on the part of its members if it is not to be destroyed as a functioning unity.

The Christian lives in the general social community, but he also is called to live in another context. This is the divine community in Christ. It is one in which the members respond to one another in a special bond of commitment to their Lord. Under the guidance of the Holy Spirit, which works within this covenant-fellowship, there is a special transforming and relating action that modifies personal demand and leads its members into greater sensitivity in their responses to others. This community—the church—does not become a perfect communion of love, because its members are human, and are also caught in the treacherous crosscurrents of a world of coercion and conflict. But the sovereign focus of its response to Christ and the divine action of the Holy Spirit within its life and worship lift it into tension with the natural communities of the world, instead of simply supporting them.

Even in this Christian fellowship, if each member claims to know the will of God in the freedom of his own conscience and adamantly insists that he can accept no compromise in common decisions with others, the fellowship splinters and falls apart. The only possible consequence is withdrawal of the members and disintegration of the group. Even in churches where authoritative creeds and theological interpretations are accepted without dissent, disagreement and conflict occur as these are translated into decisions concerning the obligation of the Christian in response to particular situations. This occurs because the gospel is not a directory of ethical rules that are unambiguously applicable in concrete situations.

The gospel is a message of what God has done and continues to do for men. It is the call to a life of response to His creating and saving action that is carried out in dialectic interaction with men and with historical events. Instead of being a set of legal prescriptions, the Christian ethic of love is a way of meeting concrete responsibilities in community through response to God.

Every decision must be a unique confrontation of God in a particular situation. Every ethical context is dynamic; each has its peculiar blockages and possibilities. An ethic of responsive love requires that a consensus must be formed in discussion and mutual decision among those participating in the situation. The outcome can never meet the exact ethical approval of all. This is why it must be generalized that all cooperative actions and decisions in groups are compromises (adjustive decisions). But, even further, we must maintain that it is ethically imperative that this be so. For the Christian, it is equally imperative that they be made worshipfully and prayerfully within the Christian fellowship in common response to God. Personal ideals, which are always tainted with rationalization and defense, must give way in compromise to the good of all in the higher synthesis of the community of love that only God creates and redeems.

THE SIN OF SOCIAL CONFORMITY

The opposite temptation—to that of refusal to act and participate in decisional processes—is to accept accommodation and conformity to the wills of others and the practices of society as normative without criticism and challenge. The pressures toward conformity are always powerful in any society, including those that claim to be free. Those who conform most enthusiastically and with the greatest demonstrations of loyalty reap popularity and advancement. Democracy has a tendency to place a high premium on voluntary conformity because of the practical necessity of winning the consent and support of majorities. Pressures toward conformity are increased in a society characterized by mass communications and large-scale organizations, which exert powerful controls over the status and advancement of large numbers.

There are strong indications that moral independence is declining and running into new forms of dishonor and resistance in our contemporary culture. Professor Riesman has argued in his much discussed analysis that modern man is becoming increasingly "other-directed,"[42] developing a kind of built-in radar-sensitivity by which his conduct is directed by the subtle signs that reveal the approvals and disapprovals of others. This is contrasted with the "tradition-directed" and "inner-directed" types of men who have predominated in other periods.

Progressive education has tended to be dominated by the goal of the adjustive personality. As was discussed earlier, the growth of bureaucratic organization in business, government, trade un-

[42] David Riesman, *The Lonely Crowd* (New Haven: Yale University Press, 1950), pp. 19-25.

ions, and so on has made it necessary for the majority of people to work in graded hierarchies, which place high value upon graciously meeting the demands of superiors and accepting organizational policy uncritically in order to attain security and win advancement.

All of this means that independent moral decision or personal responsibility and courage is stifled, or at least not strongly developed in our society. As we have already observed, the nonconformist—even on scrupulous moral grounds—is likely to be considered stubborn, uncooperative, and even dangerous. Political nonconformity is considered subversive by large numbers—if not the majority. Little distinction is any longer drawn between the self-centered and antisocial rebel or criminal and the creative nonconformist who, as a matter of conscience and in loyalty to a more demanding commitment, struggles for higher standards at high personal cost in ostracism and disadvantage. A society that cannot tolerate, even if it cannot honor, the prophet and moral critic is no longer a free society and is in danger of lapsing into stagnation and excessive coercion.

Furthermore, it provides an infertile and resistant soil in which to preach the Christian gospel of judgment and transformation under God. An acute awareness of this tendency in our society and the basic tension that the Christian faith demands in relation to the popular values of the world have led many Christians to see compromise as the besetting sin of our times. They believe that our churches are tinctured with this pressure toward conformity and are producing too few prophets and too little support for those who do dare become courageous spokesmen for the prophetic faith. We believe that we must take this temptation seriously and give full recognition to this side of the dilemma of participative adjustment versus uncompromising independence.

However, we must not overlook the fact that prophetic criticism must be more than denunciation if it is to touch human policy and become embodied in human activities. The Old Testament prophets were not scowling thunderers who took sadistic pride in the inevitable destruction of their nation and people in the hands of their God. They called for humble repentance and a return to the ways of their covenant God. They spoke for a covenant community in which the Lordship of God was commonly recognized. And they spoke especially to kings and those in authority who had power in their hands to act. Criticism that is never directed seriously toward guidance and never intended to be translated into action is less than prophetic. It is sadistic in that it is delivered to intensify human frustration and alienation and to deepen the gulf between what is and what the love revealed in Christ requires.

If the prophetic and priestly roles are totally in opposition rather than interactive, then the very term "prophetic guidance" is a contradiction. It appears that in the traditional division of the ministries of the church into the prophetic and the priestly something has been left out. This is the "ministry of administration" —of developing social strategies—which translates prophetic warnings and priestly devotion into real correctives and guides for decision among the conflicts of social existence. The Protestant doctrine of "Christian vocation of all believers" should help us overcome this omission.

Thus, we find what appears to be a dilemma with two opposite temptations to irresponsibility and unfaithfulness standing in conflict. Some Christians are more fearful of the sin of inaction and nonparticipation, shown by those who make uncompromising faithfulness the excuse for not entering into the interplay of decision in fear of being forced to do less than God demands. Another group fears the sin of conformity, of serving man rather than God, of seeking expedient ways out of hard problems rather than following the harder path of persistence and courage.

TOWARD A RESOLUTION OF THE DILEMMA OF COMPROMISE

This problem formulates one of the most significant issues in present ethical discussions.[43] One must earnestly confront the

[43] The author has seen this conflict in emphasis emerge in discussions and letters from members of the General Committee of the Department of the Church and Economic Life of the National Council of Churches concerning a study paper for that group on *Compromise in Ethical Decisions.*

question of how this problem can be faced. Because man is a being created in community and for community and because of his call from God through Christ to active witnessing, it seems clear that he must become a vital interventionist and participant rather than a critic or a neutral observer in the struggle for power and righteousness. God revealed Himself in the world through Christ, who entered the human community and faced its risks and was crucified. God Himself acts creatively and redemptively in the dialogue between Himself and the events of the world.

There is no way to influence events or to live responsibly to God except by entering the processes of interaction and accepting the restrictions of citizenship, membership, and office in the policy-forming organizations of the world.

There is no way to swim upstream without plunging into the water and getting wet. And getting wet means being contaminated to some degree by the water and its impurities and having one's course deflected by the currents, eddies, and rocks in the river. It is difficult to swim across a swift flowing stream and reach exactly the projected point on the other side. In order to get across at all necessitates an allowance for downward pull.

It must be admitted that there are situations in which the Christian witness does have an impact when proclaimed from positions outside of organizations by those who refuse to participate on ethical grounds. Even here, such a witness is dependent upon being considered and accepted by actual participants who attempt to fit it to situations, or it remains irrelevant utopianism.

There are irresponsibility and hypocrisy in insisting upon always being a "sidewalk superintendent" who offers ideal solutions and criticisms without taking the risk of conflict and compromise in application. This has been called the sniper's approach. The ethical sniper is one who sits under cover and pokes his head out from time to time to fire a burst of criticism upon what other men are doing, and then ducks again for cover with no sustained effort and no real commitment to the struggle.

The sniper, or sideline critic, seldom gains the confidence of others who must bear the burdens and risks of decision. He is labeled a dreamer who models in ethereal clay that has none of the resistances and, therefore, none of the outcomes of real media. And this popular criticism has genuine ethical support. Since the sniper has no structure of support nor channels of communication even his "advice" is bottled up in silence.

As we have already discussed, the Christian witness itself requires organization in a "body" of people who stand together in mutual support and criticism in relation to Christ as the vehicle through which the Holy Spirit moves. This body is involved in the adjustive process of consensus building, or it can never confront the world about it with unity or throw weight into the balances of opinion and power.

The church confronts the same dilemma as the individual Christian. It can "play it safe" by preaching pious individualism and by sentimentally counseling its people concerning their private frustrations without reference to the external contexts in which they occur. In this way, it can avoid all the risks of entering controversy. This will be institutionally prudent, for it can avoid offending those who desire only a culture-sanctioning and undisturbing faith. But the one thing that it cannot be—if this course is taken—is a church of influence. All issues in which there is no controversy are settled. Any settled question or activity that is reopened for the consideration of new and more ethical possibilities becomes controversial—now demanding a new response. The only way that controversy can be avoided is to accept people and social structures exactly as they are (a totally immobile and passive course). Transformation in people and social structures is always controversial, and it always places discomfiture and strain on participants. If the church is to be of any influence whatever, it must risk controversy and error. An adventuring church will be subject to error and the need of forgiveness and renewal just as the individual Christian.

On the negative side of the dilemma of compromise, it seems necessary to state rather flatly that entering the field of negotiation and controversy does imperil Christian faithfulness. It does subject the participant to serious temptations that cannot be fully resisted. However, it is unavoidable since the life of adjustment and compromise is simply the problem of being a human being in the world. Engagement in the process of adjustment provides both positive and negative possibilities—both opportunities to serve Christ and opportunities to deny Him. Like driving one's car on the highway, such an activity provides both a path to a destination and a hazard of getting killed. It is not sound advice to say that it is better to stay at home and remain less vulnerable. Staying at home forever means going nowhere and doing nothing. Nothing risked is nothing gained.

Therefore, it is important for the Christian to recognize the risks and be prepared for them. Adjustment to solutions that can be negotiated with others and with physical and social realities does provide a loophole for accepting less than might have been possible if greater alertness, wisdom, and courage had been exercised. There is always the possibility that, by yielding prejudices under a higher perspective, far higher gains could have been made if the Christian had submitted himself in prayer and openness of mind more fully to God's grace. Furthermore, it is a truism that adjustment becomes easier with practice and can reduce the tensions of the judgment of God which must be kept taut to pull upon all Christian choosing.

Another reason why there is injustice in compromised decisions is that such solutions tend to be made by a few leaders or participants in situations where many affected individuals or groups have not been represented and have been unable to insert their claims and their moral perspectives into the considerations. No negotiated policy for action represents a balanced adjustment of all claims in the whole community because of inequalities of power, shrewdness, and ability to moralize or emotionalize claims for support from others.

In an age in which many are impressed with the deterministic belief that all consequences are simply the added results of prior forces, the creative fluidity of a situation may be greatly underestimated. This may obscure creative options that were regarded as impossible from an advance analysis of the situation. The

Christian believes in taking into account the creative and redemptive activities of God in saving situations and transmuting blockages into unforseeable openings.

The Christian faith always requires adventure and risk in which decision goes beyond the prudential calculation of what the moral traffic will bear or the situational limitations allow. Christian action should rise above ordinary expediency and demand the highest possible justice that can be squeezed through situational limitations by the aid of the grace of God.

How, then, can we escape either the sin of inaction in the face of crisis or the sin of premature capitulation in the face of higher possibility? No decision can fall neatly on the razor-thin line between these two dangers, and no human judgment can accurately determine where this line is. No compromise is likely to squeeze full possibility from a situation. No submission to the will of God and the good of neighbor is complete. But, on the other hand, no resolute stand is free from pretension and defensive obstinacy.

It seems clear that an ethic that can help us stand successfully between these two temptations must be flexible and dynamic to be relatable to the context of every unique situation. Yet, it must help us to make every decision under the self-transcending claims of love that Christ has laid upon us, and under the transforming grace of God. As Paul Tillich so often asks, "How is this possible?"

An Ethic of Responsive Love in Community

What, then, is the Christian ethic, since it is one neither of rational principles nor pragmatic expediency[44]—neither of obsti-

[44] For the view of Christian Ethics that is presented here the author is indebted to several writers: Paul L. Lehmann, "Foundations and Patterns of Christian Behavior" in *Christian Faith and Social Action,* John A. Hutchison (editor) (New York: Charles Scribner's Sons, 1953); Alexander Miller, *The Renewal of Man* (New York: Doubleday & Company, Inc., 1955); Daniel D. Williams, *What Present Day Theologians Are Thinking* (New York: Harper and Brothers, 1952) and *God's Grace and Man's Hope* (New York: Harper and Brothers, 1949); H. Richard Niebuhr, *Christ and Culture* (New York: Harper and Brothers, 1951) and Yale Divinity School Lectures; and James M. Gustafson, *Christian Ethics in Economic Life* (unpublished paper).

nate adherence to one's own moral judgments nor easy accommodation to cultural and organizational pressures? This dilemma —the contradiction between what men ought to do and what they can do—loses its paralysis over decisions when we see the Christian ethic as one calling for a dynamic responsiveness to God in community. It does not close the gap, nor alleviate tension between God and man, or perfect human decision, but it does show us how to make decisions responsively in context.

Let us summarize this Christian ethic as we see it.

1. *The Christian Ethic Is an Ethic of a Community*

First of all, it recognizes that all ethics are relational, that is, having to do with the relation of men with one another in common loyalty to God. The basis of the Christian ethic is found in the Christian community. Paul Lehmann has called it a *koinonia* ethic. He says:

> The Christian *koinonia* is a fellowship called into being by God, a fellowship with His Son Jesus Christ our Lord. The *koinonia* is a fellowship of working together for the gospel. And the *koinonia* is a fellowship of organic integration and growth of its several parts, whose vitality and integrity are derived from the Head, and in which men learn the meaning and purpose of life, learn, too, what their responsibilities in life are.[45]

"The Ethics of Justification," Alexander Miller says, "constitute not a set of rational and formal principles, but a mesh of obligations determined by the relation of one member of the Community to another, and of all to the community's Head."[46] Biblical ethics, then, offer a "community of loyalty," "a covenant ethics," "a set of community mores," "a style of life."[47]

This means that the Christian in confronting the everyday world of decision must live and interact in the community of faith

[45] Paul L. Lehmann, *op. cit.*, pp. 103-104.
[46] From *The Renewal of Man,* by Alexander Miller. Copyright 1955 by Alexander Miller, reprinted by permission of Doubleday & Company, Inc., p. 91.
[47] *Ibid.*, pp. 88-89.

and worship. Here he shares in, and internalizes something of, the perspective of Christ and His responsiveness to the will of God in readiness for all decisions to come.

2. *The Christian Ethic Is an Ethic of Responsive Love*

Love is relational through and through, and it is active and dynamic. Love is not an internal motive or sentiment that a man can keep unexercised within himself as a cherished possession. It is the way he responds to others when he stands in relationship with them, when he actually confronts their needs and claims. It is submitting himself and his own interests to transformation under the claims of others. It is compromising his own interests and ideals in a higher focus that draws him beyond himself.

Often considered a principle or commandment, genuine love is intrinsically incapable of being anything but a kind of self-forgetting response to others and an identification with them. There has been a tendency of late to regard love as a kind of disinterested calculation about the good of other individuals and a disciplined response to meet that calculation. Disinterested love is a contradiction: A love that is compelled by an act of will against one's inclinations is self-discipline but it is not love. It is doubtful that love can ever be created by self-discipline. A command to love is about as fruitless an injunction as can be conceived. One cannot love by telling himself he ought to love; love is not willed. Can it be conceived that God was so unconcerned about man that He forced Himself to give His only begotten Son that sinners might be saved? Love is a simple outgoing response of the whole self to the good of the other. Whatever love a human being discovers in his life—and he seems incapable of full self-forgetfulness—comes to him by grace, not by calculation or by a rational sense that he ought to love. The latent capacity to love is already planted in man by God and is educed and infused by the action of love upon him. It is something that a man receives from beyond himself, or he does not have it at all.

Those who discuss love often forget its matrix in community. Those who have never been loved cannot discover it or create it. Love calls out the response of love. We discover love from our mothers, from sacrificial deeds poured out upon us. We can only love God in response to His mighty act of love in revealing Himself in His Son, who went to the cross for us—sinners though we are.

Love is generated in a special kind of community where some measure of outgoing concern and self-giving are experienced as one interacts in the network of relations. Love is discovered as it is practiced in community in responding to others. Men who have always lived under cold and calculating relations with one another, who have not felt the impact of love, will respond in cold and calculating responses and will not sense the claims of love upon them.

Therefore, love, which is really self-forgetting and not just self-love, comes by grace within community. Christian love, which is a gift of grace, as all love must be, is thrust upon man by the unbelievable gift of God in His supreme self-giving act of sacrificing His only begotten Son for the salvation of unmeriting sinners. This is the infusing impact of God's mighty act of love poured out upon the community of Christ. It is in this community of faith, created in this covenant-evoking event, that men come to respond to each other, as members one of another, with some small response to that love. It is in this fellowship in mutual response to that love of God, shown in Christ, that Christians find the grace to respond to each other in love and to form that love-generating context of deeper community that makes some small measure of self-giving love possible. Then from this fellowship they are enabled to carry this response of sacrificial concern into the world beyond themselves.

The Christian fellowship is never the full fellowship of love because of the inevitable hostages to the world and the sins both individual and corporate that penetrate it. Its most committed members can never fully receive the grace of love nor respond in love, as they would if their receptive capacities were greater, to one another in the love of Christ. But this community of Christ is the context in which divine love is imparted and generated, and becomes active. God's supreme act of love in Christ stands as the towering gift to which no Christian can respond with a matching response; so, in contrition he asks forgiveness and surrenders himself more deeply to God's redeeming action.

We repeat that love is social and relational at its very heart— it is a gift that no man can create. Community, at the deepest levels, is the instrument of its generation and transmission. Christians receive love as they become parts one of another in the one body in Christ. Then and only then can they even begin to love God and serve Him, love their neighbor in some measure of self-forgetfulness, and seek his good.

Love as an ethic cannot be understood outside of the context of community. Selective love directed toward particular individuals with whom we have intimate relations, even though we should rise to sacrificial heights, does not meet the requirement of love. For such love will shower special privileges on these favored few often at the expense of others. Selective love is one of the great moral problems of community. It is so tempting to squander all our love on those close at hand and have no concern left for those beyond our little horizon.

In a massive world of multitudes of men living interdependently in numerous competing groups, full impartial love can act only through interrelating and adjusting many perspectives and activities toward the balanced good of all. We must agree with Daniel Williams when he says, ". . . Christian love is the spirit which seeks the inclusive community of good."[48] Since all men live in community, the response of love is provincial and of little guidance if directed toward individuals abstracted from the whole context of relations in which all live. As Williams amplifies further, "The only way in which the goal of love can be defined so that full justice is done to the Christian appreciation of the worth of life is to say that love seeks that kind of community in which each member realizes his own good through giving and receiving in the life

[48] Daniel D. Williams, *What Present Day Theologians Are Thinking*, p. 88.

of the whole."[49] Such a community requires organized defenses of the weak, restraints upon the strong, and a balancing of powers.

In pointing out that love is not definable as a law or an imperative that can provide an advance categorical prescription for human behavior, we must make it clear that this does not mean that it is empty of meaning. Love is a definite kind of response to others in which self-interest is transcended and the good of others becomes a decisional focus. To respond by love is to act in a very particular kind of way that draws a person beyond personal anxieties and self-interest. As Julian Hartt puts it, ". . . he projects himself toward another, whose situation he penetrates sympathetically. He resolves to be for this other. He pledges himself to the other."[50] This is why it is more accurate to say that a Christian lives under a loyalty or commitment rather than a commandment. Furthermore, to say that love does not prescribe in advance does not mean that it is not rigorous and demanding in its ethical requirements. In fact, it is beyond the capacity of human beings ever to meet fully.

If we understand that love is more than a rational principle but instead a dynamic mode of responsiveness of the whole self to others under God, we can say that it is the dynamic standard of Christian behavior. It follows from this that many kinds of action contradict this kind of response.

Love can only contradict and condemn the categorical discrimination against persons of other races or groups and all the patterns and structures that exploit them. Love seeks a type of organization that gives every man the highest possible chance to participate in ethical decision in the activities in which he participates. Love seeks a community in which the barriers against sharing in giving and receiving are overcome at every possible point.

However, love cannot escape the pressures of the world, and is always restrained by tragic limitations. To fail to understand this fact is to return to sentimentality. Only God's Kingdom, which is

49 *Ibid.*, p. 93.
50 Julian Hartt, *Toward a Theology of Evangelism*, p. 50.

neither the church nor an ideal society but is working among us yet beyond us, is the true community of love.

3. *The Christian Ethic Is Contextual and Concrete*

This means that Christians must make their decisions not before they come to them but in the concrete situation. Every ethical situation is unique as a complex of pressures, participants, people who will be affected, and consequences to be produced. There is no advance ethical absolute that can determine what love-in-community requires. Every ethical decision must be made afresh. Of course, this does not mean that it is made without the resources conserved in memory and in the community of faith. But even these resources of the past take on new meaning and relevance within the perspective of the present, as new responsibility is faced.

Therefore, facts are ethically significant. Paul Lehmann quotes a pertinent statement from Dietrich Bonhoeffer, ". . . it is simply a fact, that the ethical cannot be detached from the real situation, the increasingly accurate knowledge of this situation is a necessary element of ethical action."[51] Alexander Miller presents this requirement in its Christian relationship when he says, "A valid Christian decision is compound[ed] always of both *faith* and *facts*. It is likely to be valid in the degree to which the faith is rightly apprehended and the facts are rightly measured."[52]

The Christian faith with its recognition of the power of pride and self-deception to distort facts provides a more realistic perspective for recognizing and comprehending these facts. The Christian faith, also, creates a more sensitive expectancy so that the "positive signs of the times" can be read to detect possibilities for deeper community that are opening, which those restricted to interpretation through social stereotypes would miss. Faith is a

---

[51] Paul L. Lehmann, *op. cit.,* p. 106.

[52] From *The Renewal of Man,* by Alexander Miller. Copyright 1955 by Alexander Miller, reprinted by permission of Doubleday & Company, Inc., p. 94.

perspective that helps us to make more out of what is happening. As we have already pointed out from the interpretation of Paul Tillich, religious knowledge is about the ordinary facts of the world in their relation to God. Faith looks for what God is doing in the process of challenge and response of history.

Then faith, in itself, can never be a substitute for investigation. Theoretical Christian ethics alone can never be an adequate discipline for facing the problems of decision in a complex world. An understanding of social organization, the structure of power and authority, the dynamics of social movements, the processes by which political decisions are made, the functioning of economic processes—to mention only a few broad areas of critical significance—is absolutely necessary. Those moralists who think simply in terms of a few principles and rigid situational stereotypes are incompetent to analyze complex situations and recognize the probable consequences of alternative actions.

This means that if Christians—either ministers or laymen— are to participate relevantly and constructively in social action, they must study and understand a vast number of technical elements involved in policy decisions. This requires the cooperation of many specialists and people with various kinds of knowledge to hammer out a relevant witness in practical issues. The church must understand how power is wielded and public opinion is formed and enter these processes.

Another important requirement that is derived from the contextual understanding of ethical decision is the need of identification and standing in the midst of the situation. One must know what the pressures are, what the participants are thinking and feeling, and the authority that they have or lack. What we are saying is that involvement is required to confront the issue with real identification and inside perception.

Divine ethical guidance is available to the Christian, not in the form of literal Biblical directives or ideal solutions, but in the action of God Himself upon us and upon the situation. We do not carry ready-made directives with us into a decisional situation except as a self oriented to Christ and with a sensitive responsiveness to God developed in Christian community. On the contrary, we must first plunge into the situation in confronting its pressures and its cross claims and then be prepared to respond to God and the restraints and possibilities that He opens before us. This does not mean that a Christian goes into a situation with no principles, no categories, and no memories. Without these he could not understand the situation or respond significantly. He carries with him his whole self with its present perspectives, its cherished values, its definitions of right and wrong. He carries with him his commitment to God as revealed in Christ, and his faith that God is acting to transform him.

He carries with him all that he is, in both sin and faith, in both pride and humility. But none of these things is trustworthy to guide him to understand the will of God without renewal and transformation in relation to the concrete decision.

Only when we stand in the crisis of decision and confront the alternatives, at the intersection of conflicting interests and pressures, do we fully meet our God and are we prepared to call upon Him to open our eyes to see what we must do. The Christian must be prepared to surrender definitions and predispositions under the higher community of God. He does not enter it defensively, to protect stubbornly his own position, but openly and sensitively to understand and admit into consideration as many of the complex factors as possible and to call upon God for both restraint and positive transformation in meeting them.

4. *The Christian Ethic Is Indicative Rather Than Imperative*

This is a response to what God has done, and is doing. Paul Lehmann, to whom we are indebted for a clear presentation of this view, says that it "gives primary attention to what is."[53] It is to stand "in the sphere and on the line of God's activity in the world."[54] This activity is happening in the events of the world in

[53] Paul L. Lehmann, *op. cit.*, p. 108.
[54] *Ibid.*, p. 107.

the ways that God raises up judgment and overrules the fondest plans and trusted organizations of men, and in the way He reconciles conflicts and opens unforeseen possibilities for responsive love to act in furthering the higher community. It is found whenever he girds us with the inthrust of courage to step into these paths. God is always both judging and redeeming, thwarting our selfishness and touching us with love; we always see dimly and respond with reservations, which constitute our continuing sinfulness.

Therefore, the decisions of Christians do not concentrate on the origins of ethical problems that are past control, or on remote consequences that cannot be predicted, or on utopian forms of society that are only our own biased projections, but on present responsibility in its fullest possible context. We believe with Alexander Miller that this does not remove our obligation to make "calculations" in the situation about alternative "consequences,"[55] but the precariousness of predicting consequences is recognized and the need for making new decisions as the dynamic context changes is accepted.

In other words, both motives and calculations of consequences —which ethicists see as the two alternative emphases in ethical decision—must be brought under continuous divine transformation in every new decision. To do what must be done in every situation as a response to God in the direction of true community is the Christian way of action. Daniel Williams calls this community "the order in which the members of a society are so related that the freedom, uniqueness, and power of each serves the freedom, uniqueness, and growth of all the other members."[56]

This community is God's universal community existing in Him and being created by Him. By living and entering into this community, which both is and is coming, and making every decision

[55] From *The Renewal of Man*, by Alexander Miller. Copyright 1955 by Alexander Miller, reprinted by permission of Doubleday & Company, Inc., pp. 93-94.

[56] Daniel D. Williams, *God's Grace and Man's Hope* (New York: Charles Scribner's Sons, 1949), p. 151.

in response to its Lord, Christians enter into God's action and into His formative power.

This produces the mood of sensitive expectancy, in readiness to enter into what God is doing, and this is the mood of hope in which the Christian lives. Mighty and unexpected things are always in immanence to break out of God's hand. They often dash our fondest hopes and shatter our best laid plans; they are both chastening and redemptive. Old structures are being dissolved and new situations are coming into being, calling for a new response to which we must submit ourselves again in obedience to the Lord of history.

5. *The Christian Ethic Is Absolute*

This calls for absolute obedience to God in every choice, in every kind of situation. Its only absolute is God Himself as revealed in Christ: A God who "reveals himself 'in act' or deed, rather than in the form of propositions or truths."[57] The Biblical standard is not "a law of love" nor an "infallible conscience," but the total self-giving response of Christ to God.[58] Man fulfills his commitment in responsive acts and deeds within the context of society in which he lives. This cannot be a private sentimental response in piety but is a decisional response in action.

Although it is open and unpredictive concerning what must be done—because every situation is unique—it emphasizes full relevance to every situation and also asks for full submission to God in that situation. Full confrontation of facts and full submission to God is the kind of response that cannot be fulfilled by finite and sinful men. Therefore, the Christian must live under tension and under divine forgiveness. It provides no excuses for self-serving and no loopholes for doing less than responsive love can do within the community of interdependent persons. It is never individualistic, because it calls for cooperative action within the structures

[57] John Dillenberger and Claude Welch, *Protestant Christianity,* p. 274.
[58] *Ibid.,* pp. 280-281.

of society; it is lived in the covenant community of Christ, in which the interactive gifts of love and grace are generated by the Holy Spirit and transmitted to those who share in its supreme devotion.

In the historic tradition of Protestantism, this is the way that the eternal gospel is related to the particular context of every social situation. As Alexander Miller puts it:

> The concern of biblical faith is not the sanctification of the world or any part of it, or the transcendence of the world, but the organization of the world around its true and authentic center, which is God the Creator and Redeemer, the God of love and righteousness, . . . the God and Father of our Lord Jesus Christ.[59]

KEY QUESTIONS FOR DISCUSSION

1. How has our devotion to an uncompromising heroic ethic cut us off from guidance in our daily decisions?
2. Is it possible to live by a law of total uncompromising love in an organizational world?
3. Why is an ethic of divine judgment without faith in divine transformation untrue to the gospel?
4. What is the "conversionist" view of the relation of Christ to culture?
5. Why is it true that all group decisions are compromises (adjustive decisions)?
6. What is wrong with the "sniper's approach" to participation in policy formation?
7. What is the ethical dilemma of "default versus conformity"?
8. How does the Christian ethic of "responsive love in community" help us confront this dilemma?
9. Why are facts, in addition to faith, crucial in determining what a Christian ought to do in an ethical situation?
10. What do we mean by the "indicative" character of Christian ethics?

[59] From *The Renewal of Man*, by Alexander Miller. Copyright 1955 by Alexander Miller, reprinted by permission of Doubleday & Company, Inc., p. 90.

RECOMMENDED READINGS

Ferré, Nels F. S., *Christianity and Society*. New York: Harper and Brothers, 1950.

Lehmann, Paul L., "The Foundation and Pattern of Christian Behavior" in *Christian Faith and Social Action,* John A. Hutchison (editor). New York: Charles Scribner's Sons, 1953.

Long, Edward LeRoy, Jr., *Conscience and Compromise*. Philadelphia: Westminster Press, 1954.

Miller, Alexander, *The Renewal of Man*. New York: Doubleday & Company, Inc., 1955.

Niebuhr, Reinhold, *The Children of Light and the Children of Darkness*. New York: Charles Scribner's Sons, 1944.

Niebuhr, H. Richard, *Christ and Culture*. New York: Harper and Brothers, 1951.

Tillich, Paul, *The Protestant Era,* chaps. XI-XIV. Chicago: University of Chicago Press, 1945.

Williams, Daniel D., *God's Grace and Man's Hope*. New York: Harper and Brothers, 1949.

————, *What Present Day Theologians Are Thinking,* chap. III. New York: Harper and Brothers, 1952.

CHAPTER 7

Steps in Building a Church of Influence

An effective program of Christian education helps Christians to seek the facts about complicated social problems and directs them to intelligent choices and responsible action (From Social Action in the Local Church Leader's Manual of the Department of Social Education and Action, Presbyterian Church [U.S.A.], p. 8).

I appeal to you, brethren, by the name of your Lord Jesus Christ, that all of you agree that there be no dissensions among you, but that you be united in the same mind and the same judgment (I Corinthians 1:10, RSV).

AGREEMENTS FOR ACTION

One writer has said that "there is sharp division in the church" concerning the church's responsibility for social influence. No doubt this is true concerning just what Christians ought to do, but surely there is a fundamental agreement from which we may begin. How can we be Christians at all unless we agree on three things, namely, that:

1. All Christians are called of God to serve him in every expression of their lives.
2. The church is the fellowship in Christ, which exerts the influence of His spirit in the world.

3. It is the task of the Christian and of the church to seek every possible mode of influence to transform the corruptive influences of the world into love and justice.

We must remember that Christian action is not one phase of the Christian faith or merely one department of the Christian church. It is simply the church at work as the instrument of God's grace. It is the task of bringing men into the fellowship of Christ and mobilizing this fellowship to serve faithfully in witness to the world.

In the first six chapters, we attempted to face the "why" of social action and now we must face the "how." If you are convinced of the necessity of Christian influence and alarmed at our weakness, you are "champing at the bit" and asking: "What do we do?" "How do we proceed?" These are the most difficult questions of all.

Six Imperatives for Building a Church of Influence

We believe that there are six great imperatives to guide us in building a church of Christian influence: (1) *sensitize,* (2) *organize,* (3) *investigate,* (4) *discuss,* (5) *decide,* and (6) *act.*

Sensitize

The first step is to sensitize all the people to the full meaning of the demands of the gospel. This must be done through vigorous leadership in all the ministries of the church.

Sensitizing through preaching and worship. Preaching carries a tremendous responsibility in the Protestant churches. For many Protestants, the church is simply preaching. Many of the other functions of the church have fallen away, leaving preaching to carry the load of inspiring, educating, and moving men to respond to God and to act in serving Him.

There is a great positive tradition in Protestant preaching, which is the way that the word of God is declared and interpreted. Great preaching speaks to the real situations—the tragedies and temptations of men as they face them—and it brings the grace of

God to bear upon these living situations. All great preaching is action preaching: deepening convictions, fortifying courage, and motivating men to rise above their own petty interests as they confront the world. Preaching that moves men to action is not necessarily "social issue preaching." To preach the real gospel of Christ at all is to preach the judgment of God upon our stubborn defensiveness and our conventional complacency. It is to preach the call to decisional living—the life of continuous criticism and transformation under the saving grace that girds us for action.

One kind of preaching that does not prepare for Christian action is that type of quietistic sermonizing that promises an easy "peace of mind" or "how to overcome anxiety." Henry Sloan Coffin, in commenting on such sermons, declared that they leave out "a disturbing Christ."[1] It seems that much of our preaching has grown too soft. The vigor and the "bite" have disappeared from too many pulpits, so that preaching presents a moral sedative instead of a stirring power.

Prophetic Biblical preaching is the impetus for Christian action, yet it is inadequate if it stands alone. There are grave dangers in our over-dependence upon preaching. For many people, it can become the substitute instead of the means to a deeper moral life. Many Christians can listen Sunday after Sunday to sermons that shake them to their depths and feel that in this humbling experience itself they have become prophetic Christians.

Preaching that ends with listening is power that escapes and fails to move. If we never do anything about the fire that strikes in our hearts, we are weakened rather than strengthened; we are hardened rather than made more sensitive. That is why preaching is the beginning, not the end, of Christian influence. It sends people out into the paths of decision. Moved Christians must seek mutual ways to enact their faith together within the Christian fellowship, and this is one of the greatest functions of the Christian church.

Protestants have placed too much confidence in talk—in the sheer sound of words. Even the "word of God" has sometimes been interpreted as mere sounds or letters rather than as Divine

[1] Henry Sloan Coffin, "Escapist Religion," *Christianity and Crisis* (October 31, 1949), p. 137.

power. An English church leader has declared that it is the word of God in the situation that brings the claim of God "upon us in the pressure of events."[2] The word of God becomes power when it is translated into decision.

Another great channel for the moral sensitizing of Christians is through worship. Preaching is part of worship but not all. Full worship is coming before our God in the hush of reverential silence, bowing in prayers of confession, and in the humble seeking for forgiveness and newness of life. In true worship, there are two great experiences. First, we come before our God as sinners, and we are humbled and shattered. With prejudice and pride and failure, we bow before our God to be searched and chastened. If we are earnest, none of us can escape the agony and the tension that worship lays upon us in such a time. Only then do we sense anew the saving love of God in Christ and the hope that opens up afresh to keep us on our pilgrimage. This is the second and transforming experience. Even then Christians will be misled rather than guided, if they "arise from their devotions with the conviction that their purposes are identical with the will of God."[3]

Even prayers can be arrogant and selfish, cutting us off from God rather than removing the barriers that block us from Him. The parable of the Pharisee and the publican illustrates this dramatically. Great prayers ask that "God's will be done," not ours.

Worship that sensitizes us for social responsibility is not some special kind of worship. It is any true worship that humbles and empowers us, deepening our faith to the point that we dare to act upon it, but preserving within us the humility that senses our limitations and our need for new light in every situation. Nevertheless, the great worship experiences of men, when they sense anew the mighty call of God, come when they stand together in the face of some recognized peril or some new possibility that may

[2] Hubert Conliffe-Jones, "A Congregationalist Contribution" in *Biblical Authority for Today*, Alan Richardson and Wolfgang Schweitzer (editors) (Philadelphia: Westminster Press, 1951), p. 44.

[3] Reinhold Niebuhr, "Prayer and Politics," *Christianity and Crisis* (October 27, 1952), p. 139.

soon be lost. The great pinnacles of worship are reached when a company of men bowing before God feels the mists of confusion draw back and sees the temptation to indecision stand in stark contrast to a clear way of action that can strive to right some real wrong or overcome some injustice. Such men have indeed "called upon the Lord while he is near" (Isaiah 55:6) and "hath . . . heard what he hath prepared" (Isaiah 64:4).

Sensitizing through education. We have already touched upon the religious illiteracy of Protestants in regard to the meanings of their faith. And above all we have seen that worship brings us before God in confronting decisions concerning what the Lord requires of us. Now we must consider the inadequacy of worship alone to impart the Biblical and traditional meanings of our faith. It is often asked why people who attend worship services regularly over the years have so vague an understanding of the Christian gospel.

Perhaps one of the answers may be that too much preaching is of the one-track type that merely repeats a call to Christian commitment over and over with no attempt to help men confront God in daily decisions. Or it may be the one-track preaching that promises consolation, week after week, benumbing the Christian conscience and forgetting the struggle of life. But we suspect that the answer goes deeper, and that the neglect of what some of the early New Englanders called the "ministry of teaching" accounts for our deficiency. Preaching is inspiration and devotion, reminder and praise, but not often a systematic discussion of the tradition and requirements of the faith. Someone has said that preaching is an art form, not a full teaching method. Therefore, as we saw in Chapter 5, some of the foundations of our faith are all but unknown to many church people. Under conformity to popular prejudices, the rigorous demands of the gospel have often been strained out of what preaching and teaching we do have. Important, also, is the decline of education in the church. Limited to a few minutes a week and often ending at an early age (since the decline of adult groups), the church has no chance to impart its vital meanings and attitudes to children or youth or keep them alive among adults. Furthermore, religion is no longer taught or discussed in many of our homes.

The tremendous competition for the time of people and their rigid institutional habits make the outlook for a larger opportunity to influence our people through education seem dim. But we must improve every opportunity, in the time and situations available, to develop an understanding of the full gospel, so that no Christian need be vague and unaware of the responsible gospel of our heritage.

Even though the church has developed people who feel their mission through worship and know their heritage through education, it still will fall short of its chance to exert its influence among men. For in addition to sensitivity, Christians must confront reality with their faith. They must have channels of response and ways of action. In short, the church calls men to put their hands to the plow in concrete ways, or it fails in its task.

Organize

Every church needs a group of men and women who are charged with one of the most important types of leadership in any church—leadership in ethical concern and action. Such a group can be a special committee called the "Christian citizenship committee," the "social action committee," or the "committee for Christian influence." The name is unimportant, but the function is central. So important is the task of confronting and participating in the great pressures and processes of local community and world that the whole church council (or session or consistory) should make this function one of its central concerns.

Since no church can long remain faithful to its Lord if it turns its back upon the temptations and compulsions under which its people live, it is a matter of spiritual life or death for a church to develop leaders to promote this function of exerting influence.

Church leaders who serve in this capacity must be deeply sensitive and firmly committed in their Christian convictions. Secondly, they need to be people who do not aggravate conflicts with aggressive tendencies, but who with firmness and understanding sense both the prejudices and strengths of their fellows. Thirdly, they need to be those who have the broadest possible understanding of affairs of community, economic activity, and government. In other words, here is a post that can make full use of the most balanced Christians of every congregation, and especially those with specialized competence and training in technical fields. Of course, unless they develop imagination and convictions that rise above the conventional respectabilities, they will fail to provide the leadership needed in this sensitive field.

This selected group of leaders have the task of being the eyes and ears of the church upon the community and the world of events. Let us list the functions of its members:

1. To be the social conscience of the church, not as a substitute for the responsibility of others, but as the "gentle agitator" that keeps their fellows alert to their own responsibility.

2. To discover and sift out the trends and injustices that place moral disadvantages on groups of our fellows or create an unfavorable climate of opinion in which to cultivate the Christian way of life. The members need to keep informed by reading and discussing the literature that our denominational and National Council leaders provide. They should be informed on the denominational pronouncements and resolutions and upon interdenominational reports that have grappled with many of our issues.

3. To report regularly to the larger body of the church upon their findings and concerns. They can be the leaven, working through all of the other groups and organizations in the church, to keep them alert and aware of Christian efforts in other churches and in their denomination.

4. To be, as the most prophetic group in the church, of immeasurable help to the minister. They can help him to understand the particular resistances and misunderstandings of the people and can act as the shock troops in developing a consensus of concern in the church. They can often help to overcome the

gap between the minister and laymen that was discussed earlier. It is doubtful that any minister can be effective in his obligation in this field without such lay assistance and support.

Of course, if Christian social influence is fundamental Christianity, it must be remembered that this task is not restricted to one committee. It is the work of all the other boards, organizations, and members as well. It should be a very special concern of those responsible for evangelism. Large sections of the people who are unchurched have been alienated by the neglects and discriminations of churches and church people over the years. Unless we can overcome deep-lying prejudices within our churches and demonstrate a new sense of justice and acceptance of neglected people by concrete acts, these peoples will scorn our evangelism as hypocrisy. Such people will be won by acts not words. Racial and class snobbery and "holier-than-thou" self-righteousness within our churches, unless overcome, will repel more people than all our campaigns of evangelism will ever win. Evangelism and social action must walk hand in hand if the church is to touch the lives of most of the alienated and neglected groups who are outside the churches today. Social evangelism works to remove the stones and brambles from the soil so that the "seed" may take root and grow.

A church of influence has two great aims: first, to make the church itself a dynamo of concern in which every member participates in seeking and responding to the will of God in common devotion and effort; and, secondly, to organize projects of influence in which members can find a role to play. With the church as the base for support and fellowship, it will send its people out into their vocations and responsibilities to exert every effort to be personal witnesses in every practical decision.

Investigate

When any Christian group or church has grasped its responsibility to enter the arena of social influence, its first task is to understand the situation and to discover the currents and conflicts involved. Moralists and social reformers have the reputation of letting their enthusiasms run away with them. Oftentimes, they find themselves shadowboxing with situations that do not exist. Rumor or hearsay is poor ammunition with which to enter the lists of social conflict.

Many of the great political and social issues are remote and far removed from our own personal knowledge. Often, all we know is what we read in a local newspaper, which may give a bird's-eye view of a situation, but from such a high altitude that big problems seem like specks. A distinguished historian declared not long ago "that most of us have no idea of what is really happening in the world." This is often true, even concerning events in our local cities. We hear of crimes, murders, and exposés. We hear of corruption and skulduggery in the political party or among groups that the newspaper dislikes, but often never a "peep" about the similar defects of the favored side.

Perhaps nothing is more important in facing social problems and injustices than discovering facts concerning the real situation. According to the Columbia University Centennial theme, one of the fundamental rights of a democratic society is the "right to know." This in itself is one of the great ethical problems of our times. Slanted news, jaundiced radio commentators who distort facts, false charges, and smears often stir up righteous indignation toward the side of greater justice and whitewash the side that contains the most corruption.

Since investigation is a specialized and a time-consuming task, the first step is to discover the reliable sources of research findings that are already available. Here again, the conscientious investigator must carry with him a healthy portion of Christian skepticism as an antidote to the stacked research that is so prevalent. Nearly every special pressure group and propaganda agency in the country has its own research department to sift out favorable information to support its point of view. That old adage that "figures don't lie but liars can figure" has much truth in it. The only safeguard against stacked facts is to discover reports that cite the various sides of a problem and to compare materials from opposite perspectives.

In national issues, a local group should use the recommendations of its denominational council of social progress, social action, or National Council departments for lists of materials and available studies. In fact, these groups are indispensable aids to local churches and deserve far more support than they get. If the Protestant churches of America are going to take their "failure to influence" seriously, this is a field that must be given much larger attention. The church bodies are in a better position to gather materials and investigate issues objectively than perhaps any other group. Elected church bodies, representing their constituencies, are more apt to be fair than any of the research groups with special axes to grind. They can call upon expert laymen and ministers in various fields to balance the perspective.

Thus, religious concern and technical knowledge can be combined to present as fair an approach as is likely to be found anywhere in our country. Since such groups are representatives of the broad field of our churches or our denominations (as in the National Council), they work under authority and are not likely to go far off on tangents in any direction. In fact, they are more likely to lean toward the conservative side and feel restraints that make them too neutral.

Investigation into social conflicts and social discriminations and intimidations is one of the great ethical roles that Christian churches ought to discharge in our society. It ought to be the vehicle that serves Christian citizens in "their right to know" in order to influence. This principle is one of the established precedents that the National Council of Churches inherited from the Federal Council. The Central Department of Research is one of the most indispensable instruments that the churches in America have. Its weekly publication, *Information Service,* is an invaluable aid for every Christian leader in his task of knowing what is being done and said by important groups and leaders of all types. Justin Wroe Nixon recently wrote an article of appreciation of the work of F. Ernest Johnson for his more than thirty years as director of this research department. He listed many of the great studies that have led to new achievements in the field of social justice. "Factual documentation and conclusive demonstration" are fundamental requirements in social leadership. It is based on "the idea of research as an essential element in an ethical approach to social disorder."[4] We must always investigate before we pronounce.

Every church should make sure that it is on the mailing list of its denominational council or commission, which sends out information on the larger national issues that are currently "hot" and important. It also should subscribe to *Information Service,* as well as making sure it is on the mailing list of the various departments of the Council. (A suggested list of sources is included at the end of this chapter.)

Social issues are complex problems. There are always two or more sides to every question, and those who are most unjust usually present a moral or religious justification. For these reasons, the Christian is especially anxious to keep a flexible and open attitude, until he gets the best possible picture of the situation. Only then can he safely decide and act upon the convictions that he holds.

There will also be many local issues that the individual church will need to investigate if it is to be alert to its community responsibility. Here again, it must draw upon reliable sources of facts and must use its own members who have special competence to analyze these and who, themselves, have access to situations. We shall discuss some of the methods of investigation in the local community in a later chapter.

An investigating group should assign each of its members to reading and assembling facts and materials on one phase of the problems at hand. These members can then pool their information to formulate a broader perspective. They will also want to interview people who are close to the situation and invite experts to speak to the group upon their field of knowledge. We shall de-

---

[4] Justin Wroe Nixon, "A Man and His Idea," *Christianity and Crisis,* XVIII:2 (February 16, 1953), p. 14.

scribe some concrete methods of investigation that are helpful under the various special areas in the chapters to follow.

Discuss

The next great step in influence is a thoroughgoing discussion: first, of the facts; second, of the ethical problems involved; and third, of the Christian way of confronting the problem. Discussion and confrontation are at the heart of the Christian approach to social responsibility. This is not debate, or argument, or a presentation of inflexible attitudes; but it is a coming together to confront urgent responsibility under the guidance of the Holy Spirit. It is the way in which Christians have always faced the pressures and temptations of the world from New Testament times until today. The writer of Acts tells us that "The Apostles and the elders were gathered together to consider this matter" (Acts 15:6, RSV). (In this case, it was responsibility to the Gentiles.) The Apostle Paul wrote to the Romans "to be mutually encouraged by each other's faith, both yours and mine" (Romans 1:12, RSV). He declared, "Let everyone be fully convinced in his own mind" (Romans 14:5, RSV). But he added the advice "to live in such harmony with one another, in accord with Christ Jesus that together you may with one voice glorify the God and Father of our Lord Jesus Christ" (Romans 15:5-6, RSV). In his first letter to the Corinthians, he appealed to them to "be united in the same mind and the same judgment" (I Corinthians 1:10, RSV). He encouraged them to "all prophesy one by one, so that all may learn and be encouraged" (I Corinthians 14:31, RSV). The New Testament church is one in which the members live in intimate fellowship, sharing in each other's joys and trials through continuous support and discussion.

Christians have held through the ages that where men are gathered together in the fellowship of Christ, facing their temptations and problems together in mutual concern, the Spirit moves them into greater understanding and courage. James H. Nichols, the church historian, tells us that the radical Puritans believed in and practiced group inquiry and discussion as the way of discovering God's will. They believed that new light and truth would come to believers who faced their problems in free discussion. They were convinced that the Holy Spirit would guide them into consensus and reconciliation.[5]

In early Congregational meetings, the people struggled with their responsibilities in their discussions concerning community and nation. The early Baptist covenant meetings brought together the believers to face together, under divine guidance, the temptations and pressures of the world around them. They talked things through, and stood together. The Methodist classes were times of participation in the fellowship of decision and guidance.

But how times have changed! How often today do our churches bring their members together to discuss their obligations as Christians in daily toil and in civic responsibility? From our own experience, are we not compelled to confess with Professor Nichols that our church meetings have "become miserable committee meetings on potluck suppers and the color of a new paint job in the Sunday school rooms"?[6]

How can we discover a common consensus of our responsibility through the fellowship of inquiry and discussion if Christians never meet to help one another take a stand under God on the problems that harrass them? How can we reconcile our differences and consolidate our convictions under the reconciling grace of God if we fritter away what little time we have together upon trivialities? Few churches today provide opportunities for laymen to discuss the messages of their ministers or the demands of the Gospel for confronting the world. Christians do not know their own convictions until they respond to, declare, and reconcile them in creative conversation together. Even churches that attempt to face this inadequacy often hold formal forums or panels in which a few "experts" present opposing views and answer a few questions, and the audience goes home without even an attempt to reach moral agreements.

[5] James H. Nichols, *Democracy and the Churches* (Philadelphia: The Westminster Press, 1951), p. 41.
[6] *Ibid.*, p. 239.

Educators and experts in human relations have everywhere been discussing the power in "group dynamics" to resolve conflicts and mobilize concern and action. But the Christian church, which has practiced group dynamics through the centuries whenever it has been a vital power, has let this great function wither while others claim to be rediscovering it. If Christians are to be more than spectators and casual observers of the trends of life, they must gather together to disagree and pray until they can unite upon some of the actions that God requires. It has been said that the church is the "talkingest institution in the world and that talk is not enough." We fear that Christians no longer talk, at least not upon the great issues of social policy and not in their church gatherings.

A church of influence must revive the old-fashioned and declining art of conversation and discussion. Many defunct organizations, classes, and groups in our churches could regain significance and power if they would quit running away from controversial moral questions and face up to reality under divine guidance. We live in an age when human beings are running away from creative disagreement. We suppress and avoid the controversial everywhere in our secular world: "It might hurt business or alienate friends." The two great "taboos" of conversation in contemporary times are "religion and politics"—the two primary fields in which we must discuss and decide or we are lost.

Surely the church, the last great refuge of courageous "fellowship-in-the-spirit," must not allow itself to succumb to the paralyzing fear of controversy. Here we must strive to disagree without being disagreeable. We can share and confide our convictions until the light of God draws us into a unity of expression on many great issues.

Christian discussion has four indispensable functions:

1. It is the channel through which the Holy Spirit moves in the dialectic or give-and-take of genuine spiritual intercourse to provide ethical guidance.
2. It is the way in which Christians pool their insights and

share facts, building up a larger perspective. As one writer has said: "Group discussion . . . [is not] merely a method of ventilating social conflicts. It becomes a method of liberating human beings from the limitations of their interests, their education and their experience."[7]

3. It is the great corrective in which personal idiosyncrasies and biases are softened and counterbalanced.

4. It is the intimate conversational sharing in which sympathy and identification are developed, so that in some small degree we can get over into the lives and views of others as the Christian way of love requires.

Of course, there are great dangers in a discussion that is not touched with grace and discipline. There are several kinds of discussion that cannot produce a meeting of minds or a moving of the spirit.

1. Argumentation is one of these types. It springs from aggressions within us or the desire to dominate and have the last word. It elicits hostility in others. It argues toward a foregone conclusion and does not develop the humility to see new light that develops in true sharing. Christian discussion requires the open heart and mind and the spirit of earnest seeking through which the grace of the Spirit may penetrate and lead. The dogmatic personality who believes his own inflexible conscience speaks the will of God is unable to submit himself either to divine guidance or to the reconciliation of his fellow Christians.

2. Gossip and small talk on trivial things do not provide the type of discussion that is so imperative in generating moral concern and consensus. Interest in people and daily contacts are in themselves not trivial, but they so easily divert conversation into sly malice and empty meanderings. Gossip is itself a kind of misdirected concern for others that has great potentialities for motivating constructive action, if it is steered into constructive channels.

3. Genuine Christian discussion is not quibbling over details of

[7] Bruno Lasker, *Democracy Through Discussion* (New York: H. W. Wilson Company, 1949), p. 37.

administration or property in the church. Perhaps the greatest waste of precious discussion time is found in organizational boards and committees in our churches. The author once heard the officers of a large church spend an hour trying to decide who would paint some new blocks that had been donated to the kindergarten class of the Sunday School. Many of the greatest controversies that split churches and create dissension are over problems of so little consequence that they ought never to occupy the time of Christian leaders who have the responsibility of making the church an organ of divine influence. A church of influence ought to delegate small problems to individuals and confront the great task of Christian impact in its official deliberations. We must recognize that there is a never-ending temptation to haggle over the picayune as a diversion from facing hard dilemmas.

Decide

We must never forget that discussion is a means toward the goal of decision. Discussion, no matter how honest and gracious, that does not arrive at decision is fruitless. It has been said that the occupational weakness of professors and intellectuals is that they always need to know a little more before they can make up their minds. Consequently, they postpone decision forever or until it is too late. The natural weakness of discussion groups is that they talk forever and never sum up for consensus and terminate for decision. Many Protestant groups seem actually to confuse discussion with action. If they discuss, they think that they have discharged their Christian responsibility, so that it becomes a substitute rather than an aid to common decision. If they discuss race relations, they believe they have really confronted this serious ethical issue. If they discuss temptations in the vocational world, they have the illusion that they have already faced them.

So difficult is group decision that many groups, including churches, despair of ever attaining consensus for common action. This difficulty is perhaps the origin of much of our misguided and independent freedom. Since we haven't the courage and patience to let God guide us into moral agreement, we give up and say, "Let each one make up his mind and do what he can alone." This means that the urgency and guidance that we find in common prayer and in the mutual facing of temptation under the Spirit is lost. And as individuals we are likely to drift without ever making up our minds or acting at all.

Alternatively, we may face the difficulty with impatience and after bitter disagreement and argument use the method of settling the problem by majority vote. In political elections and other broad decisions by poll, this is probably the best method that is available, but it is hardly the most appropriate way for Christians to determine what is the will of God for His children in meeting moral problems. We have already said that argument is not the Christian way of discussion, for it stirs up dissension and division, rather than generating a common will and conviction. Still less does a simple majority vote produce a unified or convincing decision out of controversy.

The Quakers, out of long experience, have a great lesson to teach the rest of us on this problem, although even they do not find that they have a neat formula that always works. They have the practice, when they face a difficult problem, of meeting together patiently in discussion with interspersed reverential silence and prayer, until they have found the "sense of the meeting." It does not mean that they always arrive at agreement, but it does mean that they come spiritually prepared to find the broadest possible agreement with a determination to find the common will of God under the Spirit. It is never a matter of vote; it is a matter of sensing the broadest common consensus upon which all can stand in their own consciences in mutual support.

When an urgent decision confronts a group of Christians after earnest and patient discussion, they must approach that great test of Christian grace: the arriving at a decision upon what their Christian commitment requires them to do. As John C. Bennett has shown, it is not so difficult to agree upon the great ethical principles of our faith, but the closer we get to action in concrete situations the more difficult it is to agree upon what the situation really is and what decision our Christian devotion requires.[8]

There are two somewhat different views being discussed currently concerning the Christian approach to group decision. One is presented by Professor John C. Bennett who suggests that Christians begin with the great ethical principles of our faith that are not so difficult to agree upon, then continue to middle axioms that carry the principle into application to a general class of cases, and finally move to what must be done in a specific situation. These steps become progressively harder because ambiguities and disagreement increase as specific action is approached.

Those who take the second view criticize this approach because it begins with abstract principles or ideals that are easy to agree upon precisely because of their abstractness. The Biblical approach to ethical decision is interpreted as beginning with a response to God within concrete situations, rather than from such principles.[9] This approach is one of open responsiveness to the activity of God in concrete confrontation and seems truer to Biblical ethics. As we declared before, Christian decision is directed by an absolute loyalty rather than an absolute principle. This loyalty is more directly relatable to pragmatic choice than principles. Therefore, in approaching decision, it is important to begin by standing in the actual ethical situation in which the conflicts of interest stand and actual alternatives are met. This will save the Christian from the "Sentimentality . . . of emotions unrelated to facts"[10] that often beclouds and blocks ethical action. The facts

[8] John C. Bennett, *Christian Ethics and Social Policy* (New York: Charles Scribner's Sons, 1946), p. 77.

[9] This view has already been presented, and is outlined by Paul Lehmann in his essay, "The Foundations and Patterns of Christian Behavior," in *Christian Faith and Social Policy,* John A. Hutchison (editor) (New York: Charles Scribner's Sons, 1953); by Alexander Miller in *The Renewal of Man* (New York: Doubleday & Company, Inc., 1955); by John Dillenberger and Claude Welch in *Protestant Christianity* (New York: Charles Scribner's Sons, 1954); by James Gustafson in an unpublished paper, "Christian Ethics in Economic Life"; and is also implicit in the works of Daniel D. Williams and H. Richard Niebuhr.

[10] John A. Hutchison (editor), *Christian Faith and Social Action* (New York: Charles Scribner's Sons, 1953).

concerning the structure of relations, the authority and power of those involved, the processes in which policies are being formed and the relationship of members to the policy makers are all of critical importance. It is always easier for insiders with authority to exert influence than outsiders who exert influence only through the external pressures of public opinion or competitive counterbalances. A group of Christians must face an ethical issue in accordance with their relations to those who are in authority to make decisions.

In local community problems, the church itself as a participating organization and its members as citizens have an already established basis or link to the problem. In other words, it is already *their own* problem in a "natural" rather than an artificial or imposed sense. As voting citizens in the community and as a group participating in the formation of opinion, they can make use of the recognized positions that they already occupy to influence decision and to use the powers already in their hands.

In political issues, democracy has provided the structure of relations of church people to elected representatives in which they can combine as a group to exert influence and moral pressure as a block of voters and as a center of dynamic opinion seeking to win others. In this context, they enter the field of contention under established responsibilities and in interaction with other forces and centers of influence.

In relation to policy in independent economic organizations, such as corporations, trade and professional organizations, and trade unions, the relations of a group of Christians are less direct because the group as a whole does not have established responsibility as direct participants. Here, only those individual Christians who are members or officers of these organizations are insiders with direct access to the factors involved and to the channels of influence. The authority of a church or a group of Christians to enter into the policy making of such organizations is not established and appears as interference from outsiders. This question, which is often asked, illustrates this situation: "What right does a church have to attempt to influence the decisions of a corporation or a trade union?" Therefore, only individual members of the church group stand directly within the context of decision.

Here the responsibility of the Christian who is also an organization member is clear and direct. He can participate as an individual Christian because of his position in the organization and can respond to his Christian insights concerning the will of God in the situation. But how can the Christian fellowship use its mutual decisions to enter such a situation except through its individual members? First of all, it can provide the individual with the focus of response to God in Christ and the insights and devotion of the supporting community of faith that he internalizes as he confronts practical decisions in his organization. Therefore, he enters the ethical situation not only from the perspective of his organization but from the perspective of the Christian community. Consequently, he does not face his decision as a private individual but as a member of "the communion of Christ." Within this community, he can seek both criticism and support as a resource from God.

However, in spite of popular prejudice against it, the faithful Christian group ought to go even beyond this way of entrance into the decisions of other organizations, because in the actual community of life there are no private corporations or organizations that are isolated from affecting the interdependent good of all. Corporate policy has a profound effect upon the lives of outsiders as well as insiders. Therefore, the church needs to criticize the policies of such organizations and develop a consensus of judgment concerning the consequences of such policies. But such criticisms also need to be proclaimed before men, so that they can enter the stream of public opinion and provide the moral pressures of restraint upon those formulating such policies.

Here, the church must be extremely sensitive to the dangers of abstract moral judgments that are made outside of the actual ethical situation. In turn, it must use the "inside" insights of those among its members who also belong to the corporate organization, and even those who are not church members, to incorporate all possible practical and technical considerations into its consensus of criticism. Paul Tillich says that it is a principle of Protestantism to respond to, and accept, the judgment of the secular world as a corrective upon itself.[11] In other words, even in the church, all abstract outside criticism must be held as "suspect," and the church group must project itself as fully as possible into an inside perspective in order to see what can be done as a response to the will of God in the particular context. If this is not done its criticisms and policy suggestions will not be valid and, we believe, will not be Christian.

Therefore, how Christians should respond to an issue depends as much upon the ethical situation and their relation to it as it does upon their loyalty to Christ. As we discussed in an earlier section, the ethical situation itself determines what an ethic of love-in-community requires. Christians have no law that can be laid down upon an issue that predetermines what must be done without relationship to the situation. The technical facts of economics or politics are ethical facts that bear upon the decision. The calculation of consequences cannot be escaped by Christians,[12] even though these calculations are always faulty and in need of revision.

When the Christian enters the decisional situation, he is prepared to respond to the action of God. He believes that God not only touches his subjective life but also transforms the objective situation in the dynamic interplay of responses that take place among all persons and groups involved.

This means that Christians receive divine guidance as they enter the situation demanding relevant response. This guidance rests upon the faith that God is constantly acting dynamically in the field of historical events, not as the mere events themselves but in a dialectic of action upon them through the judgment of restraint and through the redemptive opening of blockages. The perspective of faith gives a focus of interpretation concerning what God is making possible.

The Christian does not live by commandments but by continu-

---

[11] Paul Tillich, *The Protestant Era* (Chicago: University of Chicago Press, 1948), p. 215.
[12] Alexander Miller, *op. cit.,* p. 94.

ous responses to God as revealed in Christ. Dillenberger and Welch, in describing the directions in which theological reconstruction has been moving, say "that God reveals himself 'in act' or deed, rather than in the form of propositions or truths."[13] He has not revealed creeds or rules but Himself. The Christian lives under a supreme loyalty and in submission to the activity of God, which is not just a verbal concept but a mode of action by which God is always drawing the Christian beyond himself, breaking through his false rigidities of conscience, and transforming his limited perspectives. And the pressures and challenges of decisional situations are used by God to act upon us.

Probably few churches or Christian groups can go so far in common decision as the most outspoken members feel is necessary, and we can be thankful that by the Grace of God this is so. Yet, agreement upon many specific problems is possible when approached with humility and under divine guidance. It is imperative to have a long-suffering chairman as a leader who lets everyone express his feelings and who can continually summarize the fundamental agreements that always exist among a group of sensitive Christians. In areas where there is basic disagreement, consensus cannot be forced. The rule should be to seek the most advanced decision possible, without jeopardizing the moral unity of the group. This might be called the principle of seeking the "highest common denominator," rather than the "least common denominator." It is our obligation to exert the greatest possible influence in common action that can enlist the Christian convictions of all or nearly all the members, as they seek the will of God for concrete problems.

The ability to arrive at group decision, even on controversial issues, is something that can be developed in experience and practice. It is possible for the members of a Christian fellowship to learn the patience and persistence necessary to see difficult decisions through to a conclusion. The sense of victory in such a hard achievement and the mutual feeling of guidance by the Holy Spirit, which has softened aggressive insistences and generated harmony

---

[13] John Dillenberger and Claude Welch, *op. cit.*, p. 274.

without sacrificing the level of moral conviction, produce an experience that binds men more solidly in the bonds of Christ. Every such attainment deepens communion and makes the next issue easier to meet.

However, it is essential to point out that Christian consensus for action can never be reached without some compromise and some degree of giving in on the part of many members. Those who hold the view that it is better never to act at all, if it is not possible to attain perfect righteousness or total justice, can often block all influence and sow the dissension that makes any cooperative effort impossible. Such confirmed self-righteousness and belief that one's own method represents the will of God is unbefitting true Christian humility. No mortal man, even though he has been touched by the redeeming grace of Christ, can know the full will of God. No Christian can afford to disregard the counsel of his brothers in Christ when confronting the obligation of Christian decision.

But, after all these things are attempted, what if no consensus can be reached and no agreement upon what stand must be taken is possible? (We must be frank to recognize that this will happen all too often, even when we have struggled valiantly to form a common witness.) Then must we fall into frustration and silence or confront the world alone? Even here the possibility of acting together with those of common conviction is not lost. We cannot act as a church or a denomination to be sure, but we can gather together into a special voluntary group those who do feel the imperative to do something. Professor Winthrop Hudson calls the "voluntary committee or society to promote a particular concern or . . . objective" one of the great discoveries of the American churches.[14] Even when a handful of Christians have been unable to convince their fellows in their own church or group that there is a burning need to exert influence upon a problem that touches their consciences deeply, they can still attempt to win others and act together. Many times, when the church is slow and lethargic, such a group exerts such a persistent and convincing witness that

[14] Winthrop Hudson, *The Great Traditions of the American Churches* (New York: Harper and Brothers, 1953), p. 71.

the church itself is finally won over. This has happened both locally and on a national scale.

Every church will have a few members who are more sensitive and courageous than others. If they are gracious yet persistent, they are the greatest asset that any church can have. And even if the church does not officially use these people, they can seek each other out and be the true leaven in the loaf to lead the church to face the decisional Christianity to which Christ has called His followers.

Act

As in running a hurdle race, full achievement does not come after clearing the first hurdles, but only when the end of the course is reached. In Biblical language, only "he who endures till the end" is victorious. A church may sensitize its people, organize them for action, investigate great issues and mass temptations, discuss them graciously and earnestly, and even arrive at common decisions; but if it does not act to register its convictions and do something about them, it has dropped out of the race short of the goal. A church of influence does not hide under a bushel the convictions that it has struggled so hard to develop but seeks every possible method of registering them, so that they will enter the stream of public opinion and be brought to bear upon the seats of decision.

Since action is our special theme, we shall discuss further some of the methods and projects that have proved to be effective.

KEY QUESTIONS FOR DISCUSSION

1. Is it true that vigorous ethical preaching often short-circuits social concerns, unless ways of relating it to our daily lives are developed?
2. How does true Christian worship break down defensive complacency and self-righteousness?

3. Why is "dangling" inspiration, which is left unrelated to the context of our decisions, untrue to the gospel message?

4. Is your church organized to use its top leadership in promoting the concern of Christian influence within the membership and out into the community?

5. To keep informed on great issues, do you subscribe for and use the materials prepared by your denomination and the departments of the National Council of Churches?

6. Is your church able to draw most of its people into active discussion concerning how to confront the dilemmas and temptations of our times? Or is your church failing in its function of "talking things through" under the guidance of the Spirit?

7. Is fear of controversy a source of the moral timidity of the church? If so, how can we develop new moral courage?

8. Have you ever had the experience of participating in a controversial discussion that finally came through to real consensus and decision? Is this an experience that your church provides in the spiritual training of its members?

9. It has been said that the majority of contemporary Protestants are more like spectators than participants and that our churches assemble their people into a theatre-like crowd, rather than into a real fellowship of sharing. Is this true of your church?

10. Do you think Professor Nichols is fair when he says that most of our church discussions consider miserable trivialities like what to bring to potluck suppers, rather than great moral and spiritual issues?

RECOMMENDED READINGS

Seifert, Harvey, *The Church in Community Action.* New York: Abingdon Press, 1952.

Social Action in the Local Churches (a leaders' manual, published by the Department of Social Education and Action of the Presbyterian Church, U.S.A.). Philadelphia: 830 Witherspoon Building. $.25.

Recommended Sources for Information on Significant Issues

Bulletins from the various departments of the National Council of Churches.

Christianity and Crisis (a bi-weekly journal of Christian opinion).

Information Service (weekly of the National Council of Churches).

Interracial News Service (A Digest of Trends and Developments in Human Relations—bi-monthly of the Department of Racial and Cultural Relations, National Council of Churches).

Memo (bulletin on Congressional activity, issued by the Washington office of the National Council of Churches).

Social Action (a monthly magazine of the Congregational Christian Council for Social Action).

Social Progress (a monthly publication of the Department of Social Education and Action of the Presbyterian Church, U.S.A.).

The New York Times (daily edition).

——— (Sunday edition—"Week in Review" and magazine sections).

The Reporter Magazine.

CHAPTER 8

Exerting Influence
in the Local Community

The Church is in the community, a part and parcel of the community, but never satisfied with it. It calls upon men to repent and to prepare themselves for the "blessed community," which is always in the process of becoming. It is in constant tension with the community that is and in constant expectancy of the community that shall be. It seeks to bring the redemptive power of the gospel of Christ to every individual in the community and to transform its social institutions to make them fit instruments for the use of redeemed men and women (From Tilford T. Swearingen, *The Community and Christian Education* [St. Louis: Bethany Press, 1950], p. 27).

And we exhort you, brethren, admonish the idle, encourage the fainthearted, help the weak, be patient with them all. See that none of you repays evil for evil, but always seek to do good to one another and all (I Thessalonians 5:14, 15, RSV).

THE IMPORTANCE OF LOCAL COMMUNITY

One of the most simple yet elemental principles in Christian influence is that we must begin where we are. Each individual church must accept its responsibility to serve humanity in the immediate domain to which it is attached. The Report of the

Evanston Assembly of the World Council stated it clearly: "The Christian Congregation itself should be a visible center of community and a base for local social responsibility."[1] Here are the people who will be neglected if it does not serve them; who will drift with the tides if they do not find a guiding grace and fellowship. If the church is to be the "conscience of the community," as President Van Dusen describes it, then this is the community that must be penetrated and sensitized. Here live our own forgotten men and the groups that are exploited and discriminated against. There is always a temptation for a church to fight social injustices that are remote and that involve other people, but where the "shoe pinches" locally is where we must step forth to meet and serve our neighbors.

A saying of a professor the author once had has become almost a proverb today: "If it isn't local, it isn't real." To become real, Christian influence must take root in the soil of local community life. It is the local rocks of prejudice and brambles of corruption that thwart and choke the growth of the people we must serve. Clearing thorn bushes and planting and watering the seed of the gospel are the simultaneous tasks of a church of local influence.

When we say that the local church must begin its basic responsibility in the community surrounding it, we must not deemphasize the broader responsibilities for national problems and our mission to the remote peoples of an increasingly interdependent world. We must beware of a self-centered parochialism that is content to localize Christian concern. Even the broadest world issues have their local dimensions and are affected by local attitudes in a democracy. The crucial requirements for participating in national and world influence are to generate local opinion and then seek ways to register it at the points of broad decision.

Discovering the Local Parish

The first great requirement for an influential church is the discovery of a parish for which to be responsible. A Southern

[1] Reports of the Second Assembly, *Evanston Speaks* (New York: World Council of Churches, 1954), p. 28.

Baptist once stated that the word "parish" is a Roman Catholic term and that it has no significance for a Protestant church. But we must reply that it is a very important concept, and one that is too often neglected and misunderstood in Protestant circles. "Parish" is a religious word for the term "local community" and applies to the area of life that the church accepts as its special territory of ministry.

Because of the competitive situation in which several churches serve identical neighborhoods and because Protestant churches are gathered congregations with members often scattered over great distances, there has been a strong tendency for a church to think of itself as a collection of people rather than as an agency of ministry to a community and to all its people. There are several defects in this understanding of a church. First, it keeps the church from taking its community seriously as a basic influence under which its people live. This has a tendency to produce an in-grown church, which is content to serve insiders and fails in its mission to the unchurched and neglected who live around it. A church that works only with people who are attracted to its services and program by its reputation or the invitations of its members to their friends tends to become selective, leaving out many of the most troubled and needy people in its parish.

A church that is faithful to the "great commission" of its Lord will take upon its conscience the obligation of ministry to all the neglected souls within its territory of service. Its ideal goal should be to accept every living person who has no religious home as its charge whether or not he shows any religious interest. All Protestants, almost without exception, call upon the church at some period in their lives in times of crisis or death, and the tragedy is that so many people have no church or pastor to whom to turn. A church of influence will seek to show passionate concern for all types of people in its area. When a church says "our people," it will include not only the inner faithful but the alienated and disillusioned, the troubled and broken, and the low as well as the high. In fact, if it seeks to serve the Christ of everlasting mercy, it will expend more of its effort and concern upon these outer parishioners than upon itself. The church that deserves the title of faithful servant is not the church that squanders its work only upon itself and its own inner circle.

The church that is faithful in its stewardship will mark out its territory of responsibility and will take upon itself as the burden of its obligation to its Lord the people, the patterns of life, the conflicts, the corrupting influences, and the ways that people earn their livelihood. It will do this not as a domineering authority, tampering with other peoples' lives, but by ceaseless interest and loving concern, by persistently seeking out all who are in difficulty and who are overlooked, and by participating in the forming of community policy.

Many churches find it hard to define the boundaries of their parishes. This is especially true of central city churches that serve wide metropolitan areas. But even these churches need to recognize their territorial obligation to be the conscience of a community and to minister to a special section of humanity. Some parishes are large and some small. The larger ones have a larger obligation and must spread their influence into a broader context.

THE TYPE OF PARISH INFLUENCES THE CHURCH

Parish situations are not all alike and the community problems and the particular obstacles that are confronted will vary with the type of situation. Every parish has its unique characteristics that must be understood in attempting to face the obligations of influence. However, there are several basic types of parishes that can be described.

The Downtown City Parish

Churches in the heart of cities usually exist far from the homes of most of the residents of the city. They are surrounded by a business district, whose only immediate residents will be hotel dwellers, most of whom are transients. Beyond the central business district, in cities of any size, there will be areas of wholesale houses, warehouses, small manufacturing plants, centers of automobile dealers, and so on. Intermixed with these, there are likely to be cheap hotels, bars, and obsolescent housing where many of the most impoverished and disorganized people reside. On the margins of the business district will be found the "skid row" of homeless men, vice areas, and a general zone of deterioration and blight.

Most central churches pull most of their people from more favorable residential zones that are beyond this area. Services to the people required in this marginal zone will be so specialized, demanding the help of social workers, relief aid, and so forth, that the ordinary church often cannot carry a full program to meet their needs. The Salvation Army and such groups have developed a program and techniques of serving in such situations. Nevertheless, a central church that does not concern itself with these problems on its very doorstep and provide some leadership in facing the more unsavory aspects of city life so close to it is deliberately turning its back upon human suffering and contributing to its own insensitivity. Even though it is probably impossible for most churches to provide special social services for all these constituents, a responsible church can act in promoting adequate services and corrective measures for those who are underprivileged and are forced to live in a disorganizing setting.

As members of central churches move farther away in the general outward dispersion of city populations, such churches are often pressed to find a justification for drawing people great distances from other parishes. However, there are several legitimate reasons for the survival of the central church. It is in a better position to maintain an inclusive church that brings many types of people into intimate fellowship, cutting across class and racial barriers. Because of its strength and the spread of its membership across many types of people, it is more likely to be able to develop an influential and outspoken role in the community that isn't tied to more provincial interests; thus it can assemble stronger leaders and backing to tackle harder problems and make a greater impact upon citywide issues. It is imperative that such a church use its superior leadership and financial support, which is skimmed off many neighborhoods, to serve inner areas and neglected types of people. If it merely operates as a conventional church of upper-class suburbanites or outer-rim people who are content to serve themselves, it has probably outgrown its special function and is keeping its scattered people from working in more localized churches where a conventional program is usually more successful.

The Transitional Urban Parish

Beyond the downtown area and its margins, there is another type of situation in which a very large number of city churches find themselves. These areas are not as deeply blighted as are some of the areas closer to the heart of the city or around heavy manufacturing plants. They are often situations where many older homes are being converted into smaller apartments or rooms. There are often newer apartment buildings interspersed through such areas, ranging from lower-middle to very expensive rentals. There also tends to be a scattering of older single homes, often not too well-kept and showing their age.

We call such areas transitional because they are invaded by new apartments when old houses are razed and because of a tendency for many of the single homes to be converted into small apartments. This means older residents tend to move away, with new types of people replacing them. Therefore, such areas contain varied types of people on the economic scale. They often include concentrations of aged people, some of whom remain in their old homes but many more of whom move into rooms or small kitchenette apartments; concentrations of career women and bachelors who live in rooms and small apartments; and young married couples, starting careers, who must begin modestly.

In such neighborhoods people move frequently, take little interest in the community, have little in common with their neighbors, and live less conventional lives that are frequently lonely and troubled. From the religious point of view, they are likely to include remnants of the memberships of the great old Protestant churches; new younger Protestants, many of whom come from intimate rural and village churches; new inthrusts of Roman Catholics or Jews who may partially or almost totally displace the former Protestant residents. In addition to these, there is always a very large number of secularized and unchurched people, since the churches have found it more difficult to hold or win people in these areas than any other type of location in America.

Despite this difficult situation, a large proportion of the powerful old churches with the largest and most expensive properties are located in such transitional zones. Many of them maintain strength because of the momentum of past prestige and powerful programs that can pull people back from long distances and recruit new distant people because of their reputations. However, there is a general tendency for many such churches to weaken. With a greatly reduced number of churchgoers and usually also of Protestants, there are often too few people remaining to support the number of churches built at the height of Protestant strength.

Such churches have had an almost universal tendency to face their problem by either following their people out to a new location or putting up a last-ditch stand to pull back the same type of middle or upper-class people from other neighborhoods. Hundreds of urban churches have died in the midst of masses of unchurched people who need the ministry of the church desperately. Very few of these churches have made a systematic effort to win new types of people and to shift program and emphasis to serve their more difficult transitional situations. Many churches fail even to investigate and analyze the changing parish but continue to work under the no longer relevant stereotype of a single-home, middle-class approach.

We must not underestimate the difficulties of penetrating the resistances of people who are suspicious and defensive and who believe that the church represents cold condemnation rather than sympathetic help in time of demoralization and disillusionment.

It usually requires nothing short of a new spiritual conversion for the people in such a church for them to develop the compassion and concern necessary to serve and welcome their new and neglected neighbors.

A church that seeks to carry the influence of Christ into a transitional parish must literally reconstitute itself; it must break through its old habits and intensify its witness to the lonely, the neglected, and the secularized victims of the tides of impersonal city life.

The Single-Home Neighborhood Parish

Most of these situations are out beyond the transitional zones. Such neighborhoods are more likely to be homogeneous and stable. They may range from lower-middle class districts up through the most exclusive neighborhoods. The conventional church program (worship, Sunday School, and youth groups) is most effective in this situation since the residents tend to be of the same type and live where the more acute social problems seem remote. Such churches may suffer more acutely from contented provincialism and lack of concern for Christian social responsibility than those of other types. Often such a parish includes only an area of special favorability for normal neighborhood life. What we are saying is that since neighborhoods tend to be natural class sections, drawing people together who are alike in income, race, education and mode of life, churches restricted to serving such areas are strongly inclined to be class churches with a one-sided outlook.

The chief problem in such churches is to overcome an artificial sense of isolation from all the problems of our world, simply because most of the people live within a circle of local favorability. Outer neighborhood churches in cities are especially vulnerable to the illusion that the world is just a quiet gracious island, if only individuals would be decent and mind their own business. We call this an illusion because in reality all the pressures of blatant materialism and moral defensiveness are usually more thoroughly intrenched here than where people live under greater comparisons and see their temptations and involvements more clearly. People from such favored neighborhoods tend to be even greater addicts to the patterns of smartness and materialism set by radio, television, and mass journalism than in less favorable areas. Furthermore, in earning their livelihood they are thrust into the full hurly-burly of all the temptations of a world of special favors and difficult moral dilemmas.

We have already marshaled the evidence to show that no human being escapes the prejudices and exploitive involvements of his society, but people who live in sheltered neighborhoods and associate only with complacent people may insulate themselves from this unpleasant but basic truth. The neighborhood church may easily fall victim to this blindness and must be ever vigilant to keep alive the reminder that just because its members live on a quiet shady street does not insulate them from a hard and precarious world nor remove them from basic Christian responsibility.

Such churches need to act continuously in projects of self-giving concern for others in order to overcome the complacency and hardness of heart that resist God's spirit.

The Fringe Parish

The fringe parish is located beyond the solid suburban neighborhoods that are bedroom communities to the city. They are situations where country meets city—where city people invade the countryside and the surrounding villages and live side by side with the rural families. This often produces a situation of clash and misunderstanding. People interested in preserving intimate community life, with small local schools and small fellowship churches, find themselves neighbors to people who are more sophisticated and urbanized. These newcomers will either want to streamline and modernize local institutions, or they will remain aloof, keeping their chief contacts with city groups and friends. Many churches around expanding cities find themselves squarely in the midst of this kind of transition and conflict.

The natural solution that is likely to take place is that the old-timers will consciously or unconsciously resist intrusion by newcomers, and the newcomers will either start a new church or take over one of the older churches, thus organizing the conflict and keeping it alive. So the Christian churches, which ought to promote reconciliation and Christian understanding, become the vehicle of animosity and cleavage. The fringe parish, therefore, like other types, produces a special set of circumstances within which the church must minister and carry its great twin functions of divine criticism and transformation.

The Village Parish

People in a village live under a special structure of relationships that differs from city parishes. People know each other better, and each person has his well-established role and reputation. His neighbors know what to expect of him. Perhaps the most significant social characteristic is that all kinds of people live in the intimate neighborhood. People are not all sifted out to live only among their own kind of people as they are in cities. There will not be as big a gap between the high and the low, and there will be an acquaintanceship between the village physician and the garage mechanic, between the school teachers and the banker, and so forth. Life is more personalized and intimate.

Unfortunately, even here the churches are likely to become class churches: For instance, in a rather typical three-church village, one church served the top professional and business families; another church served the clerks and more respectable working people; and the third church served almost entirely the farmers from the surrounding countryside. And a sizeable percentage of the common people were left out entirely, along with a few of the more important people.

In such a situation it is easy for the churches not only to represent cleavage but also to promote it in many indirect if not direct ways. One rural sociologist, who is also an active Protestant church member, has said that more people "hate and misunderstand" each other because of conflicts fostered by churches than from any other source in American village life.

When this occurs the churches are deprived of being the chief local influence of reconciliation and community concern. Therefore even in small communities where community influence is so near at hand and so potent, the churches are deprived of working together as moral sensitizers and leaders in producing a responsible community atmosphere that promotes mercy and overcomes misunderstanding and injustice.

Complacency and provincialism are especially unfavorable characteristics of most small community life. The austere rejection of people in trouble, coupled with the power of gossip, makes it unusually difficult for the church to perform a saving ministry for the needy and demoralized. Often such churches find it hard to welcome even perfectly respectable outsiders and newcomers. It has been said that village churches even more than city churches "work only with the saved, and are content to condemn the unsaved," with little effort given to recognizing the Christian compassion "for all our people in our parish."

The Open Country Parish

Many of the characteristics of this type of situation are the same as in the village, except that here there is even greater homogeneity and intimacy. Nearly all the people live on farms. Even here there are distinctions between owners, renters, and hired hands, and often the church will serve only one type of the residents, letting economic distinctions deprive it of genuine responsibility for all the people and for the basic moral atmosphere of the parish.

INVESTIGATING THE COMMUNITY

If a church is to work responsibly in its community it must (1) understand its parish and (2) understand its own position in the parish in regard to whom it serves and what its position of active leadership is. Every church should conduct a running self-study to keep alert in regard to these two things. A committee formed for this special purpose or one of the existing groups should work with the minister to carry this responsibility. A church that does not do this is really "flying blind."

A church that has never thought of itself in its mission to its local parish might find a project of parish study an excellent place to begin its active outreach. Most churches will discover that they have strategic people in community life to carry out this project: people who work in public life, research workers, social workers, teachers. In smaller communities, the postmaster, school princi-pal, the local law officer, public-spirited business people, nurses, and others are among those who have contributed splendidly in such projects.

Obtaining Available Facts

The first step is to gather together the available information. In every area, much of the work is already done and waiting to be used. In cities of any size, there will be a council of social agencies, which will have maps available and much material already plotted by census tracts or other districts to show many comparative facts for the various areas. Materials from the United States Census are invaluable for the understanding of a local parish. These are available in separate tabulated form for all census tract cities and for towns and villages in tabulations for each state. They can be secured for a very nominal price from the Superintendent of Documents in Washington, D.C., but they should also be available in the local council of social agencies office and in local libraries.

The following are census facts of great significance in under-standing a local parish:

1. The population of the local tract or village, broken down into age groups, male or female, and the growth or decline by ten year periods.

2. The number and size of families and the number of people who live alone and are unrelated to families.
3. The number of foreign-born people and the country of their birth.
4. The educational level that the residents have attained, broken down into eight groups, from the fourth grade or less up through to college graduates.
5. The income of families, reported by the number falling in each of fourteen separate brackets.
6. The marital status of all people aged fourteen and over, reporting whether single, married, widowed or divorced.
7. The occupations of all workers broken down into male and female, thus showing how many women work.
8. What kind of housing people live in: whether owned or rented, whether they live in single homes, double houses, multiple apartments, and so forth.
9. When the housing in the area was built.
10. How many people there are per room, showing the degree of overcrowding.

When these factors are ranked and plotted by census tracts on maps, it is possible to see at a glance where a given area stands in comparison to the other areas in a city (or suburbs). Usually this has been done by some agency or research worker in the city and is available for the asking.

Although these materials appear in the form of cold statistics, when they are translated into the kinds of living people who reside in a parish they have great significance. For instance, if a parish has a high proportion of old people, with a large number of people living alone in overcrowded housing, much of which is old and in need of repairs, one gets a picture of a human situation that bespeaks a special responsibility to a sensitive church, not only in terms of service but also community action.

An analysis of the combination of these facts will shed much light on the situation in the midst of which a church is attempting to cast its Christian witness. But there are many other types of material that are usually available. The local health department often has available maps to show the incidence of tuberculosis and venereal diseases as distributed across the city, of housing that is below health standards, of the infant mortality rate. Experts say these are an excellent index of the favorability of living conditions in the various areas.

From courts or juvenile authorities, it is often possible to obtain maps showing the residences of adults and children apprehended for crime, indicating areas that are failing to provide an adequate environment for their youth.

From the council of social agencies, there will probably be available materials and maps showing the distribution of playgrounds and recreation and other facilities. Nearly every city has areas that are far more neglected than others, and these very often turn out to be not recognized blighted districts but older transitional areas.

In smaller towns and villages such materials as these may not be already prepared and available, but the facts concerning groups of people who live under "low chance" situations are no less important, even if one has to do his own investigating.

Conducting a Census

Already available facts will not in all probability give a full human picture of the parish. Such materials will certainly shed no light on the religious affiliation and participation of the constituency. Therefore, a church that really takes its parish to heart may feel the urgency to undertake a neighborhood census and send its workers out to interview the people to find out what kind of homes they live in, how many are Protestants, and how many attend any church. At the same time it can get a sampling of attitudes and ascertain precisely who the people are who live in the shadows of the church.

This is not an easy task. If there are other churches serving the same area, it is usually advisable to cooperate in order to make a thoroughgoing coverage. It must have careful planning and training of workers, or it ought not be undertaken at all. Tested cards and instructions are available for such a project. This type of study is not just to get names for prospects or to invite people to come to church. In fact, evangelism must come later, if the accuracy of the census is not to be jeopardized. The purpose of this type of census is to discover the parish situation. It can answer many crucial questions: What types of people are neglected in the neighborhood? Are newcomers being attracted and assimilated into the churches? Does the church have a reputation of concern for people who are new, who are in trouble, who belong to a different economic status?

A second type of neighborhood appraisal can be carried out informally by interviewing key leaders of the various social agencies and organizations to discover local problems and gaps in community services. This can cover everything from school facilities to recreational opportunities for youth or the aged. In some communities, schools have been sadly neglected and demoralized, subjected to irresponsible attack, or treated as political footballs. Under the principle of the church as cooperator and community conscience, advocated by Protestant leaders,[2] the church is interested in helping to strengthen all constructive community agencies and spotlighting all weaknesses and unmet needs. In one of the largest cities in America, the Church Federation and its leaders successfully spear-headed a city-wide drive to clean up corruption and irresponsible administration in the public school system.

There may be illegally operated taverns that are a neighborhood menace. There may be neighborhood gangs of youths who are destructive and have found few constructive opportunities. Perhaps there are inadequate playgrounds or play space. One persistent church organized quiet, sustained action and was able to remedy this problem by pressing the city officials for action in improving facilities and supervision. In many cities the most heavily blighted areas receive most of the attention and neighbor-

[2] Rockwell Smith, *The Church in Our Town* (New York: Abingdon Press, 1945).

hood services while less conspicuously needy areas are almost completely neglected.

Many of the constructive remedies for problems that are discovered can be promoted not by the organized vote of a church but by the informal efforts of groups, arising as a response to the results of investigation and concern.

WHAT MAKES A GOOD COMMUNITY?

This is a question that a responsible church must continuously ask and discuss.

The one thing that must never be forgotten is that there is a wide and uncloseable gap between the blessed community of love in which God rules over all relations and the best communities in actual social existence. The Christian church must never allow conventional definitions of good community to become the standard of appraisal in its mission. Too often the emphasis on harmony, loyalty, and uncritical cooperation obscures the Christian requirements of self-criticism, moral tension, and divinely nurtured discontent. The best community is broken by sinful cleavages, conflicts, and by unjust treatment and neglect toward its weaker and underprivileged members.

We hope that we shall not be misunderstood if we say that the role of a church is at the opposite pole from that often performed by the publicity bureau of the local chamber of commerce. A chamber of commerce emphasizes the good qualities and the splendid advantages that are the pride and joy of town or city. But the church as the conscience of the community has the prophetic role of keeping it from lapsing into complacency and pride over accomplishments that always fall far short of mercy and justice.

Nevertheless, a sensitive church, striving cooperatively toward "true community" and the highest possible welfare of all the people, must have a practical understanding of all the positive requirements for improving community life. A good community must give all its people a chance to live in a state of reasonable physical well-being. It must develop a community consciousness in which all its citizens feel a sense of belonging and a sense of responsibility. From a Christian point of view, it must produce a sense of deep concern for everyone. It must develop high aspirations and standards while maintaining humility and seeking improvement. Without condoning unethical conduct, it must hold in sympathy and give help to those in every kind of difficulty. As one writer has put it, "In a true community of love, what happens to any of the people happens to everyone." If tragedy happens to one family, others identify themselves so deeply that it happens to them, too. If some people live in housing unfit for human habitation, others suffer too, until it is remedied. This is the high Christian standard, and it is impossible to meet, especially in the impersonal life of city neighborhoods. But we must do our best to apply this kind of response in inclusive concern for all, even in the heart of cities.

The New York State Citizens' Council lists the aspects of community life that must be considered in determining a "good community" in which to live.[3] If the church is to work for the betterment of its local parish, these provide a good place to begin:

1. *Education* for all the children, youth, and adults in adequate plants with qualified teachers.

2. *Housing,* with every family decently housed. The housing, health and sanitation, and fire laws should be adequately enforced so that the health and safety of no one is jeopardized. In many cities the poorest citizens pay higher rent for condemned housing than higher income families pay for better housing, because of the pressure of shortages and the difficulty of finding anywhere else to go. This is especially true for racial groups that are restricted to limited areas and suffer a heavier competition for space.

3. *Equality of opportunity* for all groups and races in which everyone is given equal opportunities for participation in community life. All serious tensions and discrimination should be eliminated.

[3] *Scoreboard for Your Town* (Syracuse: New York State Citizens' Council, Inc., 601 East Genesee Street, 1948).

4. *Economic development,* with jobs and opportunities available for all.

5. *Cultural opportunities,* with music, art, drama, library services, and local and national news coverage available, to be used by all possible citizens.

6. *Adequate recreation,* that is, adequate playgrounds and indoor facilities to keep children and youth busy at constructive pursuits. Some neighborhoods have no place for children and youth to play and associate except streets and stores or even cheap restaurants or taverns.

7. *Health and welfare,* with adequate provision for the promotion of the health of the whole community. There should be medical care, hospitalization, and care for the underprivileged, the aged, the handicapped, and families in trouble.

8. *Community organization,* in which there is a neighborhood or community council where the representatives of all groups meet and discuss in order to overcome problems and improve the life of the community.

9. and 10. *Government and Churches,* which are receiving special treatment in our study.

These cover the basic aspects of community life. Many of these are now taken care of by public and private agencies other than the church. Therefore, it may be asked: What responsibility does the church have for schools that are publicly supported, or for housing that involves the ability of families to pay for shelter? Should the church tamper with schools? Should it try to provide housing, or medical care, or recreation? Obviously, the church cannot go into business, or perform all of these services. But *here* is where the principle of influence comes in. The church can discover and spotlight need and neglect in any of these areas. Backed by the support of its members, its leaders can work through the available channels to promote action and improvement in any or all of these fields. Sensitive church people in thousands of situations have started the ball rolling by the action of involved laymen through seeing the right people, or mobilizing public conccrn, or gently needling lethargic authorities to act more energetically.

SOME GUIDES FOR COMMUNITY INFLUENCE

The church must be a cooperator in community action. In describing a series of dramatic real-life stories of community action, depicted in a series of documentary radio programs called *The People Act,* Mary Blackford Ford said: "The difficulties these people encountered were too big for a single individual to tackle."[4] Then she describes many real victories won over tremendous obstacles through concerted community action. The same writer in summarizing these projects declared that "when people act together for the common good, their unity engenders strength. That strength, in turn, makes possible action not before dreamed possible."[5] This, of course, is the secret of genuine community influence. Someone or some group must be the initiator in any project of community betterment, but cooperation of all interested people must be mobilized from many groups to attain results.

In earlier days when America was a land of towns and villages, the church stood at the heart of the community. It was the center of the spiritual, social, and welfare life of the community. Since then, in an increasingly specialized society, many of the old functions of the church have been taken over by other agencies. Sometimes church people look jealously at these agencies as competitors and remain aloof. In this new situation the church can still be the initiator of projects of improvement in the community, but it must also act in the role of "cooperator." It must work with many outside people and agencies, recognizing that a great number of needs are satisfied by other institutions. Samuel Blizzard is right when he says, "There is a need for building rapport between the church and other community organizations

---

[4] Mary Blackford Ford, "The People Act," *Social Action,* XVII:4 (April 15, 1951), p. 5.
[5] *Ibid.,* p. 5.

and agencies."[6] The church exerts influence by developing and sensitizing leaders who are prepared to work in many cooperative efforts.

Christians must not be interested in credit but in accomplishment. It is interesting to discover how many ministers and churches were at the center of many of the projects of community action described in *The People Act* and books like *Small Communities in Action* by Jean and Jess Ogden.[7] Many of the agencies and organizations for the alleviation of human illness, poverty, and disorganization were started in America by churches or by Christian leaders, and have since become independent. The church has played the role of pioneer in launching many of the great movements and institutions for greater human welfare. In the local community, the church can still be the pioneer in discovering the areas of neglect and oversight. It can still launch efforts of its own or stimulate cooperative community action to overcome human problems and community deficiencies.

Cultivate cooperative relations with other churches on the basis of community influence. Numbers and backing count in a democratic society. Often, one church cannot mobilize the public opinion or concern to carry much weight even in smaller communities. So, if in your local church, you have discovered a situation or problem that you feel requires Christian action, often the first thing to do after developing interest in your own church is to try to enlist the cooperation of sister churches. Perhaps this can be done through the local council of churches or the ministers' association in a town that has these organizations. The difficulty with the ministers' association is that it does not include laymen, and it is of vital importance to enlist lay leadership. An interchurch committee of both laymen and ministers registers more influence, if you want to get action from public officials or instigate organizational action.

[6] Samuel W. Blizzard, Jr., "Let the Church Serve Its Community," *Social Progress* (March, 1950), p. 2.
[7] Jean Ogden and Jess Ogden, *Small Communities in Action* (New York: Harper and Brothers, 1946).

In the case of a localized neighborhood problem, it may be necessary to go to the sister churches and invite their representatives to a joint meeting. The best way of all is to organize a permanent interchurch committee that functions continuously to register the Christian concern for a better neighborhood and to back projects of improvement. Cooperative influence is always more effective than single church influence.

Cultivate friendly acquaintanceship with influential people and officials of the community. This approach is always wise, so that lines of communication will be established in advance of critical problems. It is an excellent plan to invite these people to meet with groups in your church or to be your guests at various church dinners to establish good relations. If this is impossible, the minister and lay leaders can call on them or make it a point to get acquainted with them at other functions. Let them know you want to cooperate and that sometime, perhaps, you can be of help in some problem. Some of these strategic people are the chief of police, the mayor or other civic head, the superintendent of schools or local school principals, the editor of the local newspaper, state representatives or United States representatives, the head of the council of social agencies, city councilmen or aldermen from your district, the head of your health department, the head of your county welfare department, the judge of the juvenile court, the head of your planning commission, and the head of your housing authority.

Of course, the size of your town or city will determine who these people are and how available they will be. But people in public life are always anxious to have contact with their constituencies, and you are likely to be pleasantly surprised by how available they are. It is extremely important to remember that if you are to be influential, you need to know the people of authority or be known by them as representing significant blocks of opinion. One is always in a far more favorable position when he wants help or if he wants to urge some action if friendly relations already exist.

Use the friendly face-to-face approach. Another principle,

especially important in pressing for action from those in authority, is to be sympathetic and unaggressive in every possible situation. Do not assume the unfair attitude that you are dealing with
corrupt and impossible people, or you will provoke immediate
antagonism and resistance. There are often many pressures and
difficulties that the outsider does not understand. So it pays to be
sympathetic and to listen to all objections, but to press vigorously,
yet graciously, the point of view that you represent. Of course, if
you exhaust all face-to-face efforts, sometimes it is necessary to
mobilize the pressure of public opinion. A very important rule is
always to go to responsible people and press the case before impersonal pressure is organized. Public meetings, petitions, and
pronouncement should never be used before a personal approach
is tried. Many community problems can be remedied quietly and
without building antagonism by simply urging action with the
people responsible. As one businessman once put it, "Never write
about a delicate or controversial matter; go in person and talk
it over." This also applies in community action.

Be persistent. Another cardinal principle is that of persistence.
When you take on the project of overcoming a serious community
problem, prepare for a long pull. There are so many flash-in-the-
pan efforts, soon forgotten short of any real achievement, that
politicians and public administrators no longer take them seriously. Church people so often get excited and enthusiastic about
some "cause" for a short time and then forget it entirely. Such
attempts are treated as little whirlwinds that will soon blow over.
Only determined persistence that is ready to spring back into
action whenever the old problems or laxities reappear can produce lasting results. We must remember that there are no final
victories in overcoming evils and problems. They always have a
tendency to return as before or in some new form.

Good community is a relative term. No community deserves
to be called fully Christian, for none provides a context of relations that is without injustice and corruption and vicious pressures. That is why single improvement campaigns are of short
consequence. Only permanent, never-ending surveillance and

activity can carry genuine Christian responsibility out into the patterns of community life.

Avoid the attitude of moralistic Pharisaism. The great occupational temptation of religious people is to become so self-righteous and snobbish about their own state of goodness that they actually repel others in need through pious condemnation and condescending superiority toward "sinners" and people in trouble. This danger is one of the primary themes of the New Testament Gospels, and warning after warning is issued by Jesus himself. No attitude so paralyzes the sense of mission of a church to its community as this type of Pharisaism. It benumbs its concern for others and produces an attitude that makes it suspect when it does attempt to help others or endeavors to improve the lot of underprivileged groups. It is the prevalence of this spirit that has made the term "do-gooders" one of reproach rather than honor. The Christian faith couples vigorous battle against evil and injustice with eternal sympathy for the children of God, both exploiters and exploited, who are the victims. As we insisted in an earlier chapter, no man who fails to recognize himself as a sinner is trustworthy or competent to minister to others.

Free its pastor and leaders from routine to allow them to spend the maximum amount of time to work with neglected people and situations of need. When the average minister is asked what is the most frustrating thing about his work, the most frequent reply is: "The heavy amount of petty detail and organizational routine that prevents me from doing more important things." Among these more important things are seeking out and helping unserved people who face critical needs and crises, discovering community neglect and problems, and organizing projects to meet them. The same is true of our lay leaders who are so often so overburdened with inconsequentials that the work of ministering to men is neglected.

Select projects of greatest urgency. During World War II, there was much talk about the problem of priorities; what must be done first? This is a hard moral problem that a church of influence must face. On the basis of investigation and prayerful discussion, the most critical problems must be selected and accepted as projects for action. Every church and, perhaps, every organized group within the church should embark upon some major project of active Christian witness each year. Sometimes, such urgent issues arise that other things need to be laid aside in order to spring into immediate action. Such flexibility and alertness are always required.

The great requirements of a ministry to the community can be summarized: (1) Be outspoken without being aggressive; (2) don't impute blame on others without sharing in it yourself—we are all involved in the problems that arise; (3) be fair without being soft and vacillating; (4) never be self-righteous or cantankerous; (5) be positive whenever possible, never merely negative; and (6) accept compromise gains without losing sight of the fact that a fully Christian community is always impossible and that new efforts will be continuously necessary.

A Suggested List of Community Projects

Every church or group must bear the burden of choosing where its influence is needed most. We can merely suggest a list of things that churches have done:

1. Take a parish census to discover unserved types of people. As a follow-up for action, invite a group of outside people who have something in common to have supper with a few of your own people. Make sure that your own people are in a minority so that strangers will feel it is their day. Discuss something common to all. See if they might not like to get together again.

2. Investigate delinquency in your neighborhood and facilities for the constructive use of leisure time for your youth. If there is need, get the city to open more facilities, cooperate with some other organization to expand services, or supervise an evening for youth in your own church.

3. Compare your newspaper with other papers over a period of time to see if your people are getting a full, unbiased coverage

of critical events. If you are not satisfied, select a committee of your ablest people to talk it over graciously with your editor. It might alert the newspaper, and your people, too, to a greater interest in the "right to know" in your community.

4. Take a look at housing in your community. Are people living in dwellings unfit for human habitation? Find out if health standards are enforced. Is garbage disposal adequate? Talk to the health officer. Mobilize a group to put windows or doors on the dwelling of some unfortunate family that is not protected from the weather. If there is a situation that the Christian conscience cannot tolerate, stir up the anxiety of the community. See the officials. Talk to landlords. Protest if families are paying exorbitant rents for condemned housing. Perhaps a new housing project is necessary to alleviate the situation. Small beginnings sometimes have significant endings.

5. Investigate health standards and facilities in your community. Many a village or small town is neglected in this respect. Christian citizens can spearhead action where there is need. One church group started a campaign that brought a refugee physician into a doctorless community. Are all the children in your community given a health examination each year at school? In one small community, church people started a campaign to give physical examinations to all the residents and found a high percentage of people suffering from disabilities that were not previously recognized. Find out whether health facilities are adequate for minority groups. Perhaps health officers are in urgent need of greater public support.

6. Investigate taverns, gambling rooms, and so on, in your community. Are liquor-selling establishments and places of gambling living up to the laws in your community? Is law enforcement adequate? If you are patient and persist in your pressure, you can help to keep your community sensitive to this difficult problem.

7. Start a community council that brings together representatives of all agencies and groups interested in a better community in order to discover blind spots and neglects. Many church people

or church groups have initiated such councils to work for a more sensitive and coordinated community life.

KEY QUESTIONS FOR DISCUSSION

1. Why should the church not accept the conventional standards of a good community as its own?
2. What is the role of a church as the "conscience" of a community?
3. Why is a church in a "high quality suburban community" likely to find strong resistance to its ministry of social criticism and action?
4. What are some of the moral blindnesses that seem to characterize "high quality, single-class communities?"
5. What is the concept of the "local parish" and what are its implications concerning the people that the local church ought to serve?
6. What is the responsibility of your church toward education, health, and housing in your community? Or should these problems be left entirely to educators, physicians, and real estate men?
7. What are the practical requirements of a good community?
8. What are the chief problems requiring action in your community? Talk these things over carefully.
9. Is your church interested in people whose lives are disorganized, because they are victims of untenable situations that demand correction? What has it done in response to these situations?
10. Look over your community and discuss what Christians can and ought to do as servants of Christ.

RECOMMENDED READINGS

Leiffer, Murray H., *The Effective City Church,* rev. ed. New York: Abingdon Press, 1955.

McKee, Elmore, *The People Act.* New York: Harper and Brothers, 1955.

Miller, Kenneth D., *Man and God in the City.* New York: Friendship Press, 1954.

Perry, Everett L., *Some Suggestions for Church Community Surveys.* New York: Department of City and Industrial Work, Presbyterian Board of National Missions, 1948.

Sanderson, Ross W., *The Church Serves the Changing City.* New York: Harper and Brothers, 1955.

Seifert, Harvey, *The Church in Community Action.* New York: Abingdon Press, 1952.

Smith, Rockwell, *The Church in Our Town.* New York: Abingdon Press, 1945.

Swearingen, Tilford T., *The Community and Christian Education.* St. Louis: Bethany Press, 1950. Report on Findings and Discussion of the Conference on Community and Christian Education, December, 1947; sponsored by The International Council of Religious Education, The Home Missions Council of North America, and attended by representatives of the Federal Council of Churches and other major groups, which merged to become the National Council of Churches.

Warren, Roland L., *Studying Your Community.* New York: Russell Sage Foundation, 1955.

CHAPTER • 9

Exerting Influence
Through Reconciliation

The Second Assembly of the World Council of Churches declares its conviction that any form of segregation based on race, color, or ethnic origin is contrary to the Gospel, and is incompatible with the Christian doctrine of man and with the nature of the Church of Christ. The Assembly urges the churches within its membership to renounce all forms of segregation or discrimination and to work for their abolition within their own life and within society (Resolution adopted by the Evanston Assembly of the World Council of Churches [1954]).

> *And Peter opened his mouth and said: "Truly I perceive that God shows no partiality, but in every nation any one who fears him and does what is right is acceptable to him"* (Acts 10:34-35, RSV).

THE AMERICAN IDEAL

Conflict of interests and groups is a basic fact of human existence; there are conflicts even in a family where the members love each other deeply. There are conflicts in our churches among men who seek earnestly to do the will of God. In our society, there are conflicts between great blocks of our citizens whose interests and ideals collide with one another. In fact, we live increasingly in a pressure-group world where our conflicts are not merely among individuals but among large groups or organizations with which masses of men identify their hopes and define their interests.

Conflict always endangers human existence. Since conflict generates intense loyalty toward our own group and animosity toward opposing groups, there is always the danger that it might break out into injustice, discrimination, or even violence. All civilized societies have customs and laws by which to settle conflicts peaceably. But democracy is a special way of life that attempts to set up both basic legal rights for all citizens, including minorities, and the methods by which conflicts can be controlled and reconciled through common understanding, discussion, negotiation, and, if necessary, court decision. America began as an asylum—a land of new opportunity for people who had been discriminated against and persecuted. Successive waves of migration of many types of people have made us one of the most heterogeneous nations in the world with citizens of many backgrounds and races living side by side. Our very existence as a nation has depended upon the development of common bonds of loyalty and the reconciliation of differences.

Democracies do not attempt to coerce people into conformity or to suppress conflict but rather to maintain a balance of power and justice, so that the basic values and interests of all groups can be coordinated and safeguarded. Democracies attempt to equalize justice, so that no group or class can gain power to exploit or discriminate unjustly over any other group. This achievement always falls far short of its goal even in the most sensitive democracy, because some groups always have superior power and prestige and others suffer serious disadvantages if not outright discrimination.

Our constitutional democracy is founded on the idea of providing justice for all and equality of opportunity according to individual capacity unimpaired by factors of race, color, station of birth, or religion. This is declared simply and unmistakably in our Constitution and tradition, but it is an overwhelming task requiring continuous struggle and constant readjustment. Some groups develop and increase their power to the danger point of special privilege. Racial and nationality groups derived from past and present migrations find themselves in positions of injustice and discrimination. Economic and class groups find themselves in situations where they cannot compete against the power or prestige of other groups and slump into impoverishment and disinheritance.

To provide the quality of justice and a balance of power in the conflicts of men and groups is the basic problem toward the solution of which our democratic way of life is dedicated. But this is not an automatic process, and unless we can generate an ethical sensitivity and a loyalty to a justice that transcends our own group demands, our vast interdependent society is always in danger of falling into the exploitation and coercion of the weak by the powerful. Therefore, democracy itself is dependent on the moral quality of the relations of its people and their capacity to soften self-interest and prejudice by a loyalty and power that lifts them beyond purely selfish group, class, or racial demands.

The great Carnegie Fund Study of Race Relations in America, which was summarized by Gunnar Myrdal in *An American Dilemma*,[1] found the treatment of Negroes in the United States to be utterly inconsistent with the basic ideals of our tradition. This has produced a tension and the "most glaring conflict" in the heart of the American. One-tenth of the population in America is Negro. This great mass of people was emancipated by a great war and given full status as citizens by an amendment to the Constitution, yet they are still discriminated against in our political life in many states, in public transportation and facilities of all kinds, and in economic opportunities. They are often forced to live in segregated districts, even in many Northern communities, and the vast majority of Christian churches do not admit them into fellowship or membership.

[1] Gunnar Myrdal, *An American Dilemma*, Vol. I (New York: Harper and Brothers, 1948), p. 21.

There are other sizeable racial groups that are subjected to discrimination and indignities because of the accident of ancestry. Mexicans and Puerto Ricans are growing minority groups; we also have Filipino, Chinese, and Japanese minorities that are denied many of the ordinary privileges of American life without regard to the education, capacity or degree of cultural refinement of the individual, or the dignity that democratic ideals confer upon all human beings.

In addition to such peoples who have the misfortune to carry physical characteristics of identification, there are many groups of white people, such as rural migrant workers, or slum dwellers in cities, or members of nationality groups, who are looked down upon and misunderstood by a majority of Americans who regard themselves as superior.

Despite our American tradition that abhors the distinction of class and caste, we have developed economic and occupational classes that have varying degrees of prestige, wealth, and isolation from the others. Much research in recent years has been carried on to understand this phase of our life. Nearly every village has a "wrong side of the tracks." There are employees and employers who have differing outlooks. There are businessmen, farmers, craftsmen, common laborers, professional people, and white collar workers who occupy varying positions of income and prestige. Conflicts of interest and points of view, misunderstandings, and biases grow out of these differences.

THE CHRISTIAN DENIAL OF DISCRIMINATION

Against such misunderstandings and the injustices inflicted by stronger groups upon weaker ones, the Christian faith through the ages has been the great reconciler and critic. It has never ceased to remind men that their own self-claimed superiorities are all fictitious before God. We are all created by Him, and must live unto Him in self-giving service as His children. To reconcile differences, to soften pride, to break down prejudices, to shame men for their unjust discrimination, and to gather all into the great fellowship of Christ are combined in the historic role and goal of the Christian church.

Although our democratic view in America is derived in many ways from the Christian tradition, the Biblical faith goes much farther in its protest against prejudice and discrimination. Peter declared: "God shows no partiality" and "accepts" anyone who fears Him. "So God created man in his *own* image . . ." (Genesis 1:27). "Have we not all one father?" "Hath not one God created us?" (Malachi 2:10). Jesus, himself, declared that "whosoever shall do the will of God, the same is my brother . . ." (Mark 3:35). When he was asked concerning who is a neighbor in the parable of the Good Samaritan, his example was a Samaritan from a group looked down upon by the Jews.

The great commandment of the New Testament is "love"—a love toward God and a love toward neighbor that are indissolubly linked together. Our gospel is a gospel of reconciliation and understanding. The Apostle Paul said that we are entrusted with the "word of reconciliation" (II Corinthians 5:19, RSV). Jesus quoted Isaiah declaring, "He has sent me to proclaim release to the captives and recovering of sight to the blind, to set at liberty those who are oppressed" (Luke 4:18, RSV). Neither any searching of the Biblical record nor interpretation of the Biblical faith can contradict the basic truth that God is the Father of all men without regard to race or class or nationality. Buell Gallagher states this flatly when he says that "not the narrowest of the hard-shell sects, nor the most arrogant of the Roman churchmen, nor the bluest of the blue-blooded Protestants, can find a substantial ethical basis for drawing the line of Christian brotherhood on the basis of race."[2]

Professor John Knox finds "that no single item in the historic Christian faith gives the slightest support to any attitude or act of racial exclusiveness or discrimination, but also every single item

[2] Buell Gallagher, *Color and Conscience* (New York: Harper and Brothers, 1946).

is such as to render such an attitude or act utterly . . . rebellious."[3]

In the last few years, the churches have been undergoing a major reawakening to the sin and injustice of discrimination, especially against racial minorities. The conscience of the churches has been stirred deeply. The pronouncements of the denominations have become increasingly more vigorous, and the humility of Christians over the failure of the churches has become more widespread.

The National Council of Churches sends out a message each year for Race Relations Sunday. In a recent message it declared that "a revolution in race relations has been taking place in America." But it reminded us of the widespread "denial of human brotherhood" that still exists among us and proclaimed, what we all know, that "the faith we profess condemns all racial division and directs our feet toward a new way."[4]

In tracing the resolutions of the American Baptist Conventions over the last few years, we discover a steadily rising crescendo of concern over segregation and discrimination. The 1953 Convention declared that "the American Baptist Convention has repeatedly voiced its concern regarding discriminatory practices in America, and has urged equal treatment of all citizens regardless of race, color and creed." And it resolved to call upon all of its "agencies" and "local churches to remove such practices where they exist among us."[5] The 1954 Convention resolved that "we commend the United States Supreme Court in its historic decision of 1954 outlawing segregation in public education." It also urged "American Baptists to increase their opposition in other areas of segregation—housing, employment, recreation, church participation."[6] The 1955 Convention asked American Baptists to "ex-

[3] John Knox, *The Christian Church and Race* (New York: The Federal Council of Churches, 1945), p. 10.
[4] National Council Message for Race Relations Sunday (February 10, 1952).
[5] Resolutions adopted by the American Baptist Convention (May 25, 1953); see Section IV, Article 7.
[6] *Ibid.*, adopted May 28, 1954.

amine themselves . . . and to work for the elimination of any discrimination."[7]

Several years ago the Presbyterian Church of the United States of America affirmed the goal of "a nonsegregated church and a nonsegregated society" and set up an Institute of Racial and Cultural Relations[8] to alert the churches about the facts and significance of this great issue. The General Assembly in 1955 called for "the launching of operation desegregation in our churches and church related institutions and in the communities in which our churches work and serve." It passed a special recommendation for an "inclusive church" and directed that it be sent to the stated clerk of every Presbytery, asking for a report on the action taken.[9] Similarly, the Congregationalists have made this a primary emphasis and employed a secretary to promote sensitivity and action in this critical field. The same sense of urgency has touched nearly all the Protestant denominations and spurred them to greater education and action.

The Terrible Resistance That We Face

Despite the power and clarity of the democratic tradition and the unambiguous demand of the Christian Gospel for impartiality and Christian love for all God's children, both our churches and the majority of our members practice discrimination or are tainted with prejudice. In a study of *The Protestant Church and the Negro* made by Frank Loescher,[10] it was shown that only a minute percentage of the thousands of Protestant churches in America have taken Negroes or other colored people into their membership. Only 367 churches in the Northern (American) Baptist Convention reported one or more persons of color in either attendance or membership. Of these churches 201 had only

[7] *Ibid.*, adopted May 24, 1955.

[8] *Social Progress* (Presbyterian magazine) (May, 1953), p. 3.

[9] Resolutions of the 167th General Assembly (May, 1955); reported in *Social Progress* (July, 1955), pp. 11-13.

[10] Frank Loescher, *The Protestant Church and the Negro* (New York: The Association Press, 1948).

non-Negroes of color and 166 had Negroes. Even in the churches that had Negroes the average was less than two persons per church.[11]

Four hundred Congregational Christian churches reported one or more persons of color in attendance, but two churches accounted for over half of the total number. Only 200 of the churches served Negroes, and these averaged between one and two persons per church.

In the Protestant Episcopal Church,[12] 465 churches reported Negro participation, and of those who gave numbers the average was slightly over four per church.[13] Other denominations showed much the same pattern of exclusion in the overwhelming majority of their churches.

Protestant-affiliated schools and colleges have fewer colored students than state-supported schools or private nondenominational colleges.[14] The Protestant record in church-supported hospitals and other institutions appears to be no better. These facts have led a number of authorities to say that the churches lag far behind many of our other institutions in promoting Christian reconciliation and fellowship among races. Many churches preach against racial discrimination, but when a respected Negro who has proved his Christian loyalty asks for membership they turn him away. Many a church has been rocked with dissension when one person of color has asked to be admitted to the Christian fellowship. The sad truth is that church members, like other Americans, tend to be heavily tinctured with racial prejudice and the fear of losing status if they associate with people of other races.

Since Loescher's study, another survey has been made by Alfred S. Kramer under the sponsorship of the Department of Racial and Cultural Relations of the National Council of Churches and three of the major Protestant denominations. Preliminary reports of this study show that real gains are being made,

[11] *Ibid.*, pp. 69-70.
[12] *Ibid.*, pp. 66-68.
[13] *Ibid.*, pp. 72-73.
[14] *Ibid.*, pp. 96-99.

but there is still very far to go toward approaching desegregation in our churches.

When we probe to the heart of the matter, nearly all of us have been penetrated by un-Christian and snobbish attitudes toward people who are regarded as being of lower caste or class. We are afraid that our own position or prestige will be jeopardized. We fear that our churches will not attract "better people" if we welcome such children of God into our fellowship. In our personal lives, we fear that if such people are given full economic opportunity they might compete with us for jobs or clients or a place in the sun. There is in all of us a sinful pride to want to be better than others and to enforce our superiority over those whom we want to keep inferior for our own advantage.

Prejudices run very deep in the human consciousness. They are formed early in life from the views of parents and associates before the capacity to protest has developed. They come to seem as true as the earth we walk on and become so much a part of us that we feel that our very self-respect is threatened when they are challenged. These prejudices are deepened by our anxieties and insecurities and are supported by association with those who rank our reputations by adherence to the common prejudices of class or race. Our deepest prejudices are more than beliefs; they are compulsions and emotions that rise up like butterflies in our stomachs and often take command of our behavior against our convictions. For instance, many people who have been reared under strict patterns of racial discrimination become intellectually emancipated from their biases but still find themselves emotionally unable to associate freely with people of color without qualms and embarrassment.

Racial prejudices are only the most obvious among those that infiltrate our lives. Our antipathies and superiorities cut us off from fairness and fellowship with our fellows from other walks of life and other classes. A great many facts have been gathered that show that the churches of the main denominations have been unable proportionately to serve and win the lower class of peoples in our society. The attitudes and misunderstandings of middle-class church people toward the common workers and people who exist close to the line of poverty are often unsympathetic and prejudicial. Snobbery is an ever-present temptation for all of us.

Another area of prejudice that we need to search within ourselves is found in our attitude toward delinquents and persons who have run into conflict with our customs and laws. Often we are motivated more by revenge and fear than by a mercy that seeks rehabilitation and salvation. Criminologists and experts in the field of crime have demonstrated how little good most jail sentences and punishment do in deterring crime and restoring maladjusted people to usefulness, especially among youthful and first-time offenders. But "church people" are often the chief de-manders of more severe penalties and harsher treatment rather than promoters of understanding and patient help. If we could only realize that "but for the grace of God there go I" in every person in trouble, perhaps we could live more by love than by prejudice.

METHODS OF RECONCILIATION AND OVERCOMING PREJUDICE

When the church attempts to confront this broad gap between its principles and declarations and its actual practices, it must do so with a realistic understanding of how deep and how explosive this problem is. We are facing nothing less than the ingrained bias of a whole culture and the emotional pride of man himself that is ready to erupt when challenged. Yet already much has been accomplished and, increasingly, many of the resistances are crumbling. This is a strategic time to mobilize our influence to sustain the effort of Christian reconciliation. It is becoming clearer that our whole missionary enterprise among the vast numbers of nonwhite people abroad is being endangered by our racial failures in our own land.

Discovering and Confessing our Prejudices

As soon as we see the clear Christian denial of discrimination we must search ourselves and confess our own prejudices in order to prepare ourselves for action. The standard statement of most of us is: "I have no racial prejudice, but. . . ." It is what we say after that fatal word "but" that betrays our inner qualms. "I have no racial prejudice, but I would not want to live next door to a Negro"; or "I wouldn't want to take a person of color into our church membership"; or "I would hate to have my friends know that I invited a nonwhite person to my house for dinner."

Many of us think we have no racial prejudice because we have never faced the acid test. We have never been called on to show our faith in action—to receive people of other races into our churches, or accept them into our homes or into our circle of friends. When we face the actual situation, so many of us backtrack and begin to wonder what our friends will think or what it will do to our social standing. We are clearly the victims of the influence of our world rather than carriers of our Christian mission into the society where we live.

Reconciliation Through Cultivating Fellowship

Talk rarely overcomes genuine prejudice. Preaching may change our ideas and convince us of our duties but fail to erase our feelings. However, true worship and deep religious experience can penetrate our defensive emotions and prepare us for new effort. Few people are ever talked or argued out of their prejudices because they lie deeper than mere reasoning. It is even difficult and often impossible for us to argue ourselves out of the emotional reactions and anxieties that haunt us. It has been said that a person cannot overcome his fear of spooks without screwing up his courage and walking up and shaking hands with one. There is no substitute in overcoming prejudice for cultivating the acquaintance of living human beings. Prejudice is basically not directed against real people like Sam Brown, who, perhaps, has a wife and two children; who smiles and talks about the weather; and who worries about his problems the same as we do. Prejudice is directed against Negroes or Jews or Filipinos or migrants as a whole class. It is directed largely against whole types of people whom we don't know and don't want to know.

Therefore, acquaintance in association is the only effective method of approaching the problem in ourselves and in our own churches. Every church that works near minority people who are the targets of prejudice needs to set up situations to cultivate acquaintanceship. Frequently it has been discovered in actual work situations where workers have protested the hiring of fellow workers from other races that if an initial experiment could be attempted such protests rapidly disappear. In schools and colleges where students live face-to-face with students of other races, it usually does not take long for all consciousness of dissimilarity to disappear, providing there is a normal basis for congeniality.

Of course, it must be remembered that in any racial or nationality group there are all types of people: sullen and pleasant, friendly or retiring, and so on. It is extremely unfair to generalize from one person concerning a whole race. Also, we must take into consideration that groups who have restricted opportunities in income, housing, and education will have fewer members who will have had the chance to develop broad interests and tastes. When it is said that the people of an impoverished racial group are dirty or ignorant, this is usually because of limitation of opportunity and economic status. There are ignorant, dirty, and uncouth people among the culturally and materially impoverished of every race and nationality. This means that if intimate association is to help break down prejudice, it must take place among people who have some things in common. There is little distinction among professional people, or white collar workers, or factory workers no matter what race they represent. Likewise, high school students or college students have much in common, except for differences in status that tend to establish, according to prestige, snobberies and inferiorities among cliques.

In the church, as everywhere, fellowship under inartificial circumstances is one of the great cures for prejudice. Sometimes ministers of churches of different races or nationalities exchange pulpits for a Sunday; this is a gesture in the right direction. Inviting speakers to small groups where there is opportunity for face-to-face conversations is even better. However, it is rather unfair and indiscreet to ask such people to talk on race relations, which reminds them and their audience of the very difference that is to be overcome. Such speakers should speak upon general subjects in which they are competent so that attention will be focused upon common Christian interests and experiences.

But lone preachers or speakers are, at best, presented in artificial circumstances. The most effective method of all requires a real commingling in reasonably equal numbers and in a natural social setting. Instead of exchanging pulpits on an interracial Sunday, it would be far better to exchange one-half of the congregation. Joint dinners or young peoples' meetings, mixed camps or retreats, or an informal gathering of any type is far more successful. Many successful ventures of interracial cultivation between white and Negro groups have been conducted with "new areas of friendship being opened."[15] It is usually discovered that once the "reserve" is overcome restraints and embarrassments disappear.

Another method of cultivating interracial and intercultural understanding is for Christian families to entertain in their homes some of the many college students from abroad. There are thousands of Negroes, Indians, Chinese, Filipinos, Koreans, and others in our colleges. Often they are lonely and suffer discriminating treatment. Many of these students go back to assume posts of leadership in their own countries. It is tragic if they carry back bitter experiences with them. Both hosts and guests can be the gainers in the cultivation of such friendships.

Dr. Rachel DuBois, the Director of the Workshop for Cultural Democracy, has demonstrated a simple yet effective method of breaking down barriers and creating sympathetic understand-

[15] The experience of the young adult group in the First Baptist Church of New Haven, as described in *Social Action* (January 15, 1949), p. 27.

ing.[16] She brings together people from many backgrounds, often complete strangers, into conversation fests. Some common subject like "home customs" or the celebration of Christmas is introduced as the topic for sharing personal experiences. The very variety of customs and experiences lends color and interest, yet the universality of home life or Christmas (for Christians) gives a sense of deep sharing. Dr. DuBois by homely illustrations and questions is able to help break the ice and enlist an experience of group identification that is remarkable. Churches can find in such a method a means of Christian sharing in diversity.

Many village or rural churches are situated where there are no neighbors of other races near by, yet their people absorb some of the prejudices carried in the prevailing attitudes of our culture. It may not be easy to cultivate friends across racial barriers in such situations. However, a number of churches have discovered a way to overcome this handicap of distance. Several years ago a rural church in Vermont invited a whole bus load of children from a Negro Protestant church in New York City to come up and spend a week as guests in the homes of its families. In turn they were invited to spend several days in the homes of their Negro friends. This scheme has caught on, and a number of other churches have established this pattern of intimate sharing even over considerable distances. For several years the young people of some of the churches in Cortland, New York have visited back and forth with young Negroes from New York City, staying in one another's homes and learning about one another's lives.

Until we have personal friends whose special characteristics are forgotten, we have not really overcome the "bogey" of prejudice. And until we demonstrate our friendship in free and unrestricted social intercourse, we have not overcome the sin of snobbery in race and class relations. Many people are afraid to have interracial friends because of the pressure of social ostracism; legion are the church members who let this consideration overcome their nondiscriminating comradeship with their brothers in Christ.

[16] Rachel DuBois, *Neighbors in Action* (New York: Harper and Brothers, 1950).

Reconciliation Through Drama
  and Role-Taking

Emotional identification is the bridge of reconciliation. One of the most effective ways of producing identification is through drama. Many people cannot compel themselves to enter into fellowship with people against whom they have emotional antipathies. Drama is a means of preparing the way. This is an art form that differs radically from the exhortations of preaching or the imparting of information through lecturing. It is a window into the very lives of living people who react to each other in sympathy and conflict, who suffer and hope in living situations before our very eyes. We hear their words and feel their emotions. Drama is one of the greatest vehicles of identification available, for we project ourselves into the roles of others and feel as they do.

Since our prejudices are more deeply emotional than rational, a great drama can often penetrate our defenses and shatter our resistance by throwing us into the roles of types of people we think we dislike. Even spectators can undergo soul-shaking, vicarious experiences in suffering exploitation and discrimination. In some small way they can feel what it is like to be a Negro, a poor migrant, or a Puerto Rican living in a circumscribed and hostile community.

Even more potent is the experience of being an actor in the very role itself and walking in the shoes of one who suffers the indignities that we have helped to create for others in our real lives. Role-taking is a powerful spiritual experience when done seriously. It is a method in which a person attempts to get over into the role of the other man, the discriminated, while someone else is the discriminator. This is doing what the Golden Rule really asks. "Sociodrama," as it is called, is trying to be "the other" for a time in order to be acted upon as we act toward others.

There are a number of powerful plays available, to provide the media for such experiences for both actors and audiences, that can be used as vehicles for reconciliation. Group play-reading can often provide this experience and help lift people out of themselves to a broader perspective. But what is even better is for a group to act out a situation from an issue confronted by its own members. The group can formulate the characters and the conflict representing the real problem and write its own play out of life. Then it is possible for members to play various roles and see how it feels. This will not be great drama, but it will be a great Christian experience that sometimes can produce transforming results.

What is even still more powerful is to have a mixed racial group play each other's roles in tense life situations and realistically share one another's burdens. A warning must be given, for here we approach a situation that is more than "playing," because it is fraught with an emotional explosiveness that can sometimes erupt into serious consequences. One leader in sociodrama in the interracial field found that sometimes participants would be jolted so deeply that they became ill and emotionally upset. In fact, psychiatrists are taking role-playing so seriously that it is becoming a major method of therapy called "psychodrama." This level is no field for amateurs, for in playing with deep-seated compulsions, human beings sometimes can be thrown into neurotic behavior patterns. So it is necessary to be extremely cautious in this field and to stop short of getting people too overwrought. However, this is a most significant field to explore. In this kind of interaction, the Spirit can often touch and transform prejudice into some measure of understanding and identification.

Breaking Discrimination by Group Action

There are many ways in which a group of Christians who have the courage of their convictions and are willing to risk some unpleasantness for the glory of Christ can break down patterns of discrimination. The members of one church rose magnificently to such an occasion when a young Nisei engineer and his family moved into a solidly white middle-class community. There was an immediate mobilization of neighborhood resistance with plans to make life as unpleasant as possible in order to drive them out, but a local church organized a calling campaign. For several days, one of the better-known families drove up in a shining car every hour or two to make a friendly call to welcome these new people. The campaign to drive them out collapsed and this Japanese-American family found a haven of friendship in that church.

In many communities where business establishments and public facilities are discriminatory against people of color, young people's groups have undertaken campaigns to overcome these barriers. A group of well-dressed young people with one or two members who are Negroes go together to a restaurant or theatre. Sometimes the management is too embarrassed to turn them down, and after several times the pattern of discrimination is broken. If the management does object, the most poised member of the group can ask to speak to the owner or manager and politely ask if he is refusing the patronage of members of the church group. If the group has to walk out quietly with dignity, it often does as much to crack resistance as when they are served.

It is legitimate for a group to call on various establishments to determine their policy and, if told that they accept only a white clientele, they can politely state that they are sorry but as members of the group, they will have to turn elsewhere. Many states have laws against discrimination that are sometimes not enforced strictly. If refusals to accommodate people of colored races occur, such infractions can be reported to the authorities; and if a substantial group of people insist on enforcement, action usually follows.

If churches and church organizations adopt a policy of never patronizing establishments that will not cater to all types of their people and if a significant number of individual Christians adhere to this policy, it often adds up to a weight that cracks discriminatory practices. Many major Protestant bodies in America have adopted the policy of never using for conventions, meetings, or dinners facilities that are discriminatory. Local churches and individual Christians ought to do no less.

In one segregated city a beloved church leader was to be honored upon retirement. With much publicity a dinner was planned in his honor. But all of the dining rooms big enough and adequate in service for the event refused Negroes, so this Christian leader refused to go if his Negro friends could not attend. The affair was never held, but a great many prejudiced people were deeply ashamed. This was one step toward the final breaking of segregation in many public places in that community.

Christians can do much to overcome discrimination in their vocations. Christian employers can carefully establish nondiscriminatory hiring policies. Some of the smartest retail stores in the country have discovered that well-groomed and efficient nonwhite salespeople even in conspicuous positions encounter little resistance and are easily accepted. Church people can help by making it a point to patronize such institutions and can register their conviction by going especially to colored salespeople.

In hundreds of shops and factories it has been proved that a few carefully placed workers can be introduced to begin interracial hiring. Usually the predicted resistances do not materialize or are rapidly overcome, even where they do show themselves. Christian employees can help to break the ice and befriend nonwhite fellow workers when they arrive. When Christians understand the additional burden and anxiety that colored people have to bear as pioneers in entering new openings, their Christian consciences will urge them to the rescue of their lonely neighbors.

If even a fraction of our Christians would act consistently in the ministry of reconciliation, the organized bastions of discrimination would fall.

Breaking Discrimination Through Laws

It is often argued that since racial discrimination exists in the attitudes and emotions of individuals it cannot be overcome through legislation. This is only partially true. It is certainly true that passing laws will accomplish little without the accompanying process of educating and sensitizing lives with the spirit of Christian reconciliation. Laws may not be supported by public convictions and are, therefore, often not obeyed or enforced. Nevertheless, as a method of consolidating moral gains and standardizing and protecting the freedoms guaranteed by our democratic traditions such legislation has an important place.

If the large majority of people in a society does not believe in the righteousness of a law, it will do little good. However, this certainly does not seem to apply to the general situation in America. Few people deny the free tradition of the American Constitution or the justice of a nondiscriminating way of life. The majority of our people are convinced that this is right, but are caught in a vicious circle of personal feelings and social practices without knowing how to overcome this conflict in themselves or in our society. With the exception of a few Southern states, which see in antidiscrimination laws a kind of external regional intimidation, the overwhelming majority of Americans seem ready to conform to an enforcement of what has long been our basic principle. This has been proved in the many states that have been successfully operating such laws for many years. In 1950, eighteen states had civil rights acts forbidding discrimination in places or facilities of public accommodation.

To begin with, it certainly seems untenable for our government to enforce laws to protect discriminations that are expressly denied by our Constitution. This is government acting against itself and its own highest law. Both loyal citizenship and Christian devotion should demand that as citizens we work energetically to abolish such contradictory laws. Some of the most important gains have come through court decisions that have judged state laws and institutional practices to be unconstitutional under the supreme law of the land. The Supreme Court has ruled that the courts cannot be used to protect "real estate restrictive covenants," which limit the sale of property to whites only. It would seem equally just to remove laws enforcing discrimination in the equal right of all citizens to vote and to use all public facilities and institutions. Another tyranny that certainly requires vigorous legal prohibition is lynch terror, brutality, and official condonement of those who criminally take the law into their own hands. Such intimidation by which his inferior status is driven home to the man of color is intolerable to those who believe even in the minimum kind of justice.

This far all of us ought to be able to go. As citizens we ought to register our concern vigorously and persistently and educate our Christian people to resist this travesty on American freedom.

Another area in which court decisions have attempted to bring practices into conformity with our Constitution has been in the field of public education. Through a series of decisions, beginning in 1938, the Supreme Court ruled that applicants from nonwhite races must be admitted to state professional and graduate schools. By 1953 only five state universities were still closed to Negroes. Many of the walls of segregation in higher education have been crumbling under the impact of these decisions. By the summer of 1954, thirteen private or church-related institutions, twelve Protestant theological seminaries, and twenty-five Catholic institutions in Southern states had been opened to Negroes.[17]

But the most decisive and significant court decision of all came in the historic ruling of the Supreme Court of the United States on May 17th, 1954. This was the decision declaring the unconstitutionality of racial segregation in the public schools. It reversed the doctrine allowing "separate but equal" public schools that had been enunciated by the Supreme Court in 1896. Of course, the fiction of equal public schools in the segregated state systems had become notoriously contradictory of fact with wide differentials prevailing between white and Negro schools in buildings, equipment, and teachers' salaries. Furthermore, under compulsory school-attendance laws, Negro children were forced to attend these inferior schools. The Supreme Court decision upheld the view that segregation itself imposes inequality even if the schools were equal in quality.

This history-making opinion delivered by Chief Justice Earl Warren declared: "We conclude that in the field of public educa-

[17] *Information Service*, XXXIII:23 (June 5, 1954).

tion the doctrine of 'separate but equal' has no place. Separate educational facilities are inherently unequal."[18]

The reaction of the churches was on the whole enthusiastically favorable. Even in the South a surprising number of church bodies and Christian leaders recognized the decision as just and in line with the Christian faith. The New Orleans Council of Churches passed a resolution approving the Supreme Court decision.[19] The General Assembly of Presbyterian Churches in the United States (Southern) voted for the abolition of segregation.[20] A survey conducted by the (Southern) Baptist Press Service showed that most Southern Baptist leaders "praised the decision as carrying out Christian principles." The General Board of the National Council of Churches hailed the decision "as a milestone in the achievement of human rights." It said that it "gives a clear status in law to a fundamental Christian and American principle."[21]

Public opinion and political response in the South has been mixed. Even those rejecting it tend to be on the defensive and show signs of being deeply troubled. The Tuskegee Institute's annual Race Relations Report[22] made an analysis of opinion in 140 leading newspaper editorials of the South. It found that "forty-six per cent of the editorials 'accepted' the Court's decision; twenty-four per cent rejected it; and the remaining thirty per cent were equivocal." Only 3 per cent of the rejecting editorials did so in terms of ethical principle. The moral defense has largely crumbled. Most justifications seem to take the form of calling for the preservation of segregation to prevent riots and disorder or simply for the preservation of Southern customs.

Seven governors have acted to continue segregation in the schools, while seven others have acted toward setting up programs of desegregation. South Carolina, Georgia, and Mississippi have shown the strongest resistance and have attempted to devise plans

18 *Ibid.*
19 *Interracial News Service,* 25:4 (July-August, 1954).
20 *Information Service, op. cit.*
21 *Ibid.*
22 *Ibid.,* **XXIV**:5 (January 29, 1955).

to circumvent the decision. Some Christian leaders feel that the legal attempt to overcome segregation has set back the trend toward improved race relations in the South because of the almost hysterical resistance that has been incited in some areas. Even such a distinguished Christian statesman and liberal leader as Frank Graham was opposed to the method of legal imposition. But now that the decision has come he believes it provides an opportunity for Christian leadership.[23] F. Ernest Johnson in surveying the situation says, "There is . . . a gratifying body of evidence that the South will follow the lead which the Supreme Court has given."[24] He cites materials gathered by the Southern Regional Council[25] as evidence for this belief.

It seems true that in certain states the conscience of the majority of people has not been adequately ready for compliance, and aggressive resistance has been elicited. Nevertheless, it seems that the time for decision had come to withdraw legal sanctions for a practice contrary to our traditions and our faith, and Christians must support and hail the action as upholding the Christian stand. Even in the most antagonistic states, Christians will have an opportunity to provide leadership—first, in smoothing the troubled waters; and, secondly, in building the support of acceptance among the churches.

A further question is whether we ought to favor laws to enforce nondiscrimination in employment in private enterprise. Equality of opportunity according to ability is a great ideal in America, and should be elemental in Christian justice. Why should our citizens be restricted and punished for skin color without committing any crime? The federal government enacted laws barring discrimination in war plants during the war, and a number of states have effective Fair Employment Practice laws. Both party platforms in the last national election favored laws against discrimination in employment.

[23] An address by Frank P. Graham, *Social Action* (February, 1955), p. 19.
[24] "Desegregation in the Public Schools," *Social Action* (February, 1955), p. 12.
[25] Southern Regional Council Pamphlet, *Answers for Action—Schools in the South* (October, 1954).

The experience of New York State under its F.E.P.C. law is regarded by most people as highly satisfactory. The commissioner for the New York State Commission Against Discrimination, Caroline K. Simon, declared that most discriminating employers said "they practiced discrimination because they were afraid."[26] They were afraid of trouble or that white employees would quit or that they would be considered radical. This expert says that the experience of the seven states that have enacted such laws "indicates conclusively that wise legislation creates a climate of opinion in which discrimination tends to disappear."

To do everything possible to bring our laws into support of our historic beliefs, Christian groups must study and discuss these great issues and register their witness of reconciliation in their role as citizens.

DEMONSTRATING THE INCLUSIVE GOSPEL IN THE LOCAL CHURCH

In conclusion, let us turn to the hardest but most convincing Christian witness that we can make in our time on this great issue: This is the method of making our own church open and inclusive of all types of human beings who respond to the call of Christ. The great Protestant bodies have called for "a nonsegregated church in a nonsegregated society." This cannot be accomplished unless individual local churches make this their goal. This is an acid test of our Christian faithfulness. For a church that desires to go beyond conventional routines and cut loose from sheltered defensiveness here is a real adventure, worthy of a true Christian courage that is willing to risk a demonstration of the gospel it preaches.

This is a real possibility as the growing roll of successful interracial churches shows. There are many exciting stories about churches that have successfully confronted all the hazards and

[26] Caroline K. Simon, "Causes and Cure of Discrimination," *The New York Times Magazine* (May 29, 1949).

tensions and emerged with new strength and power in their witness. The story of the declining First Baptist Church in Chicago that was able to weather the transition of its parish and open its door to all races and call to its pastorate the Rev. Jitsuo Morikawa is one of the finest of these demonstrations.[27]

The South Congregational Church in Chicago, at the very time that Negroes and Japanese Americans were flooding into the community and tensions were high, faced the alternative of dying or becoming a church for all its new parishioners. It faced the decision and became an interracial church, losing only a few of its white people and attracting to replace them many others who were excited by the appeal of this bold new approach.

The City Church, periodical of the Department of the Urban Church of the National Council of Churches, has published two stories of interracial churches. Rev. R. Francis Jones, of the Forest Avenue Community Church in the Bronx, under the title "I'm Glad to Be Pastor of an Interracial Church," tells how the transition was made in his church.[28] The other story tells how St. John's Lutheran Church in the Bronx keeps white members coming after twenty years of interracial experience.[29] In a special Race Relations Issue,[30] the Presbyterian (U.S.A.) monthly, *Social Progress,* tells how five Presbyterian Churches became interracial. It lists others that have achieved racial inclusiveness.

In a survey of what has actually occurred in the churches of three denominations as they have become interracial, it has been discovered that few members are actually lost when churches welcome colored people. Of 237,000 church members in the interracial congregations, only twenty-six individuals were reported to have left directly because of the inclusion of nonwhite persons.[31]

---

[27] Lincoln Wadsworth, "In a Changing Community," *The City Church* (September-October, 1953), p. 2.

[28] R. Francis Jones, *The City Church* (March, 1952), p. 6.

[29] William A. Dudde, "Whites Keep Coming," *The City Church* (March-April, 1953), p. 6.

[30] *Social Progress,* XLV:5 (January, 1955).

[31] *Interracial News Service,* 25:6 (November-December, 1954). Statement issued by J. Oscar Lee and Alfred S. Kramer, summary of a survey to be published.

The drastic effects that are so often feared and predicted usually do not materialize when churches actually become interracial.[32] Kenneth B. Clark in reviewing what has happened says, "The facts seem to be that white Christians, however violently they feel, are very indisposed actually to disobey the voice of their Christian consciences when in the fellowship of the church."[33]

This means that it is unnecessary and even bad strategy to delay action until the members are all convinced in their minds that they can accept people of other races. People cannot arrive at such an acceptance until they actually associate with such people, and then it is the association not the argument that overcomes the prejudice. Therefore, a church that can make a bold decision to act on faith despite heavy prejudice will usually find the grace to come through victoriously.[34]

From the experiences of others that have been successful in this transition, there are several guiding principles that can be listed for churches to follow:

1. Prepare your people with a deep understanding of the Christian ministry of reconciliation and the meaning of Christian fellowship in Christ.

2. Don't precipitate conflict before you have prepared the way.

3. Don't debate the problem of becoming an interracial church. Instead, simply begin by cultivating interracial friends and welcoming a few people into activities as the unquestioned Christian response to the church's ministry.

4. It is often easiest to begin by serving children.

5. Some of the lay leaders who see the new vision should help to lead the way, but the minister should leave no doubt concerning his convictions.

6. Remember that where interracial churches are most needed and fit the situation prejudice and tension will be the strongest.

7. Be prepared for the point when conflict will break, and when the showdown comes don't back water. Stand firm in the

[32] *Ibid.*
[33] *Social Progress, op. cit.,* 34.
[34] *Ibid.,* p. 35.

faith and through prayer and devotion let the grace of God lead the way.

8. Be sensitive to the strain upon old members and upon your new ones who have subjected themselves to the role of ice-breakers and pioneers. Do everything possible to interpret and soften these strains in the light of the gospel.

Of course many churches cannot become interracial because of their location in totally white or totally colored areas. But every church can become inclusive, welcoming all types of people in the parish. And every true church of Christ must become a church of reconciliation, softening prejudice and exclusiveness with the unlimited welcome of Christian love and understanding. We must do everything possible to carry this ministry of reconciliation into the situations in which we live and work.

KEY QUESTIONS FOR DISCUSSION

1. What is the American ideal of freedom and opportunity?
2. Why is racial and class discrimination totally incompatible with the Christian faith?
3. Why do you believe we have resisted so stubbornly our own beliefs as citizens of the American democracy and as Christians?
4. Do you agree with the analysis of Gunnar Myrdal that Americans generally live under a bad conscience because of practices in discrimination?
5. How does the Christian doctrine of sin illuminate the universality of snobbery?
6. Have you found yourself in situations where your prejudices exposed themselves and guided your actions into discrimination?
7. What experiences have helped you overcome misunderstandings and prejudices?
8. What are some of the things that you can do at once in your church to promote reconciliation?
9. Toward whom are un-Christian antipathies directed among your people: Jews, Negroes, Mexicans, Indians, members of labor unions, Italians, Polish, people in trouble?

INFLUENCE THROUGH RECONCILIATION

10. Take an inventory of your church and your community and determine what you can do about making your church an inclusive interclass and interracial church.

RECOMMENDED READINGS

"Desegregation in the Public Schools," *Social Action,* XXI:6 (February, 1955).

DuBois, Rachel, *Neighbors in Action.* New York: Harper and Brothers, 1946.

Myrdal, Gunnar, *An American Dilemma.* New York: Harper and Brothers, 1944.

President's Committee on Civil Rights, *To Secure These Rights.* Washington, D.C.: Superintendent of Documents.

Social Progress, XLV:5 (January, 1955). Special race relations issue.

The Crisis. Monthly publication of the National Association for the Advancement of Colored People, New York, N.Y.

"The Main Types and Causes of Discrimination," *United Nations Memorandum.* Submitted, 1949, to the Secretary General, United Nations Commission on Human Rights.

The following are publications of the Department of Racial and Cultural Relations of the National Council of Churches, New York, N.Y.:

Denominational Statements with Reference to a Racially Inclusive Fellowship.

Interracial News Service. Bimonthly publication.

Statements Adopted by Religious Groups Regarding Segregation in the Public Schools.

CHAPTER 10

Exerting Influence
Through Christian Vocation

The Gospel is concerned with all the activities of man, individual and social. Therefore, the Christian faith is relevant to the economic order. . . . The Church must proclaim anew the Christian concept of vocation. All work must be seen in terms of its spiritual significance as helping to make possible fullness of life for all men everywhere. The Reformation doctrine of the calling of the Christian man must be re-emphasized, and all work must be done "as unto God" (The Detroit Conference on the Church and Economic Life [1950]).

I therefore, a prisoner of the Lord, beg you to lead a life worthy of the calling to which you have been called, with all lowliness and meekness, with patience, forbearing one another in love, eager to maintain the unity of the Spirit in the bond of peace (Ephesians 4:1-3, RSV).

We have saved for our last two chapters the two areas in which Christian responsibility is most urgently needed, yet most often denied or neglected. These are the areas of economic life and politics. We have already seen that the Christian is called to live his whole life in commitment to God under divine guidance; there are no compartments of his existence where he is exempt from responsibility. This is especially true of the realm of every-day affairs where we earn our livelihood and discharge our obligations in financial affairs. Now, as we consider our responsibilities and what we can actually do in facing them, three things stand out in bold relief.

First, the faith of Protestantism has a clear and vigorous tradition based on great Biblical teachings and reinforced and clarified by the leaders of the Reformation in their most distinctive emphases.

Next, we encounter the unhappy fact that for several generations this fundamental Christian emphasis has been suffering neglect and has been running into confusion and often outright denial even by those who claim to be Christians. Many have attempted to build an artificial wall between the affairs of the world and the affairs of the Spirit, as though a human being could serve mammon most of his waking hours and God on Sunday in complete contradiction to the great saying of Jesus (Matthew 6:24).

A well-known news magazine editor, commenting on the report of the Pittsburgh Conference on the responsibility of the Church in economic life, said: "Let the Church care more for the Church . . . but let us not drag the Church into the political and economic arena." It is probably true that this secular view is reflected in the attitudes of countless church members who are not fully aware of the teaching of their own Bible and tradition.

At the North American Laymen's Conference at Buffalo, one prominent businessman, after hearing Professor Robert L. Calhoun declare that Christian vocation was a determining emphasis of the Protestant Reformation, asked with some bewilderment: "Why have I gone to a Protestant Church regularly for forty years and never heard this before?"

But a third and more heartening development has been the powerful revival in both Europe and America of the historic doctrines of Christian calling and Christian stewardship. It has been an increasingly prominent theme in all the great world ecumenical conferences. The founding Assembly of the World Council of Churches at Amsterdam declared that "the social influence of the Church must come primarily from its influence upon its members . . . whenever they make decisions . . . in any . . . vocation to which they may be called."[1]

The Second Assembly of the World Council at Evanston devoted one of its six sections to a consideration of *The Laity—The Christian in His Vocation.* The report of this section, which was "commended to the churches for study and appropriate action," should be carefully discussed by all Christians. This report declared: "It is the laity who draw together work and worship; it is they who bridge the gulf between the Church and the world, and it is they who manifest in word and action the Lordship of Christ over that world which claims so much of their time and energy and labor."[2] The report expressed the intense sense of urgency concerning the ministry of laymen in economic affairs when it proclaimed that "the time has come to make the ministry of the laity explicit, visible and active in the world. The real battles of the faith today are being fought in factories, shops, offices, and farms, in political parties, and government agencies, in countless homes, in the press, radio and television, in the relationship of nations."[3] In America we have had four great history-making conferences on Christian economic responsibility—at Pittsburgh, in 1948, Detroit, Buffalo, and again at Pittsburgh in 1956.[4] Furthermore, in 1954 the General Board of the National Council of Churches adopted a statement that had been prepared in discussions over several years by the Department of Church and Economic Life. The majority of the members of the General Committee of this Department who prepared this statement are leading laymen from business and organizations interested in economic activity. This statement, entitled *Christian Principles*

[1] Amsterdam Assembly Series Report, *The Church and the Disorder of Society* (New York: Harper and Brothers, 1949), p. 196.

[2] Reports of the Second Assembly, *Evanston Speaks* (New York: World Council of Churches, 1954), pp. 59-60.

[3] *Ibid.,* p. 64.

[4] Sponsored by the Department of the Church and Economic Life of the Federal (now National) Council of Churches.

and Assumptions for Economic Life[5] is another milestone in the development of Christian economic responsibility. It reaffirms the historic doctrines of total stewardship and Christian vocation in economic affairs. This is another great document that should stimulate earnest discussion and reappraisal among all Christians. It does not hedge on the principle that "the church should seek to influence the development of economic life in such a way that economic institutions, policies and practices are favorable to right relations between people."

Therefore, it is highly important that we discuss the meaning of our faith in this crucial field and search for methods of action in carrying it out.

The Importance of Economic Life

We are all creatures of the earth—utterly dependent upon food, raiment, and shelter for existence. Even in the most secluded cloister, man cannot escape these requirements. If it were not for the surplus of produce of the field tillers and the wood hewers, even the men devoted to the purest contemplation would be forced to engage in common toil. Production and distribution of the goods of life are the indispensable means of maintaining organic lives.

From the Greeks, we received a heritage that tended to disparage common toil and view material things as base or unreal. Philosophers spending their lives in contemplation were the most honored of men; hard toil was considered the lot of slaves.

The Hebrew-Christian tradition has a different perspective. It is often said that Christianity is the most materialistic of religions. As Elton Trueblood asserts, concerning our faith, "The true function of the spirit is not to deny matter, but rather to glorify it."[6] The Old Testament begins with the view that man

[5] Available in leaflet form from the Department of the Church and Economic Life, National Council of Churches, New York, N.Y.

[6] Quoted from Elton Trueblood in *Religion in the Day's Work* by Cameron P. Hall (New York: National Council of Churches, n.d.), p. 4.

was created out of the dust of the earth and the theme of the New Testament is that "the Word became flesh and dwelt among us" (John 1:14, RSV).

Christians are not called upon to abandon the world but rather to live in it with a focus of commitment to God for all their striving. Jesus reversed the common idea that greatness commands the respect and services of others and declared in contrast: "He that is greatest among you shall be your servant" (Matthew 23:11). The most significant thing about the Biblical view is that it does not find the root of all evil in the material world but rather in alienation from God and the sinful self-centeredness of human nature.

There are two misunderstandings that have paralyzed Christian responsibility in economic pursuits. On the one hand, many Christians have fallen prey to the notion that the occupational world is a temporary evil to endure, but with no relation to the things of the spirit to which they are committed. This view has much in common with some of the oriental religions but is far from the Biblical view.

At the opposite extreme, but having the same effect, is the almost wholly secular view that the world of production and trade is unqualifiedly good in itself; that it is the basic reality of life to which we must devote ourselves while religion deals with a vague realm of hopes and dreams that at best can give only a kind of psychological support to our material struggle. This is true materialism in which economic processes are considered supreme and under which men fall into the sin of idolatry to created things as the objects of their devotion rather than their Creator. Our religion is the sovereign devotion of our lives, and if material things become our total preoccupation we no longer serve God but mammon.

In fact, so important has economic life become in modern commercial and industrial civilization that two of the dominating philosophies of our time have elevated economic processes into total sovereignty and determining supremacy.

The first, and most antagonistic to the Christian view, is the economic determinism of Marxist Communism. It holds that morality and religion (including its God) and even the thought processes by which we criticize or defend ourselves are simply the products of economic organization. It sees all social evil, selfishness, and human exploitation as caused by the institution of private property. If it were to be abolished, they hold, good relations would automatically ensue among men and the major injustices of the world would all be eliminated.

Against this oversimple and unrealistic view, the Christian interpretation has always held that sin is not created by economic institutions, although they do make it easier or harder to discharge responsibility. It holds that sinful and selfish men need continuous transformation and divine guidance to even strive toward justice under all economic arrangements. It also believes that our Christian obligations of love and justice stand above and in criticism of all our daily activities and the institutional patterns under which we carry them out.

But there is another brand of materialism that holds that economic forces are all-controlling and supreme in the world. This is the secularistic materialism that is held and practiced by many Americans who hold intensely to the economic shell of our free economy without the ethical and spiritual resources that helped to create it and restrain its dangers. F. Ernest Johnson calls this an "economic determinism quite as crude as that which has been attributed to Karl Marx."[7] He further points out that the result has been a "divorce of the economic mechanism from its supposed moral motor power, making the economic sphere autonomous and amoral."[8]

Both of these materialisms have rebelled against the Christian gospel and its ethic. Both hold that economic processes are ultimately independent, autonomous, and self-regulating. Both tend to make economic expediency king. The holders of such

---

[7] Commentary by Johnson in Howard R. Bowen's *The Social Responsibility of Businessmen* (New York: Harper and Brothers, 1953), p. 235.
[8] *Ibid.*

views believe that Christian motives and criticisms can only interfere with and thwart the purely materialistic activities and destiny of man. To both groups religion is a "fly in the ointment," a trouble maker, when it calls men to live under the guidance and judgment of God in daily affairs. Therefore, they say that it should be kept in its place to deal with issues beyond death, beyond the daily decisions of life, and beyond the moral intimidations and temptations of the world.

The radical materialists are threatening to capture the world. But against this view stands the Christian tradition, stemming from the Biblical and basically Protestant views of Christian stewardship and Christian vocation.

Economic Life as a Great Arena of Ethical Struggle and Decision

We have reviewed the Christian denial of basic economic determinism, yet we have observed that the economic sphere exerts great pressures upon human beings and inevitably molds their lives in many ways. Only by a perspective that stands above the struggle and a divine grace that empowers us to fight back can we be more than conformists and victims. In our vocational lives, we confront many of the greatest pressures for conformity to existing standards and methods. This is true for many reasons:

1. We spend a major part of our time in our work, which tends to become the major preoccupation of our lives, coloring our interests and our outlook upon the world.

2. Our personalities are molded to a considerable degree by our occupational roles. "Who we are" in society, our status, is assigned to us largely by our occupation. To some degree we come to conform to these roles and control our behavior by the general social expectations that surround them. For instance, lawyers, businessmen, actors, musicians, bartenders, and so on come to be a good deal alike in their views of themselves, their

standards, and their behavior. Physicians may develop a permanent "bedside manner" or clergymen develop an "unctuous air" that colors their personalities. Furthermore, our occupations and income status come to control in a great many ways the kind of associates and friends with whom we converse and share attitudes and values.

3. Probably the most significant decisions that affect the lives of others and register our influence in the stream of life are made in our vocations. Here we are humbly participating in existence by aiding or blocking the activity of God. It is here that we are resisters or co-workers. We must recognize that there is resistance in our best decisions, but this does not withdraw their effects for better or worse.

4. It seems clearly evident that in the economic sphere most people are faced with many of their most serious temptations to selfishness and the exploitation of other persons. These are the great sins against neighbor in the Christian interpretation. It is easy to see why it is so popular to beg off and make the secular claim that our religious life is totally separate from the hurly-burly of the work-a-day world.

CHRISTIAN DOCTRINE OF STEWARDSHIP

One of the great Biblical doctrines of the Christian faith concerns the stewardship of the resources of the earth. This view is enunciated vigorously throughout the Old Testament and is supported and given a higher and added basis in the New Testament. It runs through the Christian tradition as attested by the writing of dominant figures of Christian history. It played a significant part in the thinking of the Protestant reformers and the Puritans of England and America.

In more recent times, it has been dressed down so that among many Christians it means little more than an appeal for church support. But, as Biblical and theological scholars widely recognize, it is a doctrine of basic economic responsibility that is at the heart of Christian teaching. Let us summarize six aspects of this Biblical view:

1. God is the creator of all the resources of the earth and all that man has is a gift of God. "The earth is the Lord's, and the fullness thereof" (Psalms 24:1, and quoted by Paul in I Cor. 10:26). "Thus saith the Lord, The heaven is my throne, and the earth is my footstool . . . For all those things hath mine hand made, and all those things have been, saith the Lord" (Isaiah 66:1-2). Dean Walter G. Muelder expresses the Biblical understanding with direct simplicity when he says, "God is the real owner; man is his steward."[9] F. Ernest Johnson, in the book on *The Social Responsibilities of the Businessman,* declares that the "Christian doctrine of stewardship is the most radical of all doctrines concerning property. It maintains that a man owns nothing; what he has he holds in stewardship under God."[10]

The statement on *Christian Principles and Assumptions for Economic Life,* which has already been quoted, affirmed this high doctrine of stewardship. It declares, "All of the resources of the earth . . . are gifts of God, and every form of ownership or use of such property should be kept under such scrutiny that it may not distort the purpose of God's creation."[11] As another scholar has stated it, "Man's authority to say of anything, 'That is mine' rests, finally, on his power to say 'I am God's.' "[12]

2. Property, being created by God, is good. There is nothing basically evil in the goods of the earth. The Old Testament is full of passages about the blessings of good crops and favors of the Lord.

3. Nevertheless, the Old Testament gives warning after warning against the pride of possession, usually with the reminder

---

[9] Walter G. Muelder, *Religion and Economic Responsibility* (New York: Charles Scribner's Sons, 1953), p. 143.

[10] Commentary by Johnson in Howard R. Bowen, *op. cit.,* p. 244.

[11] Statement adopted by the General Board of the National Council of Churches, *Christian Principles and Assumptions for Economic Life* (1954).

[12] Henry Scott Holland, "Property and Personality," *Property: Its Duties and Rights,* Bishop Charles Gore (editor) (London: Macmillan and Company Ltd., 1913), p. 192.

that all wealth belongs to God (Deut. 8:11-18, I Kings 11:1-6, Ezek. 28:2-8). In the New Testament Gospels, Jesus takes for granted these teachings of the Old Testament concerning the necessity of property but delivers some of his sharpest warnings concerning the corruptive influences of seeking wealth. Before telling the parable of the rich fool, he said, "Take heed, and beware of all covetousness; for a man's life does not consist in the abundance of his possession." And at the end, after the "rich fool" is told that "this night your soul is required of you," Jesus concluded, "so is he who lays up treasure for himself, and is not rich toward God" (Luke 12:13-21, RSV). The Apostle Paul condemns the foolishness of those who "had exchanged the truth of God for what was false and worshiped and served what he had created, instead of the Creator" (Romans 1:25, Goodspeed). The moral hazards and temptations in the pursuit of wealth form a major Biblical emphasis.

4. On the positive side, the Christian lives his life as under a divine call away from self-centeredness. He is a man under orders and under responsibility to Christ as St. Paul so often insists. All relations toward others are to be conducted under the one primary ethical orientation—love toward neighbor as revealed in Christ. Thus, the earning of our livelihood, the management and control of our property, and the way we use and spend our incomes are all to be carried out in sacred faithfulness and in trust. No Christian has a right to do with his own what he pleases unless what he pleases is pleasing in the sight of God.

5. Another aspect of the Christian view is that persons are more important than things and must never be subordinated to impersonal forces. When ambition drives men to exploit and use their neighbors for their own ends, they are sinning against their God and falling under His judgment.

6. As is often pointed out, these are high and awesome obligations that are laid upon men under the gospel of Christ. It is often said that they are impossible in a world of pressures and conflicts, and that such counsels of perfection can only bring a sense of continuing failure in the real world. Furthermore, it is

held that this Christian view runs into direct conflict with values of our culture under which the hope of selfish gain is seen as the motive power of all human effort. These things are certainly true, and that is why they are so important in keeping us all under the humility that seeks continuing forgiveness and newness of perspective and power.

Here is where the deep Christian realism about human nature is so significant. Human selfishness is universal, and, while it drives men to hard work, it also impels them to exploitation of neighbors, injustice, and preoccupation with material things. These aspects of human life are not to be simply eradicated or denied, but rather are they to be kept under criticism and softened and transformed into higher motives under God's grace as actual decisions are faced. Christians live under a higher discipline and loyalty, and it is a tragic misunderstanding, as Dr. Johnson points out, that "references to discipline of the profit motive should be confused with attacks on the profit system."[13] The development of responsibility for justice and mutual support is imperative if any system is to endure. To resist responsibility and self-discipline is the surest way to lose moral initiative and court disaster.

The Doctrine of Christian Vocation

Let us turn to the Christian meaning of vocation, which has been described as one of the most important words in the Christian vocabulary. In an earlier chapter, we discussed the New Testament Gospel as basically a call of God through Christ to a new redirected life under God's grace. In our response to this call, we take upon ourselves a new status and vocation in which all our activities and decisions become a new mission under God.

The Apostle Paul developed and interpreted this view as he helped the new converts in the early churches confront the requirements of daily living. He advised them to "work with your hands, as we charged you" (I Thessalonians 4:11, RSV). He

13 Commentary by Johnson in Howard R. Bowen, *op. cit.,* p. 244.

exhorted them to "admonish the idle" and reprimanded sharply those who were "living in idleness, mere busybodies, not doing any work" (II Thessalonians 3:11, RSV). Paul, himself, had heard and answered the call of Christ to a new vocation. But, most significantly, he translated this conception of the call into the commission to serve God in daily duties as a great focus of the faith.

W. R. Forrester says that St. Paul (I Corinthians 7) "tells us that a man's daily work may be, in fact ought to be, ordained for him by God, and that our business is to discover our calling."[14] He further says, quoting another scholar, K. E. Kirk, "It is to Paul that we owe the great Christian truth that the most ordinary and secular employment . . . should be regarded as a mission laid upon us by the Omnipotent God Himself."[15]

Thus we find that the call has two great meanings: first, the call of one's whole heart and mind and soul into a new relationship with God who continually seeks us out; and secondly, a call to a special service in daily work. These two aspects were later given emphasis by the great reformer, John Calvin.[16]

After the times of early Christianity, however, this great doctrine suffered a decline and a distinct change. Under the influence of monasticism, Christians began to think of the call of Christ as requiring an abandonment of the world into a separate religious order or a monastery. The outside world of affairs began to be regarded as secular and inferior. Only monks and priests were considered commissioned of God.

Against this view, the Reformation delivered its mighty protest and restored vocation to its earlier significance. Professor Robert L. Calhoun, who has written widely on the subject, tells us that the Reformation restored the Christian vocation for all Chris-

---

14 W. R. Forrester, *Christian Vocation* (New York: Charles Scribner's Sons, 1953), p. 34.

15 *Ibid.*, p. 35 (Kenneth E. Kirk, *The Vision of God* [New York: Longmans, Green and Co., 1938], pp. 81-82).

16 John Calvin, *Institutes of the Christian Religion*, Book III (a Compend, edited by H. T. Kerr, Jr.) (Philadelphia: Westminster Press, 1939), chap. 24, section 8.

tians and brought back the Christian esteem of committed service in daily work and the original status of laymen in the church.[17]

THE PROTESTANT TRADITION OF THE PRIESTHOOD OF ALL BELIEVERS

This view is summed up in the historic Protestant doctrine of the "priesthood of all believers." All Christians, not just clergymen, are called to live full-time lives of service and devotion to God. As Alexander Miller says, "It is commonly supposed that, at the Reformation, all priests were done away with . . . however, the Reformers had a different intention,—namely, to make all Christians priests."[18] Luther (in his Letter to the German Nobility) said, "a cobbler, a smith, and a farmer, each has the work of his trade yet they are all alike consecrated priests and bishops." In another quotation, Luther exhorts the Christian to "have a care for his own body and strive to maintain it in health and fitness in order to be able to minister to the help of those who are in need, so that the strong may serve the weak, and we may be sons of God, caring and labouring the one for the other, mutually bearing each other's burdens and so fulfilling the law of Christ."[19] Thus, we see that for Luther the true arena of the consecrated life is in the common activities of the world and not in the cloister.

John Calvin, the other towering figure of the Reformation, emphasized this same view and carried it even farther. Said Calvin, "Every one in his particular mode of life will, without repining, suffer its inconveniences, cares, uneasiness and anxieties, persuaded that God has laid on the burden . . . no work will be so mean and sordid as not to have a splendour and value

[17] Robert L. Calhoun, *God and the Day's Work* (New York: The Association Press, 1943).

[18] Alexander Miller, *Christian Faith and My Job* (New York: The Association Press, 1946), p. 27.

[19] Quoted by James Mackinnon, *Luther and the Reformation,* II (London: Longmans, Green & Co., Ltd., 1925).

in the eye of God."[20] Dean Muelder in summarizing this emphasis of the Reformers says: "Luther rejects salvation by works but nevertheless has faith express itself in work, while Calvin makes work glorify God."[21]

John Oliver Nelson, in his address to the Buffalo Laymen's Conference, illustrated this basic distinction between the Roman Catholic view and the Protestant view. He said that if a thousand Catholics were assembled for some purpose but no clergymen were present, the Church would not be there. But wherever a single Protestant works in his ordinary occupation, the church is there in the presence and in the service of this called representative of the church of Christ. He declared that the church is wherever Christians work: "The church is laymen living their lives."[22]

This historic and revolutionary Christian view of the meaning of occupational life has radical significance for the common lives of all Christians:

1. It means that there are no mere jobs or occupations for Christians. All work—worthy of doing at all—is a responsible ministry, elevated to an ordination of service to God and to neighbor.

2. It means that it is not only the clergy who are called to full-time Christian service but also all professing Christians. The layman does not serve God basically by carrying out routine obligations to the institutional church (although this is necessary), but in living the called life to the glory of God.

3. It means that there are two great questions that Christians will ask about their occupations: Can I regard my work as a divine appointment? Is the work that we ask others to do and the conditions under which they must do it such that they can recognize it as God-given?[23]

[20] John Calvin, *Institutes of the Christian Religion,* Book III (translation by Henry Beveridge, Edinburgh, printed for the Calvin Translation Society, 1865), chap. X, section 6.

[21] Walter G. Muelder, *op. cit.,* p. 42.

[22] Address in *On-the-Job Dilemmas of Christian Laymen* (New York: National Council of Churches, 1952), p. 31.

[23] Address by William G. Gallagher, *op. cit.,* pp. 43-44.

4. It means that the basic influence of the Christian church in the world is to be carried by laymen in the discharge of this calling in the sphere of their everyday duties and decisions.

5. It means, as Professor Calhoun has put it so clearly, that the Christian is called away from a life of "irresponsible self-seeking [to] take the one course in which his powers can find mature fulfillment—the way of devotion to God and to his fellow men."[24] A new "encouragement in Christ" and "incentive of love" enable Christians to strive to overcome selfishnesses and "look . . . to the interests of others" (Philippians 2:1-4, Goodspeed).

6. It means, as Dr. Nelson has described it, giving our "full life"[25] to the full capacity of our skills to others as fellow human beings, rather than to clients, customers, patients, prospects, or "suckers."

7. It means that we are in a small and humble sense "laborers together with God" in His creation (I Corinthians 3:9): that is to say, his servants in bringing new possibilities into fulfillment; in bringing food and water to the hungry and thirsty; in overcoming old wrongs and struggling for greater justices.

8. It means that as Christians we are not merely solitary competitors struggling against our fellows on every side, but that we are "members one of another" (Ephesians 4:25)—each of us playing an indispensable role to which God has called us in the community.

9. It is a call to work that gives Christians a small reflection of the sense of the divine purpose and destiny, which is shown in that passage of John about Jesus: "To this end was I born, and for this cause came I into the world" (John 18:37).

THE MODERN DECLINE OF THE SENSE OF CHRISTIAN VOCATION

When we review this fundamental Biblical and Protestant emphasis, against the situation in which we live, we are almost

[24] Robert L. Calhoun, "The Day's Work as Christian Vocation," *Social Action,* XV:12 (December 15, 1949), p. 15.

[25] John Oliver Nelson, address to the Buffalo Conference, *op. cit.*

inevitably deeply sobered and shocked. We become aware of two things: first, the extent to which we have let this basic teaching of our faith dwindle in our times; and secondly, the frightful obstructions and difficulties that the massive impersonal social structure of our society imposes upon those who dare to take it seriously. A great "crisis in work" has developed today in which masses of people conduct their labor not only without a sense of vocation but also under such impersonal and monotonous routines in vast factories and offices that a sense of purpose and enthusiasm seems all but impossible. Men work by necessity— "working to live rather than living to work," thus reversing the true vocational purpose. Masses of modern workers find few satisfactions on their jobs, much less a life purpose. They adjust to work drudgery by centering their hopes and interests upon family or often trivial diversions or distractions of leisure activities. This does not say that family and leisure activities are not part of the Christian calling, but the centering of interest in leisure activities does seem to remove the crucial work-world from the Christian calling and guidance.

ASPECTS OF MODERN SOCIETY MAKING RESPONSIBLE VOCATION DIFFICULT

Christian vocation is more than just an idea or a teaching. It involves confronting the real situation in which we practice our vocations. As Robert Michaelson insists, it also requires a "comprehensive and realistic . . . understanding of work in its social . . . setting."[26] The booklet by J. H. Oldham, *Work in Modern Society,* gives an excellent analysis of the problems imposed by modern society upon our attempts to re-establish the sense of vocation.

In the last century or more, our society has undergone a gigantic change because of the industrial and organizational revolution. This has produced an entirely new situation under which the

[26] Robert Michaelson in *Social Action,* XV:10 (December 15, 1949), p. 12.

majority of men must work as compared to the time when our republic was founded. Then, the majority of workers operated their own farms or small businesses; most people worked for themselves and could exercise considerable moral initiative and responsibility. Even those who worked for others were in close personal relationship with their employers in small groups in daily association.

So radical has been the change that today, as the 1950 census showed, 78 per cent of those gainfully employed work for someone else. This would have horrified many of our earlier statesmen and economic thinkers who believed that both democracy and a free economy required a majority of people who were economically independent and unbeholden to others. But even more important is the fact that an increasingly heavy proportion of our people work in huge aggregates and do monotonous specialized tasks under orders to meet routine requirements. This is not only true of those who work in vast manufacturing and assembling plants, but it is also characteristic of the white collar workers who work in huge offices, merchandizing concerns, or government bureaus.[27]

It has even touched the free professions. Many lawyers and physicians have become employees, working as members of large organizations under specialized functions. This organizational revolution has made enormous increases in efficiency and production possible, which have increased our material standard of living. But, at the same time, it has tended to reduce greatly the personal and moral control that the majority of men have over their own economic lives. Let us summarize this fact, using some of the points made by Dr. Oldham[28] and others:

1. Men become subordinate to machines in bureaucratic organizations. "The person becomes an anonymous, interchangeable unit"[29]—a functionary.

---

[27] C. Wright Mills, *White Collar* (New York: Oxford University Press, 1951).
[28] J. H. Oldham, *Work in Modern Society* (New York: Morehouse-Gorham Co., 1950).
[29] *Ibid.*, p. 13.

2. Work is divorced from the personal life and is carried out in a situation that is a world unto itself.
3. Work is the carrying out of instructions, leaving little scope for personal decision.
4. The majority of employees feel that they have little voice or influence over their own economic destinies in the concerns in which they work, and have turned to collective bargaining in unions or to governmental controls as a remedy.
5. Work is carried out in groups with which workers identify themselves and seek support and common purpose.
6. This modern economic organization has created a vast network of specialized interrelations in which men are more dependent upon one another and upon the tides of general economic fortune than ever before.

As a problem in incentive and vocational significance, this lack of a sense of partnership and voice has been recognized by many experts in the field of business administration. Professor Alexander Heron says: "If we want workers to work . . . willingly and well, we must give them the right to think."[30] Management must believe in the right and ability of workers "to share in the task of thinking and planning."

Perhaps the most demoralizing aspect of our society is the belief that we live in a world that operates under an impersonal momentum that cannot be controlled and in which genuine moral choice is impossible. To whatever extent this is true, it is a threat to human integrity and to our civilization.

WHAT CAN WE DO?

How can we revive the practice of stewardship and Christian vocation against all the roadblocks in our way? This is one of the great questions of our times. We can offer only a few suggestions to stir us all to imaginative effort and concern.

1. *First, we must let our people know how basic vocational*

[30] Alexander Heron, *Why Men Work* (Stanford: Stanford University Press, 1948), pp. 174, 175.

responsibility is to our call in Christ. Surely we cannot allow our members, like our businessman at Buffalo, to go to church their whole lives and never hear of one of the great issues that created Protestantism. This, like the other great responsibilities that we have discussed in prior chapters, must be preached and prayed over continuously. It must be taught in our classes and discussed thoroughly and earnestly by our people. But this is not just a task for our ministers. This is peculiarly the layman's own domain of concern; it has to do with his Christian witness in his basic life's endeavor. The minister can never fully appreciate the difficulties and tensions that the layman must encounter as he is exposed to the full brunt of the secular patterns and movements of the world.

Ministers have an obligation to understand more realistically the heavy limitations and compromises that the work-world imposes upon the most conscientious of Christians. To exhort perfectionism and belabor the layman for failure, without understanding these limitations, will neither gird the layman for the struggle nor give the leadership that is required.

2. *Laymen, themselves, must accept the call of Christian vocation.* They must struggle against all odds to cast whatever influence is possible in their work relations and decisions. They must be prepared for continual defeats and set-backs without surrender. They must learn to settle for unavoidable compromises without abandoning the sense of call and without losing awareness of what they are doing. Personal influences must be registered at every opportunity, but, in a world in which important decisions are made largely in groups and organizations and by standard procedures and institutional routines, one-man protests will be ineffective. Christians must stand together or be overruled and brushed aside.

3. *We must establish Christian vocational groups.* This brings us to a crucial requirement. Such groups are desperately needed in developing united influence to raise standards and participate in actual decisional policy in the various occupational fields. The Amsterdam Assembly Report, *The Church and the Disorder of Society,* found that "one of the most creative developments in the

contemporary Church is the practice of groups of Christians facing much the same problems in their occupations to pray and to take counsel together in order to find out what they should do as Christians."[31]

Each occupational group confronts its own peculiar temptations to irresponsibility and its own "sharp practices" that can be understood and faced only by insiders. There is a universal tendency in men to resent outside meddling, especially by those who do not have to live with the actual problems. The most effective criticism is mutual self-criticism in Christian fellowship. Furthermore, it is criticism by those who are participants and are in a position to do something about mutually discovered weaknesses.

Cameron Hall of the Department of the Church and Economic Life of the National Council of Churches has prepared a booklet on the church and economic life.[32] He recommends that businessmen, professional men, farmers, wage earners, owners, investors, and consumers gather together to investigate "relationships, opportunities, problems and responsibilities."[33] In fact, this is exactly what the North American Lay Conference on the Christian and His Daily Work did do in Buffalo in 1952. In addition to the general sessions, sixteen occupational groups met for discussion "to discover how Christians should make the decisions, meet the requirements, and conduct themselves in the relationships of their occupations."[34] The reports of these groups show how deeply self-critical and aware of ethical problems such groups can be when they meet together for divine guidance.

Since then, numerous groups have met in many sections of the country to develop a Christian response to occupational dilemmas and to bring unity into the effort of influencing our practices toward greater responsibility. But we have far to go before we give every Christian an opportunity to participate in a fellowship

---

[31] The Amsterdam Assembly Series Report, *op. cit.*, p. 196.

[32] Cameron Hall, *What Churches Can Do About Economic Life* (New York: National Council of Churches, 1948).

[33] *Ibid.*, p. 14.

[34] *Report of the North American Lay Conference* (New York: National Council of Churches, 1952), p. 7.

working toward evangelizing our occupations. Most individual churches are too small to organize vocational groups; therefore, denominational or interdenominational groups, meetings, and institutes show the greatest promise. No more lively and significant theme could be discovered for a series of men's club meetings or for the laymen's retreats that are growing in popularity.

Such movements have become far more significant in Europe than in America. The powerful *Kirchentag* movement in Germany has assembled vast Congresses of several hundred thousand laymen yearly, for several years, to attempt to promote Christian influence in everyday life. In Greece, a thousand professional and businessmen have organized a group that has developed and published a comprehensive report on Christian social responsibility. In England and Scotland, The Christian Frontier Council has been promoting the same type of effort and has organized various vocational groups who have been facing their Christian responsibilities in fresh and constructive ways.[35] These movements show us what can be done.

4. *Develop informal Christian fellowship cells among our fellow workers.* Christians who work together can form a fellowship for confronting problems and temptations and deciding how to meet them together. Why should we let Communists monopolize this ancient Christian way of influence? Of course, Christians will avoid secrecies and undercover methods. We are not suggesting separate workers' organizations or separate professional societies for Christians but, merely, a fellowship of Christians for greater participation and influence. Christians need to become vocal and energetic in working for fair policies and responsible self-criticism in labor unions, trade associations, and business and professional societies in which they participate. There is an almost universal temptation for such groups to fall into narrow defensiveness or to concentrate on special privileges and greater benefits for members, rather than to emphasize ethical responsibilities and ways of greater service.

[35] See *Professional Life as Christian Vocation* (Geneva: Ecumenical Institute, n.d.), available through the World Council of Churches.

5. *Recognize the tendency of organizations to press beyond justice*. In fact, one of the most important ethical functions of the church is to prepare all its members in the moral realism to understand that groups with the highest purposes, in the pursuit of benefits for their members, tend to press beyond the requirements of justice and infringe on the rights of others. When human interests are combined into organizations with large resources and powers and with access to the channels of communication, the balance of justice is always endangered, unless it can be counterbalanced by other groups with organized influence and the capacity to weigh the scales on the other side. This is true of business corporations, labor unions, trade associations, or professional societies. It is even true of the church itself, if it becomes too powerful in the interest of its own strength. Even the church cannot safely monopolize authority. This view is based on our Christian concept concerning the selfish tendencies inherent in human nature and the need for all men to be responsible to others who must have effective means of exerting counter claims. As Bishop Angus Dun has stated it, "The Church is heavily committed to the sobering acknowledgment that men's actual motives are far from Godly or Christian, that they are commonly selfish, irresponsible, self-centered, not only as individuals but as groups. And for that reason we need protection from other men's egoism and they need protection from ours."[36]

This principle of "checks and balances" was wisely written by our forebears into our Constitution, and it has the same applicability to our economic institutions. F. Ernest Johnson expresses this common Christian view when he says: "No person or group of persons is either wise enough or good enough to control others, except as specifically delegated to do so."[37]

6. *Support responsible occupational organizations*. Christians and churches ought to support, and criticize when necessary, such organizations as labor unions and farm organizations to enable

---

[36] Rt. Rev. Angus Dun, *The Church Has Responsibility in Economic Life* (New York: National Council of Churches, Department of Church and Economic Life, 1947), p. 14.

[37] Commentary by Johnson in Howard R. Bowen, *op. cit.*, pp. 248-249.

those in such occupations to negotiate effectively and cooperatively in a world of big organizations. Thus, workers or producers
in one occupation may not be at the mercy of the control of
others, no matter how well-intentioned they may be.

In our economy, big corporations necessitated big labor unions,
and other powerful organizations required effective farm organizations and so on. This is why Christians in service to justice and
concern for neighbor have worked for equilibrium in organizational influence. The Executive Committee of the Federal Council of Churches in 1948 said: "The Churches have been right in
giving encouragement to the development of the labor movement
both as an instrument for the securing of greater economic justice
and as a source of both dignity and morale for the worker."[38] Of
course, all such groups will be tempted to work for gains that sur-
pass justice. Christians believe in always recognizing a higher
justice that stands above their own group interests and will struggle to keep this perspective alive in all organizations in which
they participate.

7. *Work for greater voice and moral initiative.* Christians
ought to promote methods of providing men in all vocations the
opportunity to have more voice and greater moral initiative as
individuals and as members of groups in their vocations. This is
partly a technical problem that earnest laymen need to work out
under the impetus of their calling. Christians in the economic
world must have an open imagination and conscience, guided by
the Holy Spirit, to be ready to grasp new possibilities in economic
organization in order to broaden moral responsibility and freedom. This is imperative in a collective age that threatens to swal-
low up the free conscience and the self-control of men over their
own lives. Christian justice demands that no single class or group
in the economic world control our economic life, nor any ruling
party in the political sphere be allowed the power to control other
groups without their having effective means of counterinfluence.
The threat of communism against justice and freedom is so grave
because it denies the doctrine of balance of responsibility and

[38] Quoted by Cameron Hall, *op. cit.,* p. 14.

combines the state ownership of all property with dictatorial political controls in the hands of a small group that suppresses all
opposition.

There are many other specific things that the local church can
find to do toward generating a spiritual and moral atmosphere
that emphasizes this neglected area of Christian influence, but it
will not be easy in a society that has a strong tendency to honor
shrewdness and "the ability to make a fast buck." So permeated
is our moral climate with materialistic evaluations of success that,
in a real sense, Christians must go against the tide of the times.
Perhaps, the best final word comes from St. Paul when he says,
"take the whole armor of God . . . and having done all, to
stand" (Ephesians 6:13, RSV).

KEY QUESTIONS FOR DISCUSSION

1. Do you believe that the doctrine of Christian calling has been
   neglected by Protestants?
2. What is the Christian doctrine of stewardship? Look up Psalms
   24:1; Deuteronomy 1:11-18; Ezekiel 28:2-8; Luke 12:13-21;
   and Romans 1:25.
3. Discuss F. Ernest Johnson's statement that "the Christian doctrine of stewardship is the most radical of all doctrines concerning property. It maintains that a man owns nothing; what he has
   he holds in stewardship under God."
4. What are the characteristics of the modern work-world that make
   it hard to practice vocational responsibility under God?
5. What are the pressures and temptations that you confront in your
   work? List some of the hardest dilemmas.
6. What do you believe is the highest incentive to effort? Does St.
   Paul's incentive of love have any significance?
7. How common is discussion among Christians concerning their
   Christian responsibility in their employment?
8. What is your answer to the notion that our faith has nothing to do
   with our occupations?
9. What can you do in your church to re-establish Christian vocation as part of the Christian call?

10. Is there any chance for Christians to work in groups to influence economic policy and practices?

RECOMMENDED READINGS

Bowen, Howard R., *Social Responsibilities of Business Men.* New York: Harper and Brothers, 1953.

Calhoun, Robert L., *God and the Day's Work.* New York: The Association Press, 1943.

Childs, Marquis, and Douglass Cater, *Ethics in a Business Society.* New York: Mentor Books, 1954.

Fletcher, Joseph F. (editor), *Christianity and Property.* Philadelphia: Westminster Press, 1947.

Miller, Alexander, *Christian Faith and My Job.* New York: The Association Press, 1946.

Mills, C. Wright, *White Collar.* New York: Oxford University Press, 1951.

Muelder, Walter G., *Religion and Economic Responsibility.* New York: Charles Scribner's Sons, 1953.

Reports of the Second Assembly, *Evanston Speaks.* New York: World Council of Churches, 1950.

The following are publications of the Department of the Church and Economic Life of the National Council of Churches, New York, N.Y.:

Buffalo Laymen's Conference Addresses, *On-the-Job Dilemmas of Christian Laymen,* 1952. $.35.

Buffalo Laymen's Conference Report, *Report of the North American Lay Conference on the Christian and His Daily Work,* 1952. $.35.

Hall, Cameron P., *Religion in the Day's Work,* 1952. Handbook for conference and study courses. $.35.

———, *Christian Principles and Assumptions of Economic Life.* Statement adopted by the General Board of the National Council of Churches, 1954. $.10.

———, *The Christian at His Daily Work,* 1951. $.35.

CHAPTER 11

Exerting Christian Influence in Politics

The future of Western civilization depends in no small part upon the relation of American Christians to American Politics, and upon what American Christians do about American Politics. . . . We know that if religion is used merely as an emotional reinforcement of power politics it ceases to be valid or vital. On the other hand, we also know that politics divorced from religion may lead to totalitarian tyranny. It is, therefore, a matter of extreme urgency that American Christians give serious consideration to the relation of Christian faith to "politics" and feel a moral imperative to political action (Francis P. Miller, "Our Participation as Christians in Politics," *Social Action* [December, 1953]).

I was ready to be sought by those who did not ask for me; I was ready to be found by those who did not seek me. I said, "Here am I, here am I," to a nation that did not call on my name (Isaiah 65:1, RSV).

THE DUAL CITIZENSHIP OF THE CHRISTIAN

Perhaps no area of Christian responsibility is approached more gingerly or with greater confusion by Protestants than is the field of government and politics. Few church people today would claim that as citizens of Christ's Kingdom they are no longer required to be citizens of their nation. Yet, few Christians accept the positive call of God as laying upon them a new and higher responsibility as citizens of their country. But the doctrine of Christian calling means exactly that. As Augustine put it, the Christian has a dual citizenship—in an earthly city and in the City of God.

Jesus, himself, confronted this problem when asked whether it was right to pay taxes to Caesar. His answer, "to render to Caesar the things that are Caesar's and to God the things that are God's," has often been falsely interpreted to mean a complete split between the two responsibilities. The great teachings of the gospel clearly show, as we have discussed before, where our supreme devotion lies. But as Paul declared in his struggle with this problem, this does not remove our responsibilities as citizens of the world. Said he, "Let every person be subject to the governing authorities. For there is no authority except from God" (Romans 13:1, RSV). Then he goes on to say of "him who is in authority" that "he is God's servant for your good" (Romans 13:3-4, RSV). Alexander Miller says that Paul thus taught "serious acceptance of our responsibility both to respect and criticize things as they are."[1]

Of course the democratic view of the responsibility of rulers to their people had not yet been developed at that time. But in the Old Testament the prophetic judgment upon rulers and kings had become a basic tradition in Israel. As a covenant-people chosen by God, the whole community existed under God and His continuing judgment. In a time when surrounded by absolute kings, the prophets entered into open conflict with the monarchy and were allowed independence to pronounce judgment on the kings for doing evil in the sight of Yahweh.[2]

The prophet Nathan dared to point his finger at King David and say, "You are the man," and ask him: "Why have you despised the word of the Lord, to do what is evil in His sight?" (II

[1] Alexander Miller, *Christian Faith and My Job* (New York: The Association Press, 1946), p. 33.

[2] G. E. Wright, *The Old Testament Against its Environment* (Chicago: H. Regnery Co., 1950), pp. 67-68.

Samuel 12:7, 9, RSV). The great prophets all pronounced God's judgment upon the whole people and the rulers for injustice and human exploitation. As John Bright says, "Not even the king might flout the law of the covenant God with impunity."[3]

The Biblical God is the God of Nations and the Sovereign over rulers. The duty to criticize unjust rulers who fall away from righteousness is a continuing tradition in our religious history. "John Calvin held that, if any 'prince'—that is, any political ruler—ceases to act justly, he may be held of no more account than a pair of worn-out shoes; he should be got rid of and replaced by a ruler who knows his business under God."[4]

Earlier we quoted Professor James H. Nichols' description of the three great traditions concerning the relation of church and state. He traces the important religious development that brought forth the American doctrine and finds that the left-wing Puritans —the free church Congregationalists and Baptists—provided a basic tradition that came to common acceptance in America. Under this arrangement, the church is not controlled by the state but is kept free and unbeholden. Likewise, the state is not controlled by the church. Both become corrupt and pretentious when they attempt to dominate the other. Rather do the church and state coexist. Says Nichols, of this early Reformed view that later came to fruition in America, "Church and State were to be independent but cooperating bodies, distinct centers of power, in the tensions between which was to lie the greatest possibility of liberty."[5]

America established this doctrine and safeguarded against the domination of each by the other. But this did not mean a denial of political responsibility for Christians. As Nichols concludes, concerning the situation out of which our nation was established, ". . . the whole society was saturated with the fundamental Calvinist and Puritan fear of all absolutism and the sense of the

[3] John Bright, *The Kingdom of God* (New York: Abingdon Press, 1953), p. 48.

[4] Alexander Miller, *op. cit.,* p. 34.

[5] James H. Nichols, *Democracy and the Churches* (Philadelphia: Westminster Press, 1951), p. 28.

sacred obligation of political man to direct the State by the moral law."[6] This view distinguished between the spheres of nature and grace that was to miscarry later into total separation of influence as well as control. But this view was no doctrine of Christian abandonment of political responsibility. It continues the ancient doctrine that political life remains under moral judgment and is accountable to God. It is freedom *for* responsibility, not *from* responsibility.

THE GIGANTIC INFLUENCE OF GOVERNMENT UPON OUR COMMON LIFE

The state has always had great powers over the lives of its citizens. It monopolizes the powers of coercion and uses punishments to enforce its laws and regulations to keep order and preserve peace. For infractions, it deprives its citizens of their property, their freedom, and even their lives. Because of the authority and power of the state, those who wield such power have always suffered the inevitable temptations to misuse it to keep themselves in authority and to build up special privileges and gains for themselves and their favorites.

Democracy, of course, is a reaction to centuries of arbitrary power in which rulers were not responsible to the ruled nor were they removable by them. So democratic forms of government are based on the principle of self-rule in which citizens select by vote their own authorities and hold them responsible for their actions under the continuous or periodic threat of removal. Furthermore, in America we have a Constitutional Bill of Rights, which guarantees rights that even elected authorities cannot remove or disobey. In addition to this, we have three branches of government, that place checks and balances on one another. Moreover, even beyond and above these restraints to preserve justice and freedom there stands still another responsibility and judgment upon America as viewed by our founding fathers: This

[6] *Ibid.,* p. 41.

is our dependence upon God. This is the nation that traces its spiritual origins to such proclamations as are found in the *Mayflower Compact,* which declared that the new colony was "undertaken for the Glory of God," and which was covenanted "solemnly and mutually in the Presence of God." Or to the *Fundamental Orders of Connecticut,* which declared: "That there should be an orderly and decent Government according to God."

This is the nation that was founded in a Declaration of Independence, which maintained that human rights are "endowed by their Creator," that appealed to the "Supreme Judge of the World," and that placed "reliance on the Protection of Divine Providence." This is the land that Abraham Lincoln called "This Nation under God" and that mints every coin with these words raised in bold relief: "In God We Trust."

It is clear that our forebears who established our nation and its constitutional system were extremely fearful of all irresponsible power and understood well the inevitable controlling influences that even democratic power must exert over the individual lives and the patterns and practices of its citizens. As has been pointed out so frequently, the early patriots who established our republic were highly suspicious of the trustworthiness of even elected governments and of the moral vulnerabilities of all human beings who might be selected to operate them. Under such a view, the belief that "the state governs best that governs least" came to prevail.

But Washington, Madison, and Jefferson warned solemnly against parties, factions, or classes that might develop enough strength to unduly influence government toward injustices and imbalances of power. Thus, they had premonitions of the highly organized groups and interests that were to develop in a revolutionary new age of massive industrialism.

The great dilemma of government has come upon us as never before. A powerful government is always tempted to coerce and regulate its citizens and their organizations in ways that destroy freedom and allow injustices, but a weak government does not have enough power to regulate and adjust the powerful inner organizations that can promote their special advantages with resulting injustices.

The organizational revolution has produced vast centers of power in the form of giant corporations, labor unions, trade associations, farm organizations, and professional societies that exert powerful economic, political, and moral pressures upon their members, upon one another, upon society as a whole—and upon officials of government itself.

These are all what Professor Charles Merriam used to call "private governments" that have the means of exerting vast power over men. Thus, the problem of refereeing and coordinating the interests of the giants has imposed a vast responsibility upon government, if our society is not to fall into chaotic conflict.

Stronger government has been the result of necessity in the new age. Groups that want weak government in our time usually believe they are in a position to control society through nongovernmental means. Yet, stronger government is always dangerous and requires more vigilance of its citizens.

In the kind of world in which we live—in the new age of mass organizations, mass communications, and international conflict—the basic functions of government set forth in the Preamble of our Constitution become infinitely more complex. Unavoidably, the discharge of such functions has a far greater influence on the lives of all citizens.

ESTABLISHING JUSTICE

The function of establishing justice—the first stated constitutional function—was comparatively easy in the early days of our nation when most individuals and groups had reasonably equal power and the free exchange of goods and opinions was more nearly adequate to maintain justice.

Almost any conceivable policy is likely to be more favorable to some groups than others in an age when tariffs and tax policy; government procurement; the necessary regulations of transportation, trade, and communication; the maintenance of roads and of gigantic defense establishments; and the rights of labor unions and of natural or merged monopolies are all so intricate. In such a society, equity and justice become highly complex problems. Injustices and special privileges become obscure and technical considerations. Maintaining equilibrium among gigantic pressure groups becomes difficult because some groups have higher prestige, larger funds for campaigns of influence, and greater access to the mass means of communication. Large segments of the population are not organized and are not well represented in the pressure group struggle.

It is a much harder task to keep government responsible to all the people than in the simpler days. To keep some sort of order in this vast context of relations, as government has more and more regulative decisions thrust upon it, it becomes more imperative than ever that it be broadly responsible for the common good. For modern man, independence is impossible and interdependence is the chief fact of his existence. This means that the basic welfare of all is dependent on the smooth functioning and balance of society as a whole. A railroad strike in the Midwest may jeopardize the food supply in New York City. A political decision in Washington on credit policy might affect the buying power of everyone across the nation. The same is true of thousands of other policy decisions.

Political decisions are all moral decisions that affect the welfare of millions and weigh the scales of justice. Professor Schattschneider has said that politics is morals in action.[7] And this is true at the level that affects the lives of not just one neighbor but everyone.

PROVIDING FOR THE COMMON DEFENSE

The constitutional function of government in providing for the common defense has likewise become a tremendous under-

---

[7] E. E. Schattschneider, "Our Unrecognized Governmental Crisis," *Social Action*, XVI:10 (October 15, 1950).

taking in the kind of world situation in which we live. This involves not only the issues of what kind of army, navy, and air force we maintain, but also what kind of weapons we develop, such as atomic bombs, and what our policy shall be in regard to using them. It includes our diplomacy, which is our first line of defense, and what our policy shall be toward relations with other great nations. In delicate times of world tension, such decisions ought not to be made in terms of sheer national loyalty but under the awesome judgment of the God of nations. These are moral and religious questions of the highest order that are almost sure to determine the fate of our whole civilization. No argument can validly maintain that these are problems of individual conscience, for they are functions that can be carried only by government for the whole people. Whether individual conscience carries any weight at all depends on whether it is registered effectively through organization at the seats of decision.

PROMOTING THE GENERAL WELFARE

Another function of government, as stated in the Preamble of our Constitution, is to "promote the general welfare." In a society in which the majority of citizens are dependent on others for jobs, food, and clothing, they are almost totally dependent upon the functioning of social and economic processes for their security. Business cycles, decisions of management to move factories, natural catastrophes, inflationary spirals, wars and threats of wars, and hundreds of other kinds of events over which individuals have no personal control may throw them into unforeseen emergencies with which they have no private means of coping. Security becomes a great new problem in such an interdependent society.

Furthermore, our mode of life has removed many of the kinds of security upon which people used to depend in personal and family crises. In the old type of intimate rural community, if a farmer were injured or his house burned, he could count on the mobilization of neighborhood help. The family itself was better prepared to take in outside members who suffered illness or reverses. Houses were bigger; extra hands could be put to work profitably. But urbanism, the wide scattering of families, dependence upon weekly or monthly paychecks, and smaller rented housing have all made the majority of modern families immediately vulnerable to both personal misfortunes and social disruptions.

Security against inevitable emergencies has increasingly had to depend on purely monetary protections in the form of savings or insurance. But probably not more than 10 to 15 per cent of our families[8] can afford even a bare minimum of such protection against emergencies. Furthermore, our whole mass-production and high-advertising economy has built up a way of life that lures people into buying things, even on installments if necessary, rather than practicing frugal saving. The old slogan "save for a rainy day" has been displaced by a new one: "Buy to keep the wheels of progress rolling."

Therefore, providing social security has become a primary function of government. If millions of people are not to live under continuous anxiety that undermines their capacity to produce and to live stable lives, the provision of such securities is mandatory. No civilized, much less Christian, society can coldly let those who are the victims of the vicissitudes of a hazardous life suffer alone without mercy or help. A number of well-to-do people who have adequate wealth for self-protection, and others who have not understood our radically changed situation, have fought against this function of government. But the overwhelming majority of Americans now recognize it as essential. This is shown by the backing of federal social security by both political parties in recent elections. However, this trend like the others places more control in the hands of government and makes responsibility in politics even more urgent.

[8] Study conducted in one of the author's classes by David Brewer, insurance man.

SECURING THE BLESSINGS OF LIBERTY

The last purpose of government stated in our Preamble concerns "the securing of the Blessings of Liberty." This, like the other functions, has become immeasurably more complex and difficult. The threats to freedom from government coercion have grown, and the general atmosphere of suspicion and distrust has prompted many Americans to conclude that freedom is too dangerous to permit, even in the "land of the free and the home of the brave." This has been created by the world insecurity and tension, by threats of undercover Communist infiltration, and by the efforts of politicians and others to capitalize on this situation for their own ends.

Methods of browbeating and maligning Americans without the legal safeguards provided by our Constitution have come into use by some of our elected representatives and are condoned by many of our citizens. Individuals of high repute have been defamed on the basis of mere hearsay, without adequate opportunities for defense. Organizations of private citizens have taken upon themselves the prerogatives restricted to our courts and have attempted to intimidate our society into conformity with their own peculiar views. Whole departments of our government, major political parties, and even the great Protestant churches have been indiscriminately accused of disloyalty. Thus, to defend our freedoms, the methods of Communist totalitarianism have come to be favored by some of our own citizens and politicians.

This development has stirred up Protestant anxiety and protest as perhaps no other threat of our times, for it strikes at the very heart of the Protestant tradition of freedom of conscience and the right of moral criticism and action. Official statements of warning have been issued by the major religious bodies in America. As the letter of the General Council of the Presbyterian Church (U.S.A.) to all Presbyterian Churches in America declared, "A subtle but potent assault upon basic human rights is now in progress," and "The shrine of conscience and private judgment, which

God alone has the right to enter, is being invaded."⁹ This letter warned that we must use only methods "in accordance with the will of God."

The defense of our Christian and democratic liberties is one of the foremost Christian responsibilities of our times. In this field, Christians are called to cast their influence into this great struggle for which their fathers suffered in the past. And the decisive arena is finally in the field of political action. The great question is whether the weight of our political leadership will continue to protect and secure these historic liberties, or whether our political leaders will come to condone or even practice intimidation upon their own citizens to whom they are responsible.

Such issues as these test our faithfulness in our commitment to our God in Jesus Christ. Government policy and decision has a gigantic influence upon the balances of justice and the right to hold ourselves under divine judgment and guidance. No Christian can remain aloof or neutral toward such ethical obligations and be faithful to his calling.

WHY PROTESTANTS NEGLECT OR DENY POLITICAL RESPONSIBILITIES

There are six reasons why Protestants have neglected or denied political responsibilities:

1. We have already discussed the misunderstanding of the doctrine of the separation of Church and state that has caused so much mischief in America as a basis for abandoning the Christian call to responsible citizenship. Falsely viewed as a kind of permanent agreement under which Christians accept disfranchisement of influence in return for the right to freedom of worship, this notion betrays the very purpose of separation for which it was established. This bastion of religious freedom in America gives no religious organization or body a right to preferential status or governmental support or the right to use governmental

⁹ Letter issued November 3, 1953.

powers to enforce its beliefs or practices by law upon anyone else. On its positive side, it safeguards the right of religious groups to promote their beliefs under all peaceful and persuasive means as individuals and groups. It preserves the right of all Christians to work for laws and practices that are just and righteous, according to their understanding of the will of God.

As Dean Luther Weigle declared in one of our greatest modern statements on religious liberty, "[It] includes the right to dissent in the name of religious belief—[but also it includes] . . . a right greater than that of dissent; it is the right of responsible participation in the making and executing of public policy."[10] Dr. Weigle says further, in upholding this historic and Biblical view of responsibility, that "religious freedom of the citizens includes the right to hold the state responsible to the moral law and to God, and the right to labor toward this end."[11] Professor M. Searle Bates in his monumental book, *Religious Liberty*, says that it is more than absence of compulsion; "it is the opportunity to do and to be something."[12]

John Clarke, one of the earliest Baptist sufferers of state coercion in America, was told by the Massachusetts authorities that he was being sentenced not for "conscience" but for "practice." To this he replied, "Be it so, but I say that . . . practice was but a manifestation of my . . . conscience with respect unto God."[13] Conscience that cannot speak out and practice is already enslaved, for even men with no religious liberty whatsoever are free to think within themselves.

Whenever Christians or a group of Christians are told not to "meddle" in attempts to influence our political policy on the grounds of separation of Church and state, they are being challenged by the very doctrine that guarantees their right to do so.

---

[10] Luther Weigle, "The American Tradition of Religious Freedom," *Social Action* (November 15, 1947), and in a presidential address to the Federal Council of Churches (December 10, 1942).

[11] *Ibid.*

[12] M. Searle Bates, *Religious Liberty* (New York: Harper and Brothers, 1945), p. 295.

[13] *Ibid.*, p. 299.

2. There is another curious reason why many Protestants draw back from participation in political life. This is the belief that politics is dirty business and, therefore, Christians should remain aloof to keep themselves unsullied. Professor George A. Graham in his excellent book, *Morality in American Politics*, says that the American attitude is one of "mingled pride and shame in politics" with "its indiscriminate honoring of the long dead and its dishonoring of the living in the field of public affairs."[14] People who work in elections are considered "politicians" and appointed officials are "bureaucrats"—and both are among the least respected people in our society. In fact, stemming from the days of antagonism toward the British government and kings, there is a deep suspicion that all government is "inherently an evil thing."[15]

Probably another important reason for the general low view of political life has been created by the "mud slinging" tactics that have long characterized our campaigns. We need only to compare our campaigns with the dignified interchanges before elections in Britain or Canada. The American voter, while perhaps not taking our campaign oratory too seriously, has nevertheless been warned repeatedly that the members of the opposition are rascals and crooks. It can be little wonder that many people have been conditioned to believe that there is a permanent "mess" in Washington—or in Albany or Springfield or Harrisburg.

Then, of course, from time to time genuine scandals of corruption have been revealed in government. Protestants are usually properly horrified at election time, but in the long run these scandals merely confirm their notion that politics is dirty business and beneath the dignity of decent people. In 1945 the Gallup Poll asked this question: "If you had a son would you like to see him go into politics as a life work when he gets out of school?" To this question 68 per cent said No, 21 per cent Yes, and 11 per cent had no opinion.[16] We suspect that if this poll had been re-

14 George A. Graham, *Morality in American Politics* (New York: Random House, 1952), p. 5.
15 *Ibid.*, p. 4.
16 Thomas Reed and Doris Reed, *Preparing College Men and Women for Politics* (Report to the Citizenship Clearing House) (New York: Law Center, New York University, 1952), p. 108.

stricted to Protestants the results would have been even more one-sided. As the penetrating *Report on Ethical Standards in Government*[17] of the Senate Subcommittee pointed out in 1951, corrupt practices in government usually reflect common practices in the everyday world carried over by citizens into government. Such practices also show a lack of persistent concern by our citizenry as a whole.

The only possible Christian answer to this problem must be more concern and participation, not disdain and self-righteous aloofness. And, as we shall see, much greater participation in political influence does not require everyone to run for office or become a professional politician.

3. Another "prejudice" that has touched Americans rather generally is the belief that voting discharges the full duty of citizenship and is a potent way of exerting political influence. E. E. Schattschneider, a leading political scientist and Protestant layman, calls this the "old maid's view of politics" and declares, "By itself, voting is not a very effective way of influencing the course of public policy."[18] Of course, the reason for this is that critical decisions are worked out within the party structure long before elections occur. In elections the electorate is given only two alternatives by the two major parties, which offer ready-made slates of candidates and platforms. The individual voter who comes out of political hiding on election day to cast his secret ballot fails to enter the real process of the formation of policy. In a very real sense, by election day the situation has jelled; all that is left is the vote counting and shouting. This does not mean that voting is not the crucial pay-off in determining who shall govern; but the work of organization, of selecting emphases, and communicating to the people comes long before. Another way of saying this is that elections are not merely held on election day but in party caucuses, conventions, and in all the ways that issues are clarified and in which both political decision and public opinion are formed.

[17] Report of the Senate Subcommittee (Washington, D.C.: U. S. Government Printing Office, 1951).

[18] E. E. Schattschneider, *op. cit.*

4. Another great hindrance to Protestant political responsibility is the fear and prejudice against organizational effort. As any of the textbooks on government point out, elections are won by organization. Professor Schattschneider says that about 500,-000 party workers control the major political machinery of the country.[19] This makes party workers three hundred times more influential than nonworkers. Independence means a lack of influence at the levels where policy is formed and decisions made. The more people there are who adhere to lone individualism in their influence, the easier it is for organized minorities to control our political destinies. And increasingly, as we have seen, political decisions are moral decisions that have an overarching effect upon the patterns of corruption or justice, exploitation or equilibrium in our society.

Protestants have been especially fearful of organizations and cooperative effort in influencing our government policy. They have adhered to the view that Christians ought to express their influence individually. As Kenneth Underwood has pointed out frequently, this means that Protestant influence is diffused, disorganized, and feeble.[20] By default, we let other more vocal groups dominate our government policy and the climate of opinion in which we are all obliged to live.

One of the great questions that we free-conscience Protestants need to ask ourselves frankly is whether this view means that we deny ourselves the power of cooperative effort and can, therefore, no longer influence an organizational world. We have already discussed this in an earlier chapter. We strongly believe that this self-imposed isolation from the streams of influence is a betrayal of our free church tradition of voluntary fellowship in which we freely band ourselves together to seek God's will in confronting the world. We believe this strange twist that glorifies independence is an interpretation that is often promoted by secular interests, so that the guiding restraints and the transforming dynamic of Christian moral influence can be paralyzed.

[19] *Ibid.*, p. 27.
[20] Kenneth Underwood, "Some Problems Protestantism Faces in Contemporary American Society," *Christianity and Society*, 17:2 (Spring, 1952), p. 8.

5. Another reason why Protestants deny their full obligations in political influence is because of fear of controversy and its possible penalties. This is not peculiar to Protestants but is one of the basic intimidations of the world upon all people. Timid people who place self-interest above obligation are afraid that engaging in conflict might hurt business or alienate friends. It is always easier to remain neutral and in good relations with all sorts of people. We have already cited David Riesman's contention that modern Americans are increasingly controlled by what other people think rather than by their own convictions.[21] Therefore, we don't express ourselves, at least not until we find out where others stand.

This same fear of partisanship or taking sides, ironically, has produced the same noncommittal type of bashfulness in religion as in politics. These two fields are the ones that modern Americans most assiduously avoid in conversation in favor of unruffled harmony. This attitude represents one of the greatest threats to both our free churches and our democracy, which depend basically on the ability of members or citizens to discuss disagreements without engendering violent conflict and distrust. In politics, perhaps, no more dangerous development has appeared than the type of political partisanship that charges political opponents with treason. Since our parties are fairly evenly divided, if half of our people should come to suspect the other half of being traitors, our national integrity would be doomed. Because the essence of democratic politics is creative conflict, the fear of partisanship is fear and lack of faith in democracy itself.

6. The final obstruction to Protestant responsibility in the political sphere lies in the Protestant fear of compromise. Politics has been called the science of compromise. Its task is to reconcile opposing interests into the best possible balance; to attain some approximation of justice from the limited possibilities that present themselves in any situation of actual decision. The most conscientious lawmaker or political administrator often has the choice be-

[21] David Riesman, *The Lonely Crowd* (New Haven: Yale University Press, 1950), p. 22.

tween negotiating in favor of a partial solution to some problem or blocking action by unyielding insistence on all or nothing. Should he favor a bill that includes a combination of elements that both rectify some injustice and grant some unfair advantage if he believes the positive aspects outweigh the negative?

One of the best discussions of this problem is presented by Jerry Voorhis in his book, *The Christian in Politics.* Mr. Voorhis speaks as a former Congressman who has faced these issues as a Christian layman. Speaking of this dilemma of compromise, he says of the Christian lawmaker: "He will constantly be confronted with the problem of a half a loaf or none, and he will spend many a wakeful night wondering whether it is more nearly right to vote for the half loaf than to stand on principle and run the risk of getting none of it."[22] Christians who participate in the formation of policy either as officials or voluntary workers must confront this problem realistically and sincerely.

Mr. Voorhis says that the Christian's task in politics is "hard" not because you have to be a crook to get ahead, but because "no one can have entirely his own way about anything."[23] But, as we discussed in an earlier chapter, it is a good thing that we are compelled to compromise, since the best-laid plans of the best of us are tainted with some bias and need challenge and correction. Perhaps the most dangerous people of all in positions where they have power over the lives of others, such as in politics and business, are those self-righteous absolutists who insist that their own views infallibly represent the will of God for all men.

The Christian in the political arena is not a pretentious and uncompromising autocrat, armed with a new version of "the divine right of Kings" applied to himself as an elected representative. He has no vision or Biblical blueprint for justice that he can simply translate into action without confronting dilemmas. What then do Christians have for guidance that lifts them above the political expediency of secular evaluations? First of all, they have

---

22 Jerry Voorhis, *The Christian in Politics* (New York: The Association Press, 1951), pp. 26-27.
23 *Ibid.,* p. 29.

a vocation under God that provides a continuing motivation and perspective for decision under all circumstances. Secondly, as Vernon Holloway has stated, "Right action correctly understood is the action of those who know that they are wrong men," and who "know to whom they must be loyal as they struggle with the disloyalty of their society and of their own hearts."[24] Thirdly, Christians find both a criticism and renewal in the common worship and discussion within the Christian fellowship under the transforming grace of God.

WHAT NOT TO DO TO SERVE GOD IN CHRISTIAN CITIZENSHIP

On the basis of our previous discussion, let us summarize what the Christian must *not* do.

1. He must not "beg off" with excuses that Christians owe their responsibility to God and that politics can run its own corrupt and worldly course.

2. He must not be a negative citizen, merely complaining about the messes we are in and the corruption that exists. Christians believe in sharing the blame, and the less we accept active responsibility the more blame we must assume.

3. He must not expect politics to be either purer and cleaner, or dirtier and more corrupting, than the everyday world. It reflects the attitudes and values of society and the eternal temptation to misuse power for personal ends. It is especially important that he not be a partisan moralist, seeing all good on one side and all evil on the other. Both sides are always a mixture of both.

4. He must not wait until "the half-past-zero hour" of election day to cast his influence.

5. He must not be a "secret operator," never letting anyone know where he stands and always keeping his light under a bushel because declaring himself might hurt business or alienate friends. There is no way to be a Christian and avoid being a con-

[24] Vernon H. Holloway, *Religious Ethics and the Politics of Power* (New York: Church Peace Union, 1951), p. 16.

troversial figure. He must take sides and assume the risks of decision.

6. He must not be a cantankerous partisan, insisting that his own infallible view is God's perfect will. He must press for his convictions humbly without being disagreeable, while continually searching for new light from the Spirit.

7. He must avoid being a one-issue axe-grinder, believing that all human problems and sinfulness are related to gambling alone, or the liquor traffic, or racial discrimination, or war, or any other one problem. This does not mean that he can avoid ranking problems in importance, but it does mean he must see these issues in the total context of life.

8. He must not be afraid of cooperation with fellow Christians to build responsible opinion. He must not run away from organization.

9. He must not be a rubber stamp for any party or standardized point of view. Many Americans "inherit" a political party from their families or regions and never make a genuine political decision in their whole lives. They demurely go along with what is offered by their party without criticism or challenge. It is hard to see how any truly responsible Christian could fall into such a pattern.

What Can the Christian Citizen Do?

Our accent must be on the positive if we are to be citizens of Christian influence. It is not what we avoid but what we do that counts. The following is a recommended course of action.

1. First of all, the Christian must develop a Christian attitude and understanding of his call as a citizen under God. There are two great aspects of this understanding: on the one side, a humble recognition of his own biases and self-interests, which make his partisanship untrustworthy, thus requiring continuous criticism and challenge under God; and on the other side, a call to duty to

positive decision and participation under one's best Christian light on the demands of justice.

2. But a Christian attitude is not enough without being informed concerning the actual situation and alternatives under political decision. Conscientious men often decide wrongly through ignorance as well as through prejudice. As we discussed in Chapter 7, this is a baffling problem in a busy life lived in a world of propaganda and special pleading. To discover and study balanced sources of information and to share facts in fellowship offer our best hope. Here the church has a special educational responsibility.

3. The Christian citizen must register his opinion at two levels: first, in daily expression and, secondly, at the seats of power. In our society, an individual votes in hundreds of ways as he participates in the formation of attitudes, in common conversation among friends, at the barber shop, in club meetings, at union meetings, in farmers' organizations, at work, and wherever he declares himself. He votes in what he buys and whom he patronizes. He can also write letters to the editor of local papers; he can congratulate a speaker upon his stand or question his views or his facts.

Citizens, however, have a duty to register their convictions, beyond such casual means, at the seats of political power. Letters to Congressmen, mayors, and Senators carry far more weight than most people think. One of the reasons for this is that so few people take the time or have the concern to write such letters. Our government representatives receive many form letters from pressure groups and wild communications from fanatics but few sensible personal letters from their constituents. Letters that are brief, written in long hand, and state basic reasons for one's stand are taken very seriously by men in elected office. It is even better to get an appointment whenever possible and explain one's concerns in a face-to-face discussion.

4. Such efforts are important and very worthwhile, but they fail to use the potent instrument of cooperative impact. Organiza-

tion is the "great multiplier" of personal influence. It combines the greater intensity of group concern with systematic endeavors to win and educate others and to communicate the intensity of group interest to responsible representatives.

There are several kinds of organizations in which individuals may multiply their influence. The first is the voluntary group organized to meet a particular pressing issue. It may range from a few concerned individuals who share intense concern in a local church or community all the way to national organizations that appeal to all concerned people to join hands in confronting some urgent need. Professor Hudson says that the "voluntary association" is "the great discovery" and genius of Protestantism.[25] In hundreds of such organizations throughout our history, Protestants have demonstrated their belief that uncoordinated individual effort is not enough. In forming such organizations, Christians do not have to wait until they can convince the whole local church or a whole denomination that there is an urgent problem demanding action.

At the political level, such groups promote concern and education in the general electorate and act through representatives to influence legislators and to inform their own members concerning how these legislators vote. There are many general groups, such as the League of Women Voters and Independent Citizens groups, in which Christian individuals can combine with others to work in general political action. Then, too, every Christian citizen should be politically and ethically alert to do what he can to form a more just political policy in all his business, professional, and civic organizations that seek to exert political influence.

One-issue organizations are probably less fruitful and more dangerous. Perhaps there are situations that justify a mobilization of the like-minded and their converts into special political action societies on particular issues. But there are many problems and disadvantages in this approach. It takes a vast amount of effort

25 Winthrop S. Hudson, *The Great Tradition of the American Church* (New York: Harper and Brothers, 1953), p. 71.

to organize effectively, and there is the question of whether any one issue or problem warrants this kind of effort. Furthermore, such organizations draw together only those who tend to give one-sided emphasis to a single issue, thus elevating it to a dominance that obscures responsibility in other equally important fields. This has happened in various one-issue movements. Moreover, such groups often fail to adequately take into consideration the balancing perspectives of others who are outside. Then, too, the transcendent loyalty of the Christian to his God, which he places above all issues, and the continuing necessity of prayer and worship for guidance are neglected in such organizations even when most of the members are Christians.

The other two types of organizations in which Christians may multiply their influence are the great political parties that actually carry the power of political decision and the Christian church itself. Despite qualms of long standing, let us ask ourselves frankly if these are not the two contexts in which we can best discharge our responsibility for political leadership.

5. If Christians really want to exert influence in politics, there is no substitute for participation in actual political life. Instead of trying to influence others who participate in the formation of political policy, why should Christians not participate themselves? Political parties are crying for more workers, especially at the local level. People who work in political parties do not necessarily run for office. "Participation in politics is not synonymous with a career in politics." "It means work on party committees and in campaigns with a view to the exercise of influence in determining party policies and candidates."[26] It means that the worker must identify himself with the party and accept its discipline in order to win influence, but it does not mean being uncritical or swallowing everything that is decided. It is the theory of "belonging in order to influence." Professor Schattschneider says, "Few other avenues of social action open to Christian laymen in America promise so much for human welfare in this period of world crisis."[27] It has

[26] Thomas Reed and Doris Reed, *op. cit.*, p. 7.
[27] E. E. Schattschneider, *op. cit.*, p. 27.

been said frequently that the church must help take the curse off politics and help more laymen see this as a field of significant Christian service.

The same may be said of Christians actually running for office and realistically facing the dilemmas and striving persistently for the best possible action. Jerry Voorhis discussed government service as a Christian vocation at the Buffalo Laymen's Conference. Said he, "What is desperately needed is more practicing Christians in places of public trust to give their first allegiance to Christ and His Gospel. These people can find a middle way whereby they can resolve many of the conflicts that now plague us." He warned that "choices are seldom easy, seldom clear, almost never one-sided,"[28] but that one can always struggle to choose the most desirable course possible.

WHAT CAN THE CHURCH DO IN POLITICS?

Some Protestants will be horrified by the mere asking of this question. For many church people, "meddling" in politics is completely out of character for the church of Christ. But let us not be hasty in our denials or in our understanding of meddling. If the historic responsibility of Christian citizens is to keep forever burning the judgment of God upon our nation and its actions, then does not the church as the fellowship in which Christians seek the will of God have a legitimate role in this task?

The free churches in America have repeatedly expressed themselves on political issues in the common consensus of their great gatherings. It is illuminating to go through the resolutions of the official national meetings of the Baptists, Congregationalists, Presbyterians, Methodists, Episcopalians, or other major Protestant bodies. For instance, at all recent annual meetings the American Baptist Convention, which vigorously defends the separation of church and state, has conclusively demonstrated its belief in the right of the church to proclaim its beliefs and express its

[28] Jerry Voorhis, *On-the-Job Dilemmas of Christian Laymen* (New York: National Council of Churches, 1952), pp. 24-25.

judgment on political issues. At one convention (in 1953, for example), it commended the President of the United States and the Department of State for adherence to the separation of church and state in relationship to the Vatican; it voted "encouragement" and support to consecrated persons entering into public life and office after pointing out the dangers of public corruption and the shocking disregard of the public good by citizens. It commended the President for urging Congress to correct racial discrimination. It resolved "that we seek by concerted action and consistent pressure upon public agents" to safeguard the Bill of Rights and the recognized practices of jurisprudence, "whenever subversive activity must be attacked." It "deplored" the readiness of legislative committees of Congress "to credit and publicize unfounded rumors and unsubstantiated opinions to the detriment of the character of persons." It declared its "continued opposition" to Universal Military Training. It called for support of the President's recommendations for low-rent housing. It urged the revision of the McCarran-Walter Immigration Act, suppported the Point IV program and the United Nations, and called upon the President and Congress "to support and give leadership toward the establishment of peace."[29]

In addition to this, for several years representatives of the Council for Social Progress of the Convention have testified before Congressional hearings concerning these expressions of Baptist convictions as shown in their resolutions.

In the social pronouncements of the General Assemblies of the Presbyterian Church (U.S.A.), a frequently used phrase in many of the statements is "we call upon our Government to . . . continue its support of . . . Technical Assistance and so forth." And what committed Christian can deny that the Presbyterians are right when they declared in their last General Assembly (167th) that "we must take sides in the struggle between light and darkness."[30] Is not the political arena a pre-eminent battle-

[29] Resolutions adopted by the American Baptist Convention, Denver, May 25, 1953.

[30] See Social Pronouncements of the 167th General Assembly of the Presbyterian Church U.S.A., Reports in *Social Progress*, XLV:11 (July, 1955).

ground for this struggle? The Congregational Christians at the General Council in 1948 stated their views clearly: "The principle of separation was not intended to silence the church on public questions or to relieve the State of moral responsibility."

Christians from all over the world, living under many governments, declared at the Evanston Assembly: "Christians should work by active participation in political affairs."[31] This is based on the historic belief that God alone is sovereign Lord of men and nations and that "the Christian community must act as a conscience for the nation."[32]

The other great denominations and bodies have expressed similar convictions on important political issues, demonstrating their belief in cooperative Christian responsibility toward government action. This, as we have seen, is in complete accordance with the doctrine of separation of church and state, which preserves the full right of the political expression of the Christian conscience in fellowship in the church.

The church must never be partisan in the exclusive support of single parties or candidates, or deteriorate into associations of mere political controversy. Its sovereign loyalty is forever to its Lord, Jesus Christ. But there are Christian responsibilities that it must discharge as the fellowship of grace and consecration. Let us summarize these:

1. It must preach both the higher citizenship in Christ's Kingdom and the call to Christian responsibility as citizens in the nation and the whole world.
2. It must confront and discuss the ethical aspects of great political issues, seeking the widest possible information concerning all the aspects of the problem involved. Ministers, lay leaders, and denominational agencies must be prepared to help.
3. Wherever consensus becomes clear, churches, like denominational conventions, should formulate their moral judgments into expressions that can be communicated to their conven-

[31] Report on Section III of the Second Assembly, *Evanston Speaks* (New York: World Council of Churches, 1950), p. 28.
[32] *Ibid.*, p. 29.

tions, to sister churches, and to political representatives. Where basic controversies persist no such actions can be taken, but additional guidance can be sought and small groups and individuals can register their convictions with vigor.

People who belong to the Body of Christ should find new grace to confront the terrifying problems of freedom and justice, of war and peace, and of discrimination and conflict with some measure of equanimity, both when consensus can be attained and when it fails. Surely, Christians can face the baffling decisions of our times in every field more humbly and courageously under the guidance of the Holy Spirit in the fellowship of Christ than standing alone. But, finally, the Christian makes his own personal decision under his God and runs the risks of error in his struggle for faithfulness.

In one last word, we repeat our opening concern. It is not important whether you agree with the many things that we have stated in these pages. The crucial questions are: Where do you stand? What can you do concerning all these things? How can you and your church be faithful to our Lord, Jesus Christ?

KEY QUESTIONS FOR DISCUSSION

1. What is the dual citizenship of the Christian?
2. Discuss the positive meaning of the separation of church and state.
3. What does the phrase, "This nation under God," mean to you?
4. Why does the Protestant fear of organization threaten to destroy Protestant influence in our society?
5. Make a list of major political issues that clearly involve moral and spiritual considerations in decision.
6. Are there any major political issues that are not involved in ethical issues, when the full implications are analyzed?
7. How can we overcome the curse of politics so that more Christians will see it as a call to consecrated service?
8. Is it right for a church to take sides on some great ethical issue before our government if its people reach substantial agreement? If

our government should deny freedom of speech to our churches, would they be justified in mobilizing a vigorous political pressure against this threat? Should they support a political party that declared it would restore such freedoms?

9. What are the legitimate things that your church could do to increase Christian influence in our political life?

RECOMMENDED READINGS

Bennett, John C., *The Christian As Citizen*. New York: Association Press, 1955.

Graham, George A., *Morality in American Politics*. New York: Random House, 1952.

Johnson, F. Ernest, "This Freedom of Ours," *Social Action* (November, 1953).

LaRoe, Wilbur, Jr., "A Call to Militant Faith," *Social Progress* (December, 1951).

Miller, Francis P., "Our Participation as Christians in Politics," *Social Action* (December, 1953).

Muehl, William, *Politics for Christians*. New York: Association Press, 1956.

Nelson, Claude D., *Church and State*. A guide for study and discussion. New York: National Council of Churches, 1953. $.50.

Nichols, James H., *Democracy and the Churches*. Philadelphia: Westminster Press, 1951.

Report of the Subcommittee of the Committee on Labor and Public Welfare of the United States Senate, *Ethical Standards in Government*. Washington, D.C.: U. S. Government Printing Office, 1951.

Schattschneider, E. E., "Our Unrecognized Governmental Crisis," *Social Action* (October 15, 1950).

Voorhis, Jerry, *The Christian in Politics*. New York: The Association Press, 1951.

Index

307

Old Testament (*Cont.*):
property, 263-264
prophetic judgment upon rulers, 281
Organizational revolution, 37-40
and Christian concept of vocation, 270-272
iron laws, 40
Organizing, 180-182
for action, 180-182
multiplier of personal influence, 300-301
Oxford Conference, 27-28, 92

P

Parish, local:
defined, 203
discovering, 202-204
religious term for "local community," 203
types of:
downtown city, 204-206
fringe parish, 209-210
open country, 211
single-home neighborhood, 208-209
transitional urban, 206-208
village parish, 210-211
Parker, Everett C., 35
Paul, 7, 26, 69, 145, 263
Christian fellowship, 186
Christian vocation, 265-266
deeds are test of the Christian, 4
love toward neighbor, 232
man is slave to sin, 53
sensitivity to one's sinfulness, 77
the Body of Christ, 73
those in authority, 281
People Act, The, 219, 220
Personal relations, influencing through, 7-11
Persuasion, 15
mass, revolution in, 33-37
psychological techniques of, 34-35
Peter, 232
Pharisaism, 223
Philippians 2:1-4, 269
Pietistic individualism, 139-140
Pike, Dean James A., 99
Politics, 193
dual citizenship of Christian, 280-283

Politics (*Cont.*):
functions of government:
establishing justice, 285-286
promoting general welfare, 287-288
providing for the common defense, 286-287
securing blessings of liberty, 289-290
influence of government upon our common life, 283-285
what Christian citizen can do, 298-302
what not to do in Christian citizenship, 297-298
what the church can do, 302-305
why Protestants neglect or deny political responsibilities, 290-297
belief that politics is dirty business, 292-293
belief that voting discharges full duty, 293
fear of compromise, 295
fear of controversy, 295
misunderstanding of separation of church and state, 290-291
prejudice against organizational effort, 294
Pope, Liston, 81-82, 126
Power, 116-119
in group dynamics, 188
the word of God becomes, 177-178
Practical atheism, 6
Pragmatism, 132-143
Prayer, 178
Preaching:
education through, 179-180
sensitizing through, 176-179
Predestination, 26
Prejudice, 236-237
discovering and confessing, 238
overcoming (*See* Race relations)
Presbyterians:
Department of Christian Social Education and Action, 86
General Assembly, 88-90, 303
General Council, 289-290
goal of non-segregation, 234
pronouncements on social issues, 88-89
Pressure groups, 117
a society of, 37-40